MYSTERY
101

An *Introduction* to the *Big Questions* and the *Limits* of *Human Knowledge*

Richard H. Jones

Cover art: Camille Flammarion, *L'atmosphère: météorologie populaire* (1888).

Published by State University of New York Press, Albany

For information, contact State University of New York Press, Albany, NY
www.sunypress.edu

Production, Jenn Bennett
Marketing, Anne M. Valentine

Library of Congress Cataloging-in-Publication Data

Names: Jones, Richard H., 1951– author.
Title: Mystery 101 : an introduction to the big questions and the limits of human
    knowledge / Richard H. Jones.
Description: Albany, NY : State University of New York, 2018. | Includes
    bibliographical references and index.
Identifiers: LCCN 2017008962 (print) | LCCN 2017050117 (ebook) |
    ISBN 9781438468228 (e-book) | ISBN 9781438468211 (hardcover : alk. paper)
Subjects: LCSH: Knowledge, Theory of.
Classification: LCC BD201 (ebook) | LCC BD201 .J66 2018 (print) | DDC 121—dc23
LC record available at https://lccn.loc.gov/2017008962
Subjects: LCSH: Knowledge, Theory of.
Classification: LCC BD201 (ebook) | LCC BD201 .J66 2018 (print) | DDC 121—dc23
LC record available at https://lccn.loc.gov/2017008962

10 9 8 7 6 5 4 3 2 1

Contents

Preface

Sooner or later, life makes philosophers of us all.
                                                    —Maurice Riseling

At one time or another, we have all pondered at least some of the Big Questions of philosophy and science—Who am I? Why do I exist? Why does anything exist at all? Many books attempt to supply answers to these questions, but the most basic philosophical issue receives only scant attention: *Are we even in a position to answer such questions?* I will examine this basic question and support the unpopular view that we are not currently in a position to answer the really Big Questions in philosophy and science, and probably never will be. There are limits to human knowledge of one kind or another that we simply cannot get around. This leads to agnosticism. Agnosticism is commonly maligned as wishy-washy—a refusal to take a stand on an issue due to lack of interest or intellectual cowardice. However, agnosticism is a philosophically defensible stance, and I will maintain that it is in fact the only intellectually honest position for us in our epistemic situation concerning the Big Questions. In sum, the objective of this book is to expose the limits to human knowledge in the area of the Big Questions, thereby revealing that we should be more perplexed concerning the basic nature of reality than we normally suppose.

The book is written as a collection of short introductions. My approach is from a general analytic philosophical perspective rather than from one of the more specific contemporary schools (e.g., pragmatism or process philosophy). I presume some familiarity with philosophy, but not much.

I hope the positions taken here will provoke the reader to further reflection. The only thing I distinctly remember from any of my high school science classes is one day in physics class when we students were responding with the correct answers from the book. The teacher stopped and stared at us for a moment and then picked up a blackboard eraser and threw it against the wall. We students looked at each other, wondering what we had done wrong. Then the teacher said: "Why did that eraser continue to move after it left my hand? If you think it's obvious and doesn't need an explanation, then you are not thinking like scientists, and I want you to think like scientists, not just parrot back answers!" Then he gave us a brief lecture on answers to that question from Aristotle to Newton. I want this book to be like that flying eraser. I hope you start to think about the Big Questions if you haven't already done so or honestly to examine your own deeply held assumptions and any answers you have already given.

1
Philosophy of Mystery

The most beautiful experience we can have is the mysterious. It is the fundamental emotion which stands at the cradle of all true art and science. Whoever does not know it and can no longer wonder, no longer marvel, is as good as dead, and his eyes are dimmed.

—Albert Einstein

What don't we currently know about our situation in the world? And what can't we know in principle? What is unknowable in principle about reality constitutes philosophical mysteries. These are not historical mysteries that we are not in a position today to answer, nor are they like the mysteries in murder novels—they are mysteries about the fundamental nature of reality that we do not currently know even how to approach. Whether we are in the position to crack the mysteries surrounding the Big Questions of philosophy and science is the subject of this book.

One might argue that all philosophical issues are mysteries since basic issues in philosophy today are unresolved—individual philosophers may believe they have resolved the issue of, say, the relation of our mind to our body, but their opponents are not convinced and instead advance well-argued counterpositions. However, many philosophical issues do not touch the Big Questions about being human and about the natural world that most people with a philosophical bent think of when they contemplate the reality of their lives and our world; instead, philosophers today most often busy themselves with more technical matters—such as, whether propositions or possibilities are real—that are at best only very distantly related to the Big Questions. When people reflect on their existence and keep pushing for deeper explanations, they end up with these central mysteries:

- Where did we come from, and why are we here? Why do we suffer? Do our lives have an objective meaning? Are our moral, intellectual, and aesthetic values objective parts of reality, or are they only our own creations?
- What is fundamentally real in a human being? Is our apparent "consciousness" really nothing but material events? Do we survive death?
- Are all actions determined by physical forces alone, or do we have free will?
- Do we have any genuine knowledge of reality as it exists in itself, or do our claims even in science merely reflect our cultural or personal interests?
- Does a creator god or other alleged transcendent realities exist?
- Why does anything exist at all?

This book will identify today's key mysteries and some of the answers given by philosophers, but its main thrust is a deeper philosophical question: Are we capable of supplying well-grounded answers to these questions, or at least of reducing them to more manageable problems? Or are these questions we are posing questions that we simply cannot answer? That is, the objective here is not to canvas all the positions today on a given mystery and try to determine which is currently the best option, but to determine whether we have the mental and technologically enhanced capacities to dispel the mystery, at least in principle. For example, when it comes to the "meaning of life," no particular answer will be defended here; rather, the issue here is what that question means exactly, and are we in a position to know whether there is in fact a meaning of life? In short, this book asks whether we can answer the Big Questions at all. In that way, this is a work in metaphilosophy.

Mystery and Knowledge

The Big Questions provoke emotions connected to a sense of mystery—wonder, awe, and humility before reality. But mystery relates to our claims of knowledge. Mysteries arise from our attempts to understand and explain the world and our lives. Thus, they are products of our inquiring into what is real. The sense of philosophical mystery is an intellectual reaction to what we do not know. It does not come merely from ignorance—that is, the lack of knowledge or evidence—or from simply assuming that there is more to reality than we currently know. This sense of mystery can arise even if science provides answers to

Philosophy of Mystery   3

all the questions of how a phenomenon occurs: we may thoroughly understand all the steps and mechanisms by which a seed becomes a blooming flower and still wonder why reality is set up to do that and why we have a mind that can comprehend it. A starry night or the birth of a child may produce similar reactions—the "why" of the events remains after all the "how" questions have all been answered in a way that explaining how a magic trick works does not.

Not knowing something need not provoke a sense of mystery if we think that we know how generally to search for an answer or at least how to address the problem. Nor are philosophical "why" mysteries inherently religious—that is, they need not lead to a religious reaction of answering the questions in terms of a god or another transcendent reality. The majesty of the universe can cause atheists such as Carl Sagan to marvel at being alive on a planet like ours in a galaxy and universe like ours. Even when the "why" type mysteries do not provoke any sense of awe, there is still an almost visceral, "felt" quality to a sense of mystery that ordinary unanswered questions do not provoke. It is not merely the trivial point that there is always more to learn about virtually anything (including ourselves)—it is a sense that the true significance of something is being missed and that we cannot grasp it. That is, we have a sense that there is something more of significance about something that is as yet unknown and that at present we do not know how even to address trying to comprehend it. Problems get solved or at least diminished with study, but mysteries seem to get only greater and more ingrained in reality the more clearly that we see they are there.

Mystery versus Problems

Problems present matters that we do not know but that we think we know how to tackle—we may not know the answer today, but we know how to determine an answer through reasoning and experience. Problems may be difficult to solve—or even impossible to solve as a practical matter—but at least we have an idea of how to proceed against them. Thus, there are many issues in science that are properly labeled "problems," even if we do not have the technology or mathematics to solve them today. Mysteries, on the other hand, present greater difficulties. They are issues that we have more trouble grasping intellectually. We do not know how to get a handle on them, or how to formulate fruitful questions, or even how to approach them. Thus, with mysteries something is incomprehensible and inexplicable—something seems to remain hidden and to defy our attempts at understanding and explanation. We may well not possess the conceptual apparatus to see how to grasp a mystery, and thus we may have difficulty even in articulating what the mystery is. Such mysteries would then be "brute facts" for us—that is, things for which we are incapable of providing any further explanation, and thus things we simply must accept unexplained no matter how arbitrary they may seem.

Thus, the basic criterion for a philosophical mystery is our inability to know how to attack something unknown—a mystery is a puzzle about reality that we, either currently or permanently, do not know even how to address. We may never reach the far side of our galaxy, and so there may be many questions concerning our own galaxy, let alone the rest of the universe, that may remain forever unanswered, but this lack of knowledge does not grab us existentially and thus does not constitute a philosophical mystery. However, theories that postulate "multiple universes" do pull at us as a mystery: the possibility of entirely different universes affects our existence in a way that simple ignorance about other parts of our own universe does not. So too, we may speculate wildly. A classic example is H.G. Wells's suggestion that our entire universe may be only a molecule in a ring on a gigantic hand in some larger universe. Such fantasies do not provoke a sense of not knowing something that is actually real and so does not qualify as a genuine mystery. They remain a product of our imagination untied to anything empirical. But speculations around the edges of scientific theories may broach subjects that we think we should be able to master and thus may present the possibility of mystery.

Something may be an ontic mystery—something in the world that is itself inherently unknowable or paradoxical. Or something may be an epistemic mystery—something that lies beyond our ability to grasp but that otherwise is not mysterious in itself and thus knowable by beings with a different set of cognitive abilities or in a position transcending the natural universe. Our uncertainty by itself does not indicate which type of mystery may be involved or whether the issue may simply be a currently unresolved problem. So too, something may be an epistemic mystery to one person but not to another. What is a mystery also changes over time as our knowledge expands. But the subject for this book is what remains mysterious today generally in a scientifically informed culture.

Since mystery is a matter of our knowledge and understanding, one may think that all mysteries are epistemic and not ontic. Of course, there would be no ontic mysteries to the natural world for an omniscient creator god: such a being would presumably know all the basic aspects of the natural world. But mysteries may persist for all beings within the phenomenal universe, no matter what their mind or sensory apparatus is. That is, there may be aspects of the natural world that any finite beings may not be equipped to solve. Nor is it clear that all of the natural world must be expressible consistently in at least some conceptual system. Thus, there may be brute facts not only for human beings but for all beings existing within the natural universe. Such mysteries would be ontic in nature, not merely epistemic.

Either way, identifying something as a mystery is a conclusion that we are lacking knowledge where we think that something significant exists but that we are stuck on how to conquer that gap in our picture of reality. Declaring something to be a mystery does not give us any knowledge at all of the subject that we are trying to grasp—it only designates an area where our inquiries are stymied. We cannot say of something "It's a mystery" and believe we have understood or explained anything. Mystery is not an explanation and cannot be used to explain any phenomena or another mystery—it is just a blank where we want knowledge. In sum, it is a gap in our knowledge in which we believe something important dwells and that we would very much like to fill but cannot.

"How" mysteries may arise in science concerning the workings of nature. And since philosophical "why" mysteries concern the significance of a natural or human phenomenon, science may prompt "why" mysteries concerning why the world is set up the way it is. This may also lead to mysteries in metaphysics. Science has no direct control over metaphysical questions, although it has an indirect bearing since metaphysics must also account for the best current scientific findings. Chief among the metaphysical mysteries is why there is anything at all rather than nothing. The other major area of "why" mysteries relates to existential responses to our lives. Questions of meaning are foremost here and quickly lead to the entire question of whether transcendent realities exist and affect our lives.

Such philosophical mysteries arise at the limits to our knowledge. This raises the prospect of permanent limitations to our abilities to understand reality. Mysteries may point to aspects of reality that we either have no access to or that we are apparently unable to wrap our minds around. However, apparent mysteries may only be puzzles that we ourselves create by how we currently conceptualize phenomena and therefore by our questions being misguided. Many philosophers see all alleged mysteries as such misguided puzzles that will be dispelled either by science or by a conceptual clarification through philosophical analysis. But genuine mysteries are questions we cannot answer either because of the very nature of reality or because of limitations on our ability to comprehend or analyze reality. They are left standing after all scientific and philosophical analyses are exhausted.

Thus, there are several possibilities: perhaps there is no answer to a given question; perhaps we cannot even know if there is an answer or not; perhaps there is an answer, but we are incapable of knowing it because of our cognitive limitations; perhaps we simply do not know the answer at present but will eventually solve the problem. This in turn presents problems about problems: How do we know that we are currently asking questions that no amount of human ingenuity will ever be able to answer? How do we know at present what is a genuine mystery and what is a solvable puzzle? How do we know we are not artificially generating a false mystery by misconceptualizing a situation? In the case of genuine mysteries, are we so enwrapped in certain problems that we cannot get any distance from them to examine them as phenomena distinct from ourselves? That is, if we cannot separate ourselves from a problem, how can we ever explain it? Will we ever be in a position to answer definitively that something is or is not a mystery?

Identifying Mysteries

Labeling a mystery may give the illusion of understanding it. Naming a problem does help us focus and organize our attention, but labeling a problem only identifies the problem and does not increase our understanding in any way. The method in science for resolving a problem is to "seek the causes." Explanation in science is often equated with the ability to predict a phenomenon's occurrence, but more than a thousand years of accurate predictions apparently confirmed the erroneous Ptolemaic cosmology. Thus, consensus has no authority: it does not necessarily mean that we are converging on the truth. Equally important, whether prediction is always needed for a scientific explanation is open to question—geologists can explain earthquakes even though their predictions are only very rough. And it is very hard to see prediction as even possible in the case of metaphysical mysteries. Explanation more generally is a matter of giving a reason for believing something that is the case should be the case—providing an account that "makes sense" of a phenomenon to us and puts to rest our curiosity for a "why" or a "how." In our everyday lives, we do not look for an ultimate explanation of something; rather, we tend to rest satisfied once we find any connection to something that we take to be unproblematic. With mysteries, however, we do not have that option. We must reach a point where we believe that we have reached the ultimate justification for believing something and where no further explanation seems to us to be needed or even possible. Only when we are thoroughly satisfied that we have reached the bottom do we think that we have finally understood something that we previously found mysterious and thus no mystery remains. But this means that a resolution depends on our feeling content with an explanation—further study of a phenomenon or an advance in science may upset that contentment and lead to new bafflement. Thus, finding mysteries and defusing them can be open ended—what is mysterious and what is not mysterious can change with history.

Whether a particular conundrum is a solvable problem or a genuine mystery is not always obvious even after extensive study. History is full of examples of problems that were once deemed philosophical or theological mysteries that ended up being amenable to scientific analysis. Today perhaps what seems mysterious may be dispelled in the future by a new conceptual approach to the subject being studied; that is, if we conceptualize an issue differently, we may be able to formulate answerable questions and thereby enable science or philosophy to move forward. Thus, some things that seem mysterious to us today because our current reasoning cannot penetrate them may not be an epistemic mystery for all sentient beings or eventually even for ourselves.

Thus, declaring something to be "in principle beyond our understanding" is always risky. Perhaps there are no permanent, indefeasible mysteries, as many philosophers argue, even if there are no prospects for resolving a particular mystery at present. However, the starting point for addressing philosophical mysteries is our current reasoning and empirical study. Theologians may start with revelations, but to address mystery philosophically we cannot take that approach. Any conclusion that something is a mystery is the end of a discussion, not the occasion for invoking a god. (Whether revelations or invoking a god can dispel mysteries will be an issue in chapters 5 and 14.) It is affirming that there are limits to what we can know while believing that there are important aspects of reality yet to know. Identifying something as a potential philosophical mystery will depend on the circumstances of each subject-matter, but in all cases a conclusion that there is a mystery will reveal limitations on our abilities to know—not merely limitations on our current technology, but something that we cannot properly grasp at all. Our capacity to tackle basic questions may well be meager. If so, then some mysteries are indefeasible—matters that our finite minds currently and perhaps permanently cannot master. There would then be limits to our knowledge that we simply cannot pass.

Mysteries Today

It will be maintained here that mysteries surround our knowledge of ourselves and of the universe—in fact, that our big picture of things is permeated with mystery. We do not know if some well-formed questions have unknowable answers or no answer at all. This is certainly not to disparage the genuine knowledge of reality that we do have—it is not to claim "All you know is wrong!" Nor is it to suggest that we curtail philosophy or science in any way in order to preserve a domain for some mystery in our lives. Philosophy and science should be pushed as hard and as far as we can, and anyone who would attempt to limit them should not be listened to. Nevertheless, even if philosophy and science advance as far as is humanly possible, some genuine mysteries to reality still appear to remain—we cannot demystify reality totally no matter how hard we try.

But it must be noted that people generally resist any mystery in their lives—our minds try to explain anything unfamiliar to keep puzzles away so that we can proceed with our daily work. So too, people who are not philosophically minded can simply ignore the whole matter and proceed with their lives undisturbed. (It is worth remembering what Sören Kierkegaard said: one way God punishes people is by making them philosophers.) Moreover, it must also be noted that today philosophers in general hate mysteries: all legitimate questions of reality can in principle be answered either by science or by philosophical analysis. To them, claiming "It's a mystery!" is defeatist. Granted, the conclusion that something is a mystery does end conversations and thus leads only to silence—again, a mystery is not an explanation of anything but only an indicator of a hole in our knowledge where we think something important should be. For many philosophers, a mystery is at best only an attempt to put a positive spin on our ignorance, and to discuss it further only shows a willingness to plunge forward into something that we admit we cannot know. At worst, mysteries are an admission of the defeat of the intellect or an attempt to obfuscate something that can be addressed clearly and defused—any question is meaningless if we cannot know how even to begin to address it, and so any question leading to a claim of mystery can be dismissed out of hand. Thus, the place to begin to determine whether the Big Questions end in mystery is to examine how philosophers have dealt with mysteries in the past.

2

Do We Create Our Own Mysteries?

The point of philosophy is to start with something so simple as not
to seem worth stating, and to end with something so paradoxical that
no one will believe it.

—Bertrand Russell

History of Mystery in Philosophy

Socrates can be credited with making us aware of our own ignorance
in philosophical matters. In the *Theaetetus*, Plato has Socrates say that
wondering about something is the point where philosophy begins. It is
realizing that we do not actually understand what seemed unproblematic. To Socrates, what was "self-evident" to his fellow Athenians
was ripe fodder for analysis. To Plato, we should remain in the state of
wondering about things since this opens up inquiry—it is an unsettling
state, but we should remain open to the inscrutable in the everyday
world. Plato's student Aristotle also stated in his *Metaphysics*: "It is
owing to their wonder that men both now begin and first began to
philosophize." But Aristotle advocated the countervailing trend of
closure: ending wonder by finding the causes of the subject of our
wonder. He valued wonder only as a preliminary step—wonder is
ultimately eliminated by knowledge.

Aristotle's position came to dominate Western thought. By the time
of Thomas Aquinas, remaining in a state of wonder and amazement
was only a sign of sloth: we should keep pressing until we know all the
causes except the one unknowable cause (God). By the beginning of the
modern period, René Descartes listed wonder in *The Passions of the Soul*
as the first of all passions, but he too insisted that this was only a means
for gaining knowledge of things and that an excess of wonder is always
bad—one stuck in astonishment is not apt to investigate causes. And
he believed that his method of analysis would replace all wonder with

9

comprehension. He thought that those who understood his work would see that in the end there is nothing at which to marvel, and thus wonder would cease: his doctrine of "clear and distinct" perception implied that if we understood a thing at all we understood it completely.

Descartes's search for certainty and clarity shaped the modern philosophical quest: since the Age of Enlightenment, a campaign to banish all mystery from the world has been waged in the West. The objective is to maximize our vision and minimize mystery. Of course, many philosophers continue to wonder at the world. For example, Immanuel Kant wondered at "the starry heavens above me and the moral law within me." But the anti-mystery sentiment of most analytic philosophers of the last hundred years is expressed by the logical positivist Moritz Schlick: "No meaningful problem can be unsolvable *in principle*"; "a genuine question is one for which an answer is logically possible"; "in principle there are no limits to our knowledge"; "there is no unfathomable mystery in the world." He could still maintain that "the more we know of the world the more we shall marvel at it" and that "if we should know its ultimate principles and its most general laws, our feeling of wonder and reverence would pass all bounds," but nevertheless he believed that all mysteries will be banished under the glare of reason. Any real question will have a logically possible solution, and scientists—at least in principle—will be able to find it. All we have to do is to formulate the right question with the appropriate concepts. Conversely, if scientists cannot possibly answer a question, there was no real question there in the first place. The only limits to our knowledge are the practical limits of science. To logical positivists, the alleged deep philosophical mysteries of reality do not fall into that category because no observation could in principle solve them—e.g., how could we possibly tell if the world is ultimately mind or matter, and what would it matter to us if we could tell? There is nothing "unsayable" about the real world, and thus no genuine mysteries.

But the positivists' solution failed: they never succeeded in reformulating scientific theories into sentences about sense-experience alone with no theoretical commitments, and without being able to do that, their way of dealing with mysteries rang hollow. Trying, in effect, to produce a new language in which metaphysical questions could not be formulated failed. However, the idea that all mysteries are to be clarified by philosophers and the remaining empirical matters are to be resolved by scientists did prevail. As Ludwig Wittgenstein said in the preface to his *Tractatus Logico-Philosophicus:* "What can be said at all can be said clearly; and whereof one cannot speak, thereof one must be silent." In the body of the work, he states: "When the answer cannot be put into words, neither can the question be put into words. *The riddle* does not exist. If a question can be framed at all, it is also *possible* to answer it." "Everything that can be known can be expressed in the propositions of science." And he ended the *Tractatus* with the famous last line: "What we cannot speak about we must consign to silence." This did not prevent Wittgenstein from expressing "wonder at the existence of the world," although he thought this expression was a misuse of language (because he believed that we cannot imagine the world *not* existing). The philosophers' job was to solve the conceptual problems resulting from, to use Wittgenstein's phrase from his *Philosophical Investigations*, "the bewitchment of our intelligence by means of language." Philosophical questions are of the form "I am in a muddle; I don't know my way," and the purpose of philosophy is "to show the fly the way out of the bottle." Thus, the objective was not to offer a solution to a mystery but simply to show that it never existed in the first place.

By the middle of the twentieth century, the philosophical analysis of ordinary language in Anglo-American philosophy was going strong. Certainly, ill-formed questions lend themselves to being clarified and then revised or discarded. To give a simple example, consider the old question, "What happens when an irresistible force meets an immovable object?" This can be easily resolved by a philosophical analysis: if there is an irresistible force in reality, then by definition there cannot be any immovable objects—anything can be moved; conversely, if there is an immovable object, then there cannot be irresistible forces. Thus, the two cannot meet—if the one thing exists, then the other cannot—and hence the question of what happens if they meet is only a muddle. The question may sound meaningful, but it is as meaningless as asking "If 2 + 2 = 4, what happens when 2 + 2 = 5?" Once the muddle is cleared up, nothing remains, and the apparent mystery vanishes.

Thus, that question had an implicit contradiction revealed by philosophical analysis. For a simple example of how science and philosophy work together in an analysis, consider another old question: "Does a tree falling in the woods with no one around make a sound?" This comes down to what we mean by "sound"—if we mean "the generation of sound waves," then of course the falling tree makes a sound; if we mean "the sensation resulting from the impingement of sound waves on an ear drum," then of course no sound is generated (the sound waves simply dissipate unheard). All that is left after the analysis are scientific accounts of the generation of sound waves and the generation of the sensation of sound in a person and a decision on how to use the word "sound."

Under ordinary language analysis, all alleged mysteries once again would be reduced to empirical problems for scientists or conceptual problems for philosophers—all legitimate questions would be answered. That is, the alleged misuse of ordinary language was seen as the cause of philosophical problems, and the philosopher's task was to point out the confusion—and the alleged mysteries would then evaporate. Unfortunately, the ordinary language movement also did nothing to resolve mysteries: the Big Questions have not proved to be amenable to such dissolution. The mind/body problem and free will were especially popular targets, but the philosophical community finally accepted that these issues, like the other Big Questions, required substantive arguments.

Mystery in Philosophy Today

Nevertheless, the negative attitude toward mysteries persists today. For example, Daniel Dennett states that "[a] mystery is a phenomenon that people don't know how to think about—yet." Mysteries, he claims, are tamed once we know how "to tell the misbegotten questions from the right questions." Alleged mysteries are still divided into two groups: empirical puzzles that scientists either will solve or will at least reduce to "in principle" solvable remainders, and philosophical mistakes generated by our conceptual systems that philosophers will unravel. All that is required is the proper analysis. Thus, the only legitimate unanswerable questions about reality are those that scientists as a practical matter cannot address, but nothing remains obscure in the sense of exceeding our ability to comprehend in principle. We may still feel awe and astonishment about some phenomena or reality itself, but all legitimate questions about reality will have been tamed.

However, there is a surprising lack of consensus among professional philosophers today on any of the Big Questions.[1] As Peter van Inwagen notes: "Disagreement in philosophy is pervasive and irresoluble." And philosophers also change their mind on major issues, as with Antony Flew over whether there is a transcendent deistic source to the natural world. This does not mean that there has been no progress on addressing the Big Questions or that any of the Big Questions are necessarily mysteries—perhaps some philosophical positions maintained today are correct and perhaps arguments may be forthcoming that will convince most opponents. Certainly, the disputants do not take the lack of consensus as a sign of mystery—each believes that he or she and like-minded colleagues have solved a particular alleged mystery or at least have made important strides toward cracking it. But the field is divided up into competing camps rejecting the others and defending their own claims. The competing answers do help to clarify current issues, but the relative lack of progress toward any consensus does suggest that these issues are not simple problems. (And remember the Ptolemaic astronomy problem: consensus does not guarantee moving toward the truth. Here, closure may be no more than a way to quiet our questioning mind rather than the truth.) In science, there are empirical methods to resolve conflicts, and disputes usually are eventually resolved as long as further research is possible. But philosophy has no resolution protocols, and the lack of any way to resolve the disputes may mean that we are stuck with mysteries.

Still, the prevailing view among philosophers today, to the extent they think of mysteries at all, is that there cannot be ontic mysteries: mystery is obviously only our problem—it is a matter of our lack of an ability to know and understand. Epistemic mysteries may remain but only because of the limitations to our mental and technological capacities. On the other hand, perhaps everything is in fact comprehensible with our rationality and technology—since we are a product of nature, our rationality may eventually be able to unravel all of it. If so, it is only a matter of time before we know everything fundamental about reality. Either way, for most philosophers nothing is truly mysterious about reality itself: it must be rational—how could reality have any intrinsic mysteries or paradoxes?

Few books or articles have been written on the subject in philosophy since the rise of logical positivism. Indeed, mysteries are seldom mentioned in most works in epistemology and metaphysics, even just to mention unraveling one. (One exception: the term "mysterians" was applied as an insult by the opponents to one position in the mind/body field, but advocates of that position happily adopted it.) Part of the problem is simply that mystery is not a subject for direct assault—it is the residue remaining after an analysis. Philosophers cannot get the type of closure that they like to get in their arguments when the topic is so murky. Thus, the very idea of "mystery" has fallen into disfavor.

Conceptualization and Mystery

However, the analytic philosophers' assault on mystery does raise an interesting question: do we in fact create mysteries where there are none simply by the way we *conceptualize* situations? Concepts are innately vague, and this can lead to unanswerable questions. For example, should a given stone be classified as a "pebble" or a "rock"? Or the "paradox of the heap": how many straws can we remove from a bale and still have a "bale"? Or consider the ship of Theseus, the legendary founder of Athens, that the Athenians kept in good repair: if we replace broken parts of a ship one by one, when do we no longer have the original ship? What if the original ship was insured and the ship now consisting entirely of new parts is in a wreck—does the insurance company have to pay? What if someone builds a ship by refashioning all the discarded pieces—which ship is now insured? Perhaps pushing philosophical analysis on any subject far enough leads to all things looking fuzzy and mysterious.

We do create puzzles here, but no one considers these to be real mysteries—they are only products of, for example, applying our discrete "digital" concepts to a continuous "analog" world, and no one but philosophers linger over the resulting problems. But conceptualizations can present deeper problems. Consider how our conceptualizations play a role in seemingly straightforward empirical questions. For example, the question "What is the longest river in the world?" seems simple enough—we just get a globe and measure all the rivers in the world and see which one is longest. As things stand, the Nile River is the longest. However, Mark Twain in *Life on the Mississippi* mentions something relevant here. The Mississippi was originally mapped by Europeans north to south from its headwaters in Minnesota down to Louisiana and the Gulf of Mexico. Thus, when the Mississippi met a big body of water flowing in from the west, that body was considered a separate river—the Missouri. But if the Mississippi had been mapped south to north, then when the mappers reached the confluence of the two bodies of water the mappers would have considered the Mississippi as turning west since that was the larger branch. This means there would be no Missouri River but only a much longer Mississippi and a "new" river heading north (perhaps called the "Minnesota River"), and the revised "Mississippi River" would then be the longest river in the world. Thus, how we conceptualize the situation—how we label the rivers—determines the answer to an apparently simple empirical question.[2]

Or consider the famous paradoxes of the ancient Greek Zeno. By arguments that are now familiar he showed, for example, that a rabbit, no matter how fast, could not catch up to a tortoise with a head start, or that an arrow shot from a bow could not move. We know from experience that these situations are not so, but the point is that we can conceptualize things in such a way that shows them to be *impossible*—we create a false "mystery" by how we conceptualize a situation. This leads to an unsettling question: how do we know that our conceptualizations and questions are not so totally misguided that they create problems where there are none, just as with these paradoxes? Perhaps, as many philosophers believe, all philosophical mysteries are in fact no more than by-products of our misrepresenting reality, and all we need to do is to devise concepts that better reflect the nature of reality. We can revise concepts—for example, in the Copernican revolution, new meanings were given to earlier astronomical terms—and that may be all that is needed to dispel deep-seated mysteries. In the mind/body field, perhaps what we need to do is to devise a conception of ourselves that does not reflect a dualism of "mind" and "body" and our sense of not understanding will disappear.

More generally, what we consider things to be depends on how we conceptualize things, and when a paradox arises we may be able to figure out another conceptual scheme that avoids the conflict of ideas crystalized in the paradox. For example, the ancient Egyptian word for "south" literally means "to go upstream" and the word for "north" means "to go downstream," reflecting the northerly flow of the Nile River. So when Egyptian soldiers encountered the Euphrates River, which flows south, they had to call it, paradoxically, "that circling water that goes downstream in going upstream." The physical situation itself was obviously not paradoxical—the soldiers could clearly see the direction that the Euphrates was flowing—but their language simply could not handle what they saw. We now have conceptual systems that consistently handle the situation with more abstract concepts of "north" and "south" that are not tied to local phenomena and thus avoid the paradox caused solely by the ancient Egyptian language.

This suggests that at least some paradoxes are of our own making: they are only the result of how we conceptualize situations. But all paradoxes arise only when our *concepts* conflict with each other, not necessarily because of the way reality is. Our ideas then seem to produce absurdities. Paradoxes often occur at the limits of knowledge on a given subject. They can also occur directly from our conceptual systems, as shown by the paradoxes of self-reference—the most famous being the Liar's Paradox ("This sentence is false"—if it is true, then it is false; if it false, then it is true). Paradoxes in science lead to attempts at reconceptualizing reality. But if we cannot get around a paradox, we are left with a mystery: reality may in fact involve paradoxes or perhaps we simply cannot see reality clearly enough or think deeply enough to develop a system that circumvents the problem. If we are left with a paradox, how can we tell if the problem lies with reality itself or is only a by-product of our all-too-human conceptualizations? Conversely, are we routinely imposing consistent order where there in fact is none?

We accept the Aristotelean laws of identify (x is x and not not-x), noncontradiction (nothing can be both x and not-x), and the excluded middle (anything is either x or not-x with no third possibility), and we think that a contradiction in a statement about the world indicates that one of two conflicting claims must be wrong. That is, we believe that the universe cannot contain paradoxes because we believe that any self-contradictory statement cannot be true. We would not know what to believe in a self-contradictory description of anything. If someone said, "Both the Mets and Yankees won last year's World Series," what are we supposed to believe when we know that only one team can win it? But why are we unable to accept two halves of a contradiction simultaneously? Is it because of the way our brain works, and so we are incapable of thinking any other way? Or is just the rules of how any language must operate to be intelligible? Or is it because reality itself cannot be contradictory?

For most philosophers, the laws of logic are only a matter of the relation of our statements—they are a restriction on our statements and do not constrain reality in any fashion. Claiming that something is both "x" and "not-x" tells us nothing whatsoever about that thing or about anything else and thus is meaningless. But philosophers routinely draw a consequence of this without any discussion: reality must be logically consistent—it must conform without any contradictions to some set of concepts that we can devise. However, it is not clear why reality must conform to our concepts without contradictions or how we can be certain that contradictions among our ideas must be only the product of our conceptual systems.[3] Why must reality be capable of being fitted consistently into some conceptual scheme that beings with our particular brains can devise? In fact, the consequence of the laws of logic being only a matter of our statements is that logic in no way compels anything to be logical or prohibits reality from being illogical. Perhaps there may be aspects of reality that lie outside of any conceptual horizon that any beings existing inside the natural universe could conceive. Indeed, many philosophers throughout history have accepted limitations to our ability to understand reality. For Plato, the fact that we inhabit an imperfect material world limits our ability to comprehend the real world of the realm of perfect forms: we are like prisoners in a cave who can see only moving shadows on the cave walls caused by real people walking by a fire—we cannot see the reality causing the shadows. So too, for Immanuel Kant (as discussed in the next chapter): our mental abilities cannot comprehend the world-in-itself. But it is not clear how we can resolve this matter of logic and reality.

One final issue about the nature of conceptualizations must be noted: may our conceptualizations not only create apparent mysteries but also *shield* us from a genuine mystery? That is, do we supply a conceptualization or explanation to what is in fact a genuine ontic mystery that only makes us erroneously feel that we understand it? Do our conceptions obscure much of reality? For example, do reductive explanations completely miss nonphysical factors at work in nature? This leads to a troubling bottom line: even if we think that we have solved a mystery or reduced it to a solvable problem by a reconceptualization of a situation, how can we be sure? Or does our perennial view of something that never seemed mysterious miss something vital that would expose a deep mystery? Perhaps future conceptualizations will open up new mysteries. And does this mean that our conceptualizations are too impermanent to determine today whether there are genuine mysteries to reality? Do we simply open and close "mysteries" by our very fragile conceptualizations? Or, are all human beings endowed with an unrevisable set of concepts that conditions us to see things as paradoxical when there are none? Does an irresolvable paradox or other mystery indicate something profound about reality or only show that we are way off the track for a proper understanding of reality and that we need a new way of looking at things? How can we ever tell what is the true situation?

Asking Questions and Demanding Answers

It is often said that the questions asked in philosophy are more important than the answers proffered at any moment. But the questions reflect how we see reality, and particular questions may be faulty: how do we know that we are asking questions that will lead to genuine final knowledge? Perhaps we are closing off aspects of reality by our questions. The limits of our language may not set the limits of our world, as Ludwig Wittgenstein thought, but language does encode what we take to be real and how we conceptualize the world.[4]

William James spoke of "our indomitable desire to cast the world into a more rational shape in our minds than the shape into which it is thrown there by the crude order of our experience" and that "[t]he world has shown itself, to a great extent, plastic to this demand of ours for rationality." Looking for a "because" for our "why" questions is a sign of rationality, but philosophers may also suffer from a compulsion: trying to dispel all mystery by demanding reasons for mysteries *even if there are none*. The mindset to resolve all mysteries at all costs is the "philosopher's disease"—that is, the belief that, even if we do not have the correct answer today, we can be certain that one is forthcoming because there must always be a sufficient reason that we can find for anything. Talk of mystery simply covers up confused thinking. Looking for a reason must be pursued, but this approach becomes counterproductive when the assumption that there is always a reason will not be given up under any circumstances—when one is certain that there must be a "because" no matter what. Even if as a matter of simple logic there must be a "x" or "not-x" answer to any meaningful question, it is another matter to assume that that answer must be available to us.[5] Such a predisposition may distort our ontic and epistemic situation in the world—the demand can lead to dismissing legitimate questions and forcing erroneous answers and fraudulent reasons where there are none. It may lead to accepting a partial understanding as a sufficient or total understanding. At a minimum, this creates conceptual barriers between us and reality by directing our attention away from direct contact with reality and focusing it on the conceptual products of our mind. And why the universe must be transparent and free of paradoxes or mysteries to finite beings such as ourselves would also be an issue that must be addressed. And if the universe does indeed turn out to be transparent, that itself may turn out to be a mystery. But perhaps our rationality cannot be celebrated as all-encompassing—genuine mysteries in fact would then become only deeper and more entrenched as we study more of reality.

Unless we can prove that all well-formed "why" questions must have a "because" (and that appears hard to do), we should remain immune to the philosopher's disease and should remain open to the possibility of indefeasible mysteries to reality. Whether the basic philosophical mysteries of the Big Questions will ever be resolved as science advances is a real issue. Conceptual clarification by philosophers would of course be helpful at any point in history, but some questions that we accept at a given time as well formed may be unanswerable by us even in principle. That they are unanswerable does not make them literally meaningless even if we not are in a position to know how even to begin to answer them—in fact, they may be of utmost importance to us. So too, when studying mysteries, we must remember the danger noted above that we may only be fooling ourselves by the answers we provide: we may never be in a position to guarantee that there are no genuine mysteries to reality—we may simply be supplying conceptualizations that quiet our mind but that do not reflect reality. This is a mystery about mysteries that is always present.

Notes

1. A 2009 survey of professional philosophers shows the lack of consensus on any major philosophical topic (Chalmers 2015: 351–352). For example, on the mind/body problem, 57 percent accepted or leaned toward physicalism, 27 percent nonphysicalism, and 16 percent other; on the question of God, 73 percent accepted or leaned toward atheism, 15 percent theism, and 13 percent other. Only a "nonskeptical realism" about the external world reached over 80 percent support (82%). David Chalmers believes that new insights, methods, and concepts may finally lead to answering the questions because all truths are logically entailed by fundamental empirical truths concerning fundamental natural properties and laws discovered by scientists—none are

inscrutable. But he acknowledges that not all philosophers today (e.g., Colin McGinn and Peter van Inwagen) are so optimistic: they believe that some answers may be unknowable because the lack of progress on the Big Questions shows that human beings do not have "the level of intelligence" to answer some of them (ibid.: 368–369).

2. Today, the Nile is once again longer because engineers have straightened the Mississippi by cutoffs.

3. It should be pointed out that most of us operate normally with contradictions permeating our everyday thought. Many of us do not try to make all our beliefs consistent with each other but simply accept dilemmas unresolved. F. Scott Fitzgerald opined: "The test of a first-rate intelligence is the ability to hold two opposed ideas in the mind at the same time and still retain the ability to function." But that is not the issue here—here the issue is the theoretical possibility of a consistent conceptual system reflecting the basic nature of reality.

4. Bryan Magee correctly points out that the limits of what we can apprehend determine the limits of what is linguistically intelligible to us, not vice versa.

5. Badly formed questions can distort situations. Even apparently simple "yes or no" questions may have a background that entails implicit claims that make a question ill-formed. For example, the classic question, "Have you stopped beating your wife?" cannot be answered "yes or no" by a husband who has never beaten his wife.

3
Do We Know Anything at All?

Calculate what man knows and it cannot compare to what he does not know. Calculate the time he is alive and it cannot compare to the time before he was born. Yet man takes something so small and tries to exhaust the dimensions of something so large! Hence he is muddled and confused and can never get anywhere. Looking at it this way, how do we know that the tip of a hair can be singled out as the measure of the smallest thing possible? Or how do we know that heaven and earth can fully encompass the dimensions of the largest thing possible?

—Zhuangzi

Do we have any real knowledge of the world, or is everything a mystery? Was the oracle at Delphi correct in calling Socrates the wisest of all men because he claimed to know so little? When it comes to the fundamental nature of reality, we may feel that we know little or nothing, but in everyday matters we are confident that we know things—I know whether it is raining outside my window right now, how many people there are in my room right now, and so on. So too, we have solid scientific knowledge, even though we readily accept that knowledge of things may be inexhaustible—there is always more to learn about virtually anything (including ourselves). But the issue here is the basic question of whether we can in fact truly claim to know anything at all. To know something rather than merely to believe it involves objectivity and certainty—it is a type of universal true belief.[1] However, can we be certain about any of our claims of knowledge?

Pushing Our Search for Knowledge

As discussed, the question of unresolvable mystery arises when looking at our claims to know and understand, especially in our claims to give a final explanation to what we consider known phenomena. An explanation is more than merely identifying the cause of something—it is establishing that we think we understand how or why it exists. Normally we can stop at intermediate explanations: we do not need a PhD in physics to repair a household electrical problem—we can stop with lesser understanding to live our lives in the everyday world. But that is not an option when we deal with philosophical matters. It is when we push to our final understanding of a phenomenon that the issue of mystery arises.

Our knowledge-claims are oriented toward our needs and reflect our points of view. Thus, they are not free of presumptions. No description or explanation is dictated by reality in a simple and straightforward empiricist manner but reflects our interests and how we see things. Science presents a particular point of view on how questions are to be answered; individual scientific theories add more restrictions. This does not mean that our claims are necessarily wrong but only that our knowledge is not necessarily a reflection of reality. Moreover, changes in theories throughout the history of science usually represent progress, but this also means that scientific knowledge-claims today are most likely transient and so should be held only tentatively. In particular, our view of reality on the subatomic and cosmic scales may be very different in a hundred years.

So too in philosophy: what is "self-evident" changes as knowledge advances. Few today would agree with Descartes that since the idea of God as a substance that is infinite, eternal, immutable, omniscient, and omnipotent is the "most true, most clear, and most distinct of all the ideas that are in [his] mind," God must exist. Similarly, the changing methods and positions in philosophy in the last century do not inspire confidence that final knowledge-claims are being attained. Overall, as David Chalmers puts it, "arguments for strong conclusions in philosophy (unlike in science and mathematics) almost always have premises and inferences that can be rejected without too much cost," and arguments from even "consensus premises are relatively powerless to settle the big questions of philosophy." Basic premises may be wrong, and in what is known as Frank Ramsey's maxim, chronic philosophical disputes commonly rest on mistaken assumptions that are shared by all the disputants. So too, Gary Gutting points out that intuitions of what is "self-evident" play a greater role in philosophy than is normally thought, and there is a surprising lack of rigorous argument even in contemporary philosophy. George Lakoff and Mark Johnson argue that metaphors grounded in our embodied experience in the world permeate our thought and are not merely literary devices—we have no "pure reason." Our reasoning also typically reflects cognitive biases and logical errors. The role of emotions, attitudes, and personal background in our evaluations and decision making is also gaining attention in philosophy today. All of this leads many to endorse a fallibilism in which we must continually reevaluate our conclusions in light of the danger of unnoticed prejudices and ungrounded intuitions.

Thus, paradoxically, as our knowledge increases, our confidence and sense of certainty in basic claims has decreased.

Explanations and Brute Facts

Another issue is how we can be certain that an explanation or justification is in fact final. There is always the danger that we may have stopped looking for a complete or ultimate explanation too soon. More importantly, as Karl Popper argued: "There is no explanation that is not in need of a further explanation." When it comes to the Big Questions, nothing ends until we think that no more explanations are needed. But for any explanation, we can always ask "why that?" Every premise must be supported by some reason, and the process of justifying any conclusion never ends and thus is never complete. In a trilemma named in honor of Baron von Munchausen, philosophers as far back as the Greek skeptic Agrippa have asserted that all arguments end in one of three ways: circular reasoning, an infinite regress of justifications, or unproven assumptions. The only way around this is finding foundations that need no further support, but philosophers today discount that as even a possibility: nothing is self-justifying or self-explanatory. So too, the contingency of all intuitions rules out the possibility that something is truly "self-evident." All arguments that end in an ultimate explanation involve accepting something as a brute fact—that is, something that simply must be accepted without further justification or explanation and thus whose existence is itself a mystery. Because of this incompleteness of any argument ending in a brute fact, such facts present mysteries and are not the foundation for any certainty in knowledge—one cannot appeal to what is accepted as unexplained as a premise for an argument for complete knowledge.

Thus, our claim to know or understand definitively never ends in closure. We have to admit that our knowledge is not complete. Philosophers may be dissatisfied with this and discuss it very little, but brute facts limit all our efforts at being thoroughly rational. (As noted in the last chapter and below, many philosophers insist that reality cannot be irrational—that is, it must meet our standards of reasoning all the way down.) To accept mystery is to admit there are brute facts but to refuse to accept any temporary intermediate point as a final answer. Even the prospect that what is currently unexplainable will someday be explained only leads to new brute facts. Indeed, how in fact do we know when we have reached a true brute fact that "just is" and thus is incapable of any further explanation? Are we actually only fooling ourselves with our current explanation of a mystery? Have we allayed our curiosity only by connecting a mystery to something from our ordinary experience that really is no explanation at all? How can we be sure that what satisfies us today is indeed the final answer removing a philosophical mystery? In science and mathematics, what seems certain in one generation is sometimes overthrown in the next. Do we have enough information at this date for any final answer? Our curiosity may be laid to rest, but how can we ever really be certain that we know that our alleged explanation is correct? Perhaps with more information we may reconceptualize what we deem real and remove the problem that led to a sense of mystery concerning some fact. Nevertheless, the "subjective" element that explanations necessarily rely upon—our experience and our understanding—must always be part of the picture.

Problems on the Path to a Final Explanation

There are also limitations on human experience and our ability to reason that must be contended with. Even when extended by technology, there are limits to what we can sense on submicroscopic and astronomical scales. This limits what we can ever see of reality. Henri Poincaré asked the interesting question of what our physics would be like if the sky were permanently overcast and we could never see through the clouds. By extension, we must ask whether whatever we are able to see on scales outside the everyday world is not also limited and incomplete.

Scientists also raise issues related to whether we can believe our eyes. We like to think that we normally see the external world "as it really is," but neuroscientists have found otherwise. Some issues are these: the subjectivity of our perception of objective light waves, illustrated by color blindness and by the puzzle that if I could tap into your optic nerve would I perceive what you call "blue" as what I call "yellow"; that animals experience different ranges of the light spectrum; whether synesthesia (e.g., seeing numbers as having color) suggests that we might have seen the world very differently if we had evolved differently; the experience of phantom limbs; and why some optical illusions persist even when we know that they are illusions. But the principal problem is broader: there is evidence that our conscious and subconscious mind *creates* images of the world, not merely filters or structures sensory data. Experiments show that our mind "corrects" and constructs things (e.g., filling in visual and audio blind spots). Apparently, our mind automatically creates a coherent, continuous narrative out of all the sensory input it receives. What we actually "see" is a reconstruction of the world, and this leads to the question of whether our visual world is only a "grand illusion." According to the neuroscientist Andrew Newberg, the mind seems overall to have difficulty separating fantasies from facts—it sees things that are not there and does not see some things that are. The mind does not try to create a fully detailed map of the external world; instead, it selects a handful of cues and then fills in the rest with conjecture, fantasy, and belief. Our brain constructs one subconscious map that relates to our survival and another that reflects our conscious awareness of the world.

Obviously, we must have some reliable knowledge of the world if we are to survive, and we can utilize technology for more objective observations, but the issue of the "grand illusion" survives concerning our overall picture of reality. We must ask by what independent source we can verify our claims as ultimately true, especially for the fundamental matters of the Big Questions that are not related to immediate survival. We cannot step back from the world and check whether there is an accurate correspondence between our claims and the world.[2]

Immanuel Kant in his *Critique of Pure Reason* presented another troubling prospect: we never can experience the world "as it is in itself" independent of our senses. Rather, our minds are active in constructing the world of appearances: we see only phenomena—that is, the noumenal world as structured through mental concepts such as space, time, substance, and causation—and can never know what the world is like in itself independent of the structuring that our mind necessarily employs. Appearances are created by our subconscious imposition of a priori categories of understanding upon what is real.[3] Such ways of organizing the world are innate to all human beings and are not derived from experience or thought—we are born with them and cannot get around them. Even "mind" and "external world" are appearances and not part of the world in itself. Thus, what our common sense says is real is not in fact reality as it exists apart from us. Even space, time, and substance are not part of the noumenal realm—they do not exist in their own right but are only "species of our representations." Our reason may posit noumena, but even our "pure reason" cannot reflect the nature of noumenal reality but only the world of appearances. All we know of noumenal reality is that it is not like the phenomenal world of our experience. Our minds cannot reach the noumenal realm in any sense, and thus we have no conceptions of it—it is only an inference we make to explain why we have experiences. And we also create a false realism by reifying the content of our sense-experience into an external world: if all conscious beings ceased to exist, the entire phenomenal world—including all of space-time—would also cease to exist since that realm is dependent on us.

But if we cannot know "true reality," what is truth? Yet Kant did not deny that we have genuine knowledge of a real world: there are certain ways that things-in-themselves appear to beings with our cognitive structures, and true claims reflect those appearances. He argued only that this knowledge is packaged in forms we ourselves supply—the *content* of knowledge derives from our experience of the real world, even though we impose the *order or form* upon that content. Nevertheless, appearances always remain different from reality, and sense-experience cannot get us to that reality. And trying to think about reality-in-itself only leads to unresolvable antinomies (e.g., whether the universe is eternal or not, or whether it is made up of simple parts or not): advocates of each horn of a given antimony claim that the other one leads to absurdities. We cannot even speak of it as one or many. Contradictions reveal nothing inherent in the reality-in-itself but only reveal the limits of our understanding. Reason is confined to more practical matters within the phenomenal world.

Thus, if Kant is correct, there is an impasse: the real world is cut off from our cognitive abilities—the real world is simply unknowable and thus unconceptualizable by us. Similarly, we cannot know the self, the subject of consciousness: it is what observes (the "transcendental self") but cannot itself be observed. The noumenal realm hence is unknowable in a different way that some distant part of our galaxy may forever be unknowable to us. For Kant, "Human reason has this peculiar fate that in one species of its knowledge it is burdened by questions that, prescribed by the very nature of reason itself, it is not able to ignore, but that, as transcending all its powers, it is also not able to answer."

This unknowability of the noumenal realm solidifies a place for mystery in Kantian thought. Moreover, one can ask where the categories of our mental life (time, space, and so forth) come from. Aren't they also real? The spaceless and timeless noumenal reality is forever inaccessible, forever hidden behind a veil of appearances that we have no choice but to create. Our knowledge is limited to the phenomena that we ourselves partially generate: we know only the world of sense-impressions and according to Kantians these tell us nothing of reality-in-itself. In fact, we can only infer its existence at all. In the end, we are left with a complete mystery concerning the realm of reality existing independent of our mind and senses. Thus, if Kant's thought is accepted, mystery is permanently established in all our thought and experience.

Reasoning about Reality

Even if we reject Kant's position, there may well be limits to what embodied, evolved beings such as ourselves—indeed, any finite being within the universe—can understand of the universe, whether we are created by nature or a god: there may be limits to what our reasoning can achieve even if we are the product of what we want to understand. All evolved animals are limited in their cognitive abilities, and we are no different. We might like to think that our minds are unfettered and limitless, but our consciousness has evolved so that we can interact with our environment (the surface of one planet) more effectively in matters of survival, even if it also participates in the reality that generated it. As Bryan Magee says, our bodily apparatus has evolved without contact to most of what we know exists, and it would be a sheer coincidence if we had the capacity to know *all* of it. Even if our consciousness does participate in reality, we have reason to believe that we are not able to come up with correct ideas for all ultimate how-mysteries. Moreover, how can we ever know answers to the ultimate why-mysteries of reality when we cannot turn all of reality into objects for examination? As noted in the last chapter, there is no reason to believe that the universe must be transparent to beings such as ourselves or that all of the universe's features must be expressible consistently in one of our conceptual systems.

So too, even to start reasoning we must presuppose that reasoning works. But can we trust our reason? There is no abstract "reason" but only our concrete reasoning, and our reasoning is not as firm as we usually believe. Such reasoning changes with cultures and history. Aristotelian laws of logic may be transcultural standards that apply in all valid arguments, but all arguments depend on different premises and rules of what constitutes a valid deduction. (Lewis Carroll in one of his more serious works also showed that the justification of inferences itself involves an inference.) Premises may hold hidden assumptions that we do not see. Consider the "A white horse is not a horse" paradox formulated in China about 300 BCE. It can be schematized as follows:

(1) A black horse is a horse.
(2) A white horse is not a black horse.
(3) Therefore, a white horse is not a horse.

No one doubts the two premises, and the conclusion does follow. This bedeviled Chinese logicians for some time. The problem is that the first premise is ambiguous depending on what the meaning of "is" is—"is" can mean either identity (all horses are black) or being a member of a class (a black horse is one type of horse). With the first meaning of "is," the conclusion does follow; with the second, it does not. How do we know that deductions that hold as valid today are not similarly loaded or have other problems that we simply do not see? Indeed, today's quintessential deduction actually involves circularity:

(1) All men are mortal.
(2) Socrates is a man.
(3) Therefore, Socrates is mortal.

The problem is that we cannot know that the first premise is true unless we already know the conclusion is true. That is, the first premise is not a matter merely of definitions, such as "All bachelors are unmarried men," but an observation based on our experience of human beings, and so we must already know that the conclusion is true (since Socrates is part of "all men") before we can adopt the first premise.

Why we have rationality at all—that is, the ability to recognize valid arguments and reasons—needs explaining. Reasoning about everyday matters is one thing, but gaining scientific knowledge about aspects of reality outside our everyday world is another. So is being able to develop abstract mathematics. Philosophers debate whether our reason can be relied upon at all if it is only the product of our highly contingent evolution—why should the fallible ravings of what Charles Darwin called a "monkey mind" reveal any truths at all? If determinism is true and our thoughts are only the deterministic output of our brain, how can any reasoning be valid? Or are there independent standards that assure that our reason can reveal something of reality? We may not embrace empiricism, since there is little reason to suppose that sense-experience must be the only source of knowledge for beings with minds like ours—especially when our reason must correct optical illusions and when we do not know whether sense-impressions reflect reality-in-itself—but we also should be cautious in what we think that the reasoning of our particular evolved brains can accomplish.

One common position in philosophy today is that rationality demands that in principle there are no barriers to our knowledge and nothing can end in unknowable mysteries—ultimately there can be no mysteries to the world. If we know that something exists, we must know something about it, even if there is always more to learn about it. The thing must have some characteristic that distinguishes it from nothingness or we would not know it exists at all—if it did not, there would be no difference between believing it exists and believing it did not. But this line of reasoning leads to the "paradox of knowability": common sense tells us that there probably are truths that human beings will never know, but logically it is impossible to know that there is some statement that is true but unknown to anyone. That is, if a given truth is in principle knowable, then it is in fact known to exist—to know that it is unknowable, we would already have to know it. Thus, there can be no unknown truths: if a true statement were in principle unknowable, then it is unknowable that it is a truth that is not known. Other philosophers argue that there are statements that must be either true or false, but (following Gödel's theorems in mathematics) it is impossible to tell which: there are pairs of propositions that are knowable, and one must be true and one false, but because of the limits of our knowledge, we can never tell which one is true and which one is false.

Skepticism

Also consider the specter of skepticism—that is, that we have no grounds to consider any claim to be true about the external world or about any alleged reality other than our present state of mind. The word "skeptic" comes from the Greek "to investigate," and the result of their investigations is that all our claims to knowledge are unfounded and only opinions. According to Sextus Empiricus, skeptics do not make any firm claim of the truth of anything they assert—they merely accurately report each thing presented to their senses at a given moment. Skeptics present arguments attacking the very root of knowledge and leading to one conclusion: all knowledge-claims can be doubted—there is no convincing argument for believing that our mental capacities thoroughly and accurately reflect reality since we cannot prove the reliability of the means we employ in our apparent contact with the external world. There is nothing that we can be sure about, and by traditional standards we can have no knowledge at all without certainty. Skeptics can ask of any explanation or justification that we advance "How do you know?" and this process would go on *ad infinitum*. So too, we need a criterion for truth, but then we would need a criterion establishing that criterion and so on *ad infinitum*. The same applies to any proofs. But this does not mean that skeptics dogmatically assert that all empirical beliefs are necessarily *false*—we cannot know that either. Since statements about the experience of phenomena are accepted, while any statement, pro or con, about the underlying nature of things is denied, this leads to accepting a conventional social life but to suspending all judgments of truth or falsity of beliefs about the world or values. Thus, all belief-commitments are eliminated. (According to Pyrrho of Elis, this neutral state of belief leads to peace of mind.) Philosophical skepticism is not the practical skepticism of scientists in which their theories are treated as tentative and open to revision—indeed, skeptics deny there is any progress in knowledge. Rather, it is the universal questioning of all evidence for claims about the external world.

Such skepticism arose in the West with the ancient Greeks, and in searching for absolute certainty, Descartes in his *First Meditation* firmly planted a version of skepticism in modern philosophy. His attempt to find irrefutable foundations upon which absolutely certain knowledge could be built led to his famous *cogito ergo sum*. He thought that the only certainty we can have is from the innate ideas God implanted in our minds that we see clearly and distinctly. That is, all we truly know are only those matters about which it is impossible for us to be wrong. However, he could not get past the possibility that we may be dreaming or that an "evil demon" may be misleading us about what our senses seem to be telling us about the world. (Like many others, I once was discussing Descartes's point, assuring a listener that I knew with absolute certainty that I was awake and that nothing could convince me otherwise, only to wake up to find that I was dreaming all along.) Today the analogies are to the possibility that we are no more than a brain in a vat hooked up to a computer on some other planet with more advanced technology than ours, or that we are all only characters in the world of *The Matrix*.[4] But there is no way we can know or test whether this is the case or not: nothing that occurs in our phenomenal world can show us that we are a brain in a vat or not. (Thus, G.E. Moore's appeal to common sense in response to skepticism does not work—we would be just as certain of the world if we were a brain in a vat.) All we can be certain of is that even in those circumstances we are conscious and therefore must exist at this moment—*cogito ergo sum*—not anything about what our mind and senses deliver.[5]

Thus, philosophical skepticism is a product of the quest for certainty. Some philosophers today change the standard of what constitutes "knowledge" in response to skepticism, but most concede that such skepticism cannot be refuted. Skepticism would avoid all possibility of error, but philosophers dismiss taking it seriously since it requires a standard for knowledge that is beyond unrealistic—this standard is impossible in principle to satisfy since refuting it would require that we stand outside of the world. Most believe that we should trust our senses and rationality until they are proven unreliable. But as long as realism is accepted, the possibility that we are profoundly wrong in our claims about the world cannot be gotten around.

However, philosophical skepticism is a theoretical point. It is a second-order claim about the nature of our first-order knowledge-claims about the world: it does not mean that all our first-order knowledge-claims are necessarily wrong or that we do not know anything—it means only that we do not have absolute foundations upon which to assert the certainty of claims. (If skeptics claimed to know nothing about the world, they would have to admit that they know at least that they do not know this—but, like skepticism, that claim would be a second-order claim about our first-order knowledge-claims about the world necessarily being wrong.) Thus, we can accept the skeptics' assault on the certainty of first-order claims and still go about our lives as before. We do not need irrefutable proof that the world or other persons exist in order to proceed with life. As David Hume said, radical skepticism about the world's existence cannot be refuted, but it is not a *live* option—we cannot live as a total skeptic.

To deny the first-order knowledge-claims themselves leads to solipsism—the belief that only you exist and that the rest of the apparent world is an illusion—and, as with Pyrrho, to renouncing all practical living. Nevertheless, today Peter Unger does advocate a scorched earth skepticism that leaves nothing standing: we have no grounds to believe our senses or our reasoning about claims based on our sense-experience; and since no one can ever know anything, nobody can ever be justified or even reasonable in believing anything or ever be happy about anything or regret anything. We have no assurance that there is any as yet unknown reason for believing or refuting any claim, and so all first-order claims must be denied. But Unger admits that he has trouble living up to this creed.

Most philosophers today think that there is no good reason to accept skepticism. They simply shrug their shoulders and move on to topics they find more interesting. (Robert Fogelin says that East Coast skeptics are deeply troubled by realizing that their knowledge is limited, while West Coast skeptics find the idea liberating.) We can still accept the second-order claim of skepticism that we cannot give a definitive reason for believing the "real world" is so but go on living in it. So too, we can live denying solipsism even if we concede that we cannot logically refute it.[5] Thus, we are in the paradoxical situation in which we can affirm the principle of skepticism while recognizing that we must actually live as if it were untrue.

This leads to the question of whether skepticism is really a reason for accepting mystery about the existence of the external world at all, rather than merely being a theoretical point about our inability to attain certainty. Nevertheless, the value of radical skepticism is that it reveals that we have no certainty on the basic ontic topic of the reality of an external world.

Thus, the thrust of skepticism is that we are left with mystery about the fundamental nature of what is real. We are deluding ourselves when we think that we truly know with confidence anything basic about reality beyond that we exist and have mental states. This has the valuable effect of countering any dogmatic assertions or unsupported metaphysical accounts of the nature of reality, but it goes further: most broadly, skepticism means that we cannot guarantee any knowledge-claims for a reality independent of our present state of mind, and thus that we cannot be certain that any alleged outside world does not ultimately remain a mystery to us.

Agnosticism

But even if we dismiss skepticism as requiring too much certainty, we still must consider *agnosticism* about our knowledge of the world. Agnosticism also involves believing that we cannot be certain about things that many people accept. It is not confined merely to whether God exists; it can include other topics such as free will or what is the best available interpretation of quantum physics. It need not be global like philosophical skepticism. And unlike skeptics, agnostics accept that there are good arguments for or against the existence of something: in most matters of our alleged knowledge, one side will have the stronger argument about whether something exists or not, but for some matters there currently are no *compelling* arguments one way or the other, and thus we are left unable to affirm or deny the claim. (Thus, agnosticism is not, as commonly portrayed, indifference.)

In sum, agnostics deny that we have enough knowledge on a particular subject to commit one way or the other to its existence—there is no way to tip the scale to belief or disbelief. Either we cannot know the truth or we in fact do know it but we are not in a position to know that we know. Strong agnostics assert the impossibility of knowledge of some subject in principle, and other agnostics assert there is a lack of sufficient knowledge of it at present to make a determination. Further evidence may cause agnostics to change their position on a given topic, if we are able to gain more evidence. That something is unknowable does not necessarily require agnosticism—Kant was not agnostic about the existence of the noumenal realm. So too, agnostics need not suspend judgment in practice: they may adopt one position (e.g., they may have little doubt that the external world exists and thus have a high degree of confidence in acting on the assumption that it exists), but they admit that their position is not epistemically superior to that of those who adopt the opposite position. They may also disagree on what counts as "good enough" or "sufficient" or "compelling" evidence for a position.

Agnostics may try to remain neutral on a given topic of vital importance to our lives, but that is often hard to do—for example, whether there is free will or life after death. Should one believe without sufficient evidence? Does one have the epistemic right to do so? This brings up the ethics of belief. William Clifford argued that it is always wrong in every situation for anyone to believe anything upon insufficient public evidence.

William James responded that a "leap of faith" is acceptable on issues of human existence that are "forced, live, and momentous" when the evidence is inconclusive and the issue unresolvable—we are forced to make a decision, and so we must choose. Are we compelled as a practical matter to take a side on such issues as whether there are transcendent realities, free will, or life after death once we are presented with the issues even if neither camp is in a better epistemic position? Can we actually suspend judgment even in the face of a lack of evidence one way or the other? In short, is agnosticism not a real option for us on the Big Questions? Or is it instead in fact the default position on mysteries?

The Limits of Knowledge and Reason

For the different positions on evidence, consider a balancing scale: believers on a given issue think that the scale tips one way, disbelievers think the scale tips the other way, agnostics think that the scale is balanced (or at least that it is not definitively tipping one way or the other), and skeptics believe that there is no real evidence to place on the scale to begin with. The option of agnosticism and the irrefutability of skepticism may lead to accepting less than certainty as our standard for knowledge. Pragmatists and reliabilists have no problem accepting a lower standard. And we do know at least that we exist in some fashion, and we do have what appears to be genuine knowledge of the world. Nevertheless, we are left with mysteries: reality apart from our experience is largely unknown (if Kant is correct, it is completely unknowable), the knowing self has its own mysteries, and the process of conscious experience itself introduces other problems. We have difficulty accepting that conclusion. Many philosophers deny that there are any intrinsic ontic mysteries to reality, but some are willing to accept that there may be limits to our knowledge and thus that epistemic mysteries will remain. For many philosophers, our reason demonstrates the limits of itself. As Blaise Pascal put it: "Reason's last step is the recognition that there are an infinite number of things that are beyond it."

The role of philosophy here is not to produce new knowledge but *to understand* the status of our existing claims of knowledge of what is real. But whether there also may in fact be philosophical knowledge about the nature of reality in metaphysics is the next subject.

Notes

1. Postmodernists deny the entire enterprise of searching for objective and universal knowledge, reasoning, and justification. For the objection that postmodernism's perspectivism (relativism) involves

a self-contradiction (i.e., postmodernists make claims that they themselves see as objective and universally valid) and other problems, see Nagel 2003.

2. The alternative to a "correspondence theory of truth"—a "coherence theory"—has its own problems: it is based on a consistent web of beliefs, but for total consistency the web must be detached totally from the world, and how to root any web of beliefs based only on coherence in the world in a way that guarantees truth is hard to specify. That is, if statements only refer to other statements, how do they connect to the world?

3. Constructivists go further and argue that cultural categories also structure our perceptions. Thus, there is no "pure experience" untainted by thought. As Willard Quine puts it, experience is not "a medium of pure unvarnished news." Conversely, Kant points out that concepts without experiential content are empty. He gives the analogy of a dove complaining about the air interfering with its flight, but without the air it could not fly, and without nonconceptual constraints, our concepts could not fly either but would be out of control.

4. For another angle, consider Bertrand Russell's remark that we could not prove that the universe was not created five minutes ago. Of course, we would have to have been created with our present memories and physical condition, trees would have to have been created with rings, and light from stars would have to have been created in mid flight, but nothing we could observe could confirm or refute the possibility. He did not advance this for serious consideration—he added that "[l]ike all skeptical hypotheses, it is logically tenable but uninteresting."

5. Descartes himself was not a skeptic, but the resulting Cartesian skepticism is actually stronger than Greek skepticism. Cartesian skeptics present arguments against perception providing knowledge of the external world, while Greek skeptics remained more neutral on whether perception can provide knowledge. Greek skeptics readily accepted everyday beliefs—their main target was the dogmas of the "professors."

6. There is a joke about a woman walking up to Bertrand Russell and saying "I'm a solipsist, and I don't know why everyone isn't one also!" But if we take solipsism to be a *second-order position* like philosophical skepticism, that is not quite as silly as it sounds: she may have meant that there is no rational way to justify fully any metaphysical realism beyond solipsism even if, as a practical matter, we all but must reject it in our lives.

4
What Is Reality?

Metaphysics is the finding of bad reasons for what we believe on instinct.

— F. H. Bradley

Metaphysics and Metametaphysics

When you walk into a wall, you get a certain sensation of reality. But what exactly is *reality*? This Big Question precedes even "first philosophy"—metaphysics, that is, the delineation of the basic categories of what is real. The objective in metaphysics is to identify the irreducible realities behind appearances. For example, are matter, mind, time, or causation real? What are the fundamental realities, what depends upon those fundamental realities, and what is actually only an illusion? Today, metaphysicians try to identify the best language in which to take inventory of the fundamental furniture making up reality.

But the more basic question is a metametaphysical one: what exactly constitutes "*reality*"? That is, what makes something *real*, and what is its nature? That is the main topic for this chapter, but it should be noted first that epistemic and perhaps ontic mysteries surround many of the traditional topics of metaphysics. Not all metaphysical issues generate real mysteries. Some come only from studying the nature of our conceptualizing. For example, philosophers debate whether a mountain is a separate entity from its surrounding earth since we have the term "mountain." (This issue takes on importance concerning "persons" and theoretical "entities" in science.) So too, the issue of universals versus nominalism comes only from arguing over the nature of our conceptualizing. Some philosophers dismiss such disputes as unanswerable because the questions are ill-formed. But many metaphysical issues seem more substantive. Consider time. Why does reality change—that is, why is there a flow that we call "time"? Change occurs and it has causal order, but is the time by which we measure it only an illusion—a fabricated extra element to reality that we imagine "flows"? If time moves, what does it move in? So too, with "now"—that elusive moment "in" time that Ludwig Wittgenstein called the image of eternity in the phenomenal world. "Now" is not part of the measurement of time but is the space on the temporal continuum within which we are aware of reality. Since "now" is not part of scientific equations, is it actually not part of objective reality? Or consider order. Are the laws of nature real? Or what is the nature of causation? How do causes bring about effects? When a cause occurs, why must an effect follow? Do conditions bring about a cause?

Such questions are the epitome of the questions that logical positivists found meaningless since these are questions about the world with no empirically testable answers, and even if we could find an answer that, say, time is unreal, it would not affect our lives. Many philosophers today working in the foundations of metaphysics want to dismiss all metaphysics for the same reason. They ask whether these questions actually have answers, and, if they do, whether the answers are substantive or merely a matter of how we use words. Many treat all metaphysical questions like they treat the question of whether a statue "really exists" in addition to the gold it is made of—unanswerable or pseudo-questions because nothing real is truly at issue. To them, it is like asking when there is a cup and a saucer, is there an additional third object—a cup-and-saucer? We all should agree that a term for an entity consisting of a mailbox, a piece of toast, and a walrus does not "cut nature at its joints" or help us understand the nature of things, but are all "entities" no more than our conceptual creations? Or should the basic inventory of the world even be in terms of entities (tables, statues, and so forth) rather than the distribution of the material that things are made of (carbon, gold, and so forth)? Many metaphysicians today believe that quantum physics has shown that there are no things but only structures to reality. Many also deny that there is a "logically perfect language" that carves nature at its joints. That would avoid the issue of whether the conflict of different inventories is a pseudo-mystery produced only by our conceptual systems and not by reality since they see no empirical matters at issue and thus no determinate truth-value of "true" or "false" for claims about them.[1] Some question whether existence-claims about entities such as subatomic particles or persons have a determinate truth-value. At best, they want to revise how terms are used.

Other metaphysicians try to naturalize metaphysics by restricting it to unifying the results, practices, and presuppositions of science: "speculative metaphysics" is rejected, but the search in "scientific metaphysics" for the basic structures of reality is permissible as long as the inquiry is based on the content of science and not on a priori posits based on intuitions.[2]

So too, philosophy must use the methods of science to solve its problems. Thus, any "speculative ontology" has no place in a scientific understanding of reality. Philosophers must engage scientific problems to add anything of value to our knowledge of reality.

The tables (as it were) have turned from the heyday of "ordinary language" analysis. However, according to David Manley, most analytic philosophers working in metaphysics today are "robust realists." Even if such metaphysics involves speculation, realists accept that substantive questions about the nature of reality are at stake—they believe that there is a true inventory of what is real in the universe, and that is so even if we may not be able to determine it.

Another problem for all metaphysical views of reality is this: our brain receives sensory signals that we interpret as being from "objective" reality—we do not experience reality directly and immediately. For example, light from the sun takes six to seven minutes to get here: the sun itself is always a little to the west of where the image our mind creates appears to place it—we never see the real sun. We posit something as producing the effect, but, as with Kant's noumenal world, we can never experience that posit. Indeed, every visual signal takes enough time for the brain to edit the input and produce a representation. George Berkeley's idealism (in which the world consists of ideas in the mind of God) could get around this problem only by positing that perception works without sensory signals.

What Is Reality?

Commonsense realism starts by treating as real what apparently exists independently from our mind plus the consciousness of the subject. In such realism, the world does not depend for its existence on the mind of an individual conscious being—something exists independently of our consciousness and so if all conscious beings were removed from the universe, something would still remain. In short, such realism is merely anti-solipsism: the natural universe is not a subjective illusion—there is a universe that has existed for billions of years before any conscious beings existed within it and will continue after we are gone; and now there is also a mind that is real, if perhaps dependent on the body. That is, there is an "objective" reality—a "something out there" when no one is experiencing it—plus consciousness as a part of what is real in the final analysis. In short, what is real is the natural realm of matter and energy, space-time, and consciousness. Many will add transcendent realities to the list. Within this context, metaphysicians try to determine what is "fundamentally" or "ultimately" real (i.e., what is not dependent upon anything else), what is derivatively real, and what is unreal.

This leads to a more basic issue: how do we determine what is real? Is it what can produce a causal effect? Is it what grounds experience? Traditionally, philosophers East and West have believed that something must persist throughout change to be real, but must something last *forever* to be deemed real? Is there only one way to "be," that is, only type or mode of being, and thus everything real exists in the same way? We may agree that what is real is what cannot be denied in our final analysis of things—that is, a nonnegotiable feature of the universe that we cannot get around in leading our lives, in scientific findings, and in our theory of things. It is what cannot be analyzed into anything simpler or more fundamental or dismissed as illusory. Naturalists who are structural reductionists see the real in terms of matter and energy only—"matter in motion."[3] Idealists see the fundamentally real in terms of consciousness. Another basic divide is between naturalists and transcendent realists: the former accept only what is open to scientific analysis as real, that is, space-time and its contents (although, somewhat inconsistently, many naturalists add mathematical entities as realities in order to make science work); the latter also accept realities transcending this realm.[4]

But still, whatever stuff is finally deemed "real," what is it to be real? What makes something *real*? What is its nature? If we think that the stuff of the world is matter, fields of energy, consciousness, "spirit," ideas (or computer simulations) in "the mind of God," or God himself, we still must ask what the ontic nature of that stuff is. The question is not answered by scientists identifying the smallest bits of matter—the question of what is the basic ontic nature applies as much to matter as anything else. Even if there is something in the universe that gives particles their mass (e.g., a Higgs particle or field), we still have to ask what gives that reality its being and what is the nature of its being. The same is true of alternatives to matter, such as energy or space-time. As the physicist Richard Feynman remarked: "It is important to realize that in physics today, we have no knowledge what energy *is*." Or what is the nature of a "field" from which matter arises? Calling it a "state of space," as Michael Faraday did, does not explain all of its nature.

All in all, the nature of the "stuff" of the world is unknown. The physicist John Wheeler saw this problem and argued that today "we are no longer satisfied with insights only into particles, or fields of force, or geometry, or even space and time. Today we demand of physics some understanding of existence itself." He proffered a "participatory universe" in which later observers somehow participate in the creation of the universe that permits the reality of those observers. But this still does not explain "existence itself." Indeed, no science will help do that: as discussed in chapter 8, scientists deal with the structures responsible for the interaction of things, not the medium in which those structures are embedded or what gives those structures their reality. Physicists do not deal with "substance" or "matter" but only study certain structures of reality that can be measured by the interaction of things. This is true even for mass: it is measured only by interactions and not otherwise analyzed. If matter is ultimately quantized in small packets, it is still the interactions of the packets that physicists study, not the nature of the "stuff" in the packets.

In short, scientists identify structures, not being. Physics is called the "science of matter," but a better title would be the "science of the most general level of structures." It is not the "science of being": being cannot be tested by pushing and pulling since it is uniform to everything—there are no parts, and thus no way to measure it through the interactions of parts. Indeed, matter/energy is much more of a mystery than we usually recognize. The universe is made of something about which we know nothing scientifically. We do not know even where to begin to ask about the nature of matter, despite it being the most familiar "thing" we experience. It is simply the medium in which structures are embodied. Calling being "matter" only reveals our prejudice in metaphysics toward our common sense (here, solidity and weight). Perhaps we should follow the idealist scientist Arthur Eddington and start instead with what we all really know as real—our minds and sense-experience.

Being

So what constitutes "being"—that is, the "power" of things (including matter and energy) to be? Labeling it "substance" as a substratum that carries properties or otherwise grounds or sustains things does not help much—we only end up with John Locke realizing that it is "something we know not what." Analytic philosophers have little interest in the question. What the world is made of in a metaphysical sense (as opposed to a scientific issue of the most fundamental entities and fields) is no longer a major topic in philosophy. Rather, the question becomes reduced to another: whether "being" is a *property* that things have simply because they exist. To logical positivists, the immediate givenness of experience is not amenable to further analysis, and any speculation on the ultimate nature of being is the paradigm of meaninglessness since no scientific finding is relevant to determining its nature. To most philosophers today, "being" is either an empty term or denotes merely the sum of all objects. The question of being is either considered ill-formed—a puzzle arising only because we have terms denoting "existence"—or overly ambitious since science cannot answer it. Neither empiricists nor the more rationalist-minded are concerned with it. To Willard Quine, "to be is to be the value of a variable." Beyond that, philosophers occupy themselves with such issues as whether abstract objects are real or not. The focus is not on what gives anything existence. Being simply is—at best, the mystery of being is only the mystery of the existence of the world.

However, one can still ask what constitutes "being"—the sheer "is-ness" of things or the "power" of things to be—of both the stuff being ordered and the structures doing the ordering. What is the nature, in Buddhist terms, of the "such-ness" of the natural world apart from our conceptual division of it into objects? This is a prime instance of the mysteriousness of the ordinary: in Buddhist terms, there is both the "form" of objects and their "emptiness" (i.e., objects are empty of anything that would give them an independent existence and permanence). Being is not undifferentiated matter but is what gives matter its existence—along with mind and whatever else is part of the universe. The philosophical mystery of "matter" is not to identify the lowest level subatomic particles or any issue related to how the world is—those are subjects for science. Rather, it is to identify what is the being of "matter." What gives matter its power to be? Is the being of living or conscious beings something different than the being of atoms or that of numbers or truths? Even if being has some inherent properties (e.g., mass or consciousness), still what is it? What is a superstring, or whatever is the smallest bit of matter, apart from the structures it embodies? And how do the structures of nature (e.g., gravity and electromagnetism) relate to the stuff on which they operate?

Can we explain anything about *being*? What can we say beyond that it is whatever gives things existence? How can we get any distance from it to analyze it? All attempts to grasp or express the nature of being transform being into a distinct object. But these attempts must fail since being is not a particular object among objects but something common to all objective and subjective phenomena. Examining an object will not suffice since being is not an object—to grasp being as an object, we would have to step outside the universe (and outside of ourselves), which obviously we cannot do. If being is beyond all possible analysis, how can we say anything about its nature? Doesn't the question of its nature lose any frame of reference and thus become devoid of sense? To most philosophers, there is only a perplexing and ultimately nonsensical question with which we plague ourselves and which we should set aside.

But one philosopher, Milton Munitz, has seriously examined the question of being. He asks whether we can even *speak* of being since it is not an object or set of objects. Being, Munitz notes, never presents itself as a phenomenon—it "shines through" the known universe but is not identical with it. It is not an entity of any type—not a thing, a combination of things, or the totality of things. Unlike an object, it is not "conceptually bound." It has no properties, qualities, or structures to discover, nor is it a cause, source, or creator—it has nothing to describe. Nor does it perform any actions within the phenomenal universe. It is utterly unique in that it is not an instance of any category (since categories encompass more than one thing). It is beyond all conceptual analysis and rational comprehension. It can be characterized only negatively as "not this, not that." To be aware of being is a level of human experience unlike any other; recognizing it is a basic experience that cannot be analyzed into anything simpler or more fundamental. Thus, being-in-itself is unintelligible, since intelligibility requires the applicability of descriptive or explanatory concepts or laws. That is, we see trees and cars, not "being," and we cannot formulate propositions about it. We live in a world of differentiated objects and see and speak only of those objects. Being itself remains beneath any of the conceptual maps that we apply to the world in order to create order. Once we start speaking of being—or even just naming it—we make it one object among objects, which "it" is not. (Note the similarity between what Munitz says about being and what introvertive mystics say about the reality they allegedly experience.)

If Munitz's position is correct, any understanding or explanations of the being of our world would be foreclosed. As Ludwig Wittgenstein ended his *Tractatus*, there are things that manifest themselves (and hence that we are aware of) but are unutterable and incapable of being conveyed in language; and what we cannot speak of, thereof we must remain silent. This would apply to our awareness of the being of the world. If this position on language is correct, we are left with only mystery about the very being of the world. That is, being cannot be "captured" by any language, and thus its nature is unconceptualizable and inexpressible—it is essentially unknowable and thus a permanent mystery.

So is the being of the universe indeed beyond our understanding? One issue is how exactly we are aware of being. We experience our bodies, tables and chairs, the wind, and so forth, but do we experience *being*? When we walk into a wall, do we experience the being of a wall or just its structured objectness? If we are aware only of objects, is our sense of beingness only a product of reflection, that is, a posited reality that we infer beneath what we actually sense? But being does not seem to be inferred—it seems experienced immediately and constantly in our awareness even if we only *know* objects. Is our own awareness of being conscious any closer to being than sense-experience? Do mystical experiences put us in contact with being per se free of our conceptualizations? Or is the being of reality completely unknowable? But we cannot avoid the presence of being even if we could successfully confine our lives just to a world of the objects that we conceptually differentiate.

Indeed, being is self-evident even if we have no idea of what it is except that we are continually aware of it, strange as that might sound.

But again, as a constant in all experience, we cannot step away and examine being. This means that we realize that there is something very basic to reality that we experience in some sense and yet cannot comprehend. We end up asking a question that is not answerable: "What is the nature of being?" It is this reflection on what we are aware of that creates the mystery of being.

A related mystery is our sense of both permanence and impermanence—of timeless "being" and constant temporal "becoming." Their relation remains a mystery. In fact, why there is any *change* at all is puzzling. We think being is pure and undifferentiated but also unchanging and hence static; yet the world is dynamic, a realm of perpetual change. Mustn't change itself be explained in terms of something that does not change, and yet how is that possible since change is not changeless? Is why there is any change at all in the universe an intractable mystery? Should we follow Parmenides and claim that in the final analysis change is unreal? Or is change primary? Does only the dynamic "becoming" exist, and is the idea of changeless "being" simply an illusion that our mind has created? Is it like our sense of an unchanging personal identity that persists through the constant changes as we age?

So too, we must account for the *structures* that scientists study. These order the changes in the stuff that is structured: the commonality of being provides one unity to everything, and structures provide a common order. The distinction of these two dimensions of reality goes back to Aristotle, but since most philosophers today are not interested in being, the issue of their relation is rarely broached. The "power to be" is common to both, but how are the reality of the organizing structures and the stuff being organized related? And is one component—what is structured or the structures—more fundamental? Can the structures be "more real," since, as Ernest Gellner asked, what is so great about weight and substance anyway? Structures have at least an equal claim with matter to be real. After all, natural structures appear to show the same unchanging permanence as the stuff underlying the shifting configurations of the universe that they structure. Indeed, one can argue that in fact structure is more fundamental—the stuff of the universe is merely a medium here only to support the structures that really run the show.

The Problem with Metaphysics

Philosophy helps to clarify our situation in the world, but does all of this mean that there is no genuine metaphysical knowledge? We human beings have a stubborn desire to form visions of the world, but are all metaphysical systems merely shields against the unknown to quiet our mind? We may accept that based on our experience in the world and the success of our reasoning in science that we have the epistemic right to speculate at least a little on what is beyond science. The insight of empiricism is that we should keep thought as close to experience as possible and that the further we stray from the check of experience the greater the risk that we are fooling ourselves. That nature is constantly surprising scientists should give metaphysicians pause about their projects when they think that they can know the fundamental nature of reality by basically a priori thought alone. What "seems plausible to us" changes for scientists over time, and this will indirectly affect metaphysics. But if theorizing beyond our immediate experience is totally prohibited, we could never get beyond solipsism and would have to conclude that there is no external world and no other persons.

However, we must always remember that theorizing is our thought and that, unlike in science, there is no way to test either through experience or reasoning which metaphysical theories are best and which are off track, and thus there is no finality to be attained. We cannot even determine if there is an objectively correct answer. Moreover, we must be cautious in our intuitions about what is real: the unreliability of intuitions has been shown as science has advanced.[5] So too, what a naturalist deems to be "self-evident" about what is real is obviously wrong to a theist and vice versa. This affects all our reasoning in the field—justifications in metaphysics often end up being circular. This in turn leads to adopting an agnosticism about the truth of whatever metaphysics one endorses.

Not only is the Big Question of what is the nature of reality left unanswerable, we cannot proceed on the assumption that our cognitive resources are adequate to assure that we are in touch with the fundamental things making up reality on both the everyday and exotic levels of reality. Metaphysicians may assert that reason demands that we can discern the underlying structures of reality and produce a thorough account of them. But those not suffering from the philosopher's disease do not find that claim compelling. There may be more to reality than our conceptual packaging can capture—not only may there be more to reality than is dreamt of in any philosophy, but more than we are capable of dreaming of. In addition, Immanuel Kant pointed out that the same conceptual apparatus that gives order to our experience inevitably leads to confusion when it is applied to matters beyond our experience. Thus, tentativeness in metaphysics is not merely wise but mandatory. Metaphysics has changed through the centuries, but whether it has advanced in the sense of resolving the issues is another question. (The history of metaphysics can be seen as a series of valuable insights blown out of proportion.) Nor has philosophy uncovered new information for theorizing—when a theory leads to anything empirical, a new science is born and takes things from there. Philosophy itself, however, cannot be fully "naturalized" as being continuous with science as long as philosophers advance untestable theories.

Notes

1. The idea of "essences" results from thinking that something in nature must correspond to our unchanging concepts. This creates the puzzle of how an "essence" persists through changes to a thing. But the real philosophical question is whether a concept applies to something that is constantly changing rather than whether that thing has an unchanging substance-like essence.

2. How to ground the philosophy of naturalism (and also scientism) by means of science without a circular argument is far from clear since naturalists by definition accept only what can be studied in science as being real. However, science is only a filter—one way of looking at reality—and naturalists go further than the practice of science itself and reduce reality to only what that filter reveals. But that a scientific ontology exhausts reality is itself a *metaphysical claim* that cannot be justified by any scientific experiment or observation.

3. Identifying what "matter" is is harder than might be supposed. Carl Hempel identified the dilemma: if we define matter in terms of what is discovered in physics, then a problem arises since the theories of physics change—we cannot equate matter either with the posits of current theories because they will be superseded or with an ideal theory without admitting that we do not currently know what matter is.

4. Scientism is the epistemic correlate of naturalism: only science can give us knowledge (including knowledge of the nature of knowledge). It would require that true knowledge of oneself depends on scientific analysis and not on subjective "self-awareness." How many people actually subscribe to this "ism," consciously or subconsciously, is a matter of debate.

5. For an example of how our intuitions fail when we extend them into exotic realms, consider the infinity of natural numbers (1, 2, 3, 4, . . .). If we remove all the odd numbers from the list, we are left with only the even numbers (2, 4, 6, . . .), and so we are left with only half as many numbers, right? Wrong—we have just as many numbers as we began with, as counterintuitive as that may seem. To see why, go back to the original list of numbers and double the value of each entry; now we have the list of only the even numbers, but we have not deleted a single item from the list (we have only doubled each item's value), and so we have as many numbers as we began with.

5

Why Is There Something
Rather Than Nothing?

THE RED KING: "What do you see?"
ALICE: "Nothing"
THE RED KING: "What good eyes you have!"
— Lewis Carroll, *Through the Looking Glass*

Why is there anything at all rather than nothing? This is one of the biggest Big Questions of them all. Gottfried Leibniz, reflecting a philosopher's demand for answers, put the matter more fully: "Why is there something rather than nothing? For nothing is both simpler and seemingly easier to comprehend than is something. And once you start with nothing, how do you get from nothing to something?" Perhaps there could have been nothing, but now something definitely does exist. Is there a reason for existence? The physicist John Archibald Wheeler wrote, "I know of no great thinker of any land or era who does not regard existence as the mystery of mysteries." Martin Heidegger considered this question the fundamental question in metaphysics. But Buddhists find the question to be only a distraction from focusing on the goal of ending our suffering, and the question is not foremost to many people who take the universe to be eternal. Nevertheless, the contingency of the world's existence does produce existential angst and astonishment in many persons—Paul Tillich's "ontological shock" of sheer that-ness.

Nothingness

Let's start with nothing. Indeed, philosophers make much ado about nothing. But Friedrich Schelling's question "Why is there not nothing at all?" is hard to think about since we inevitably end up forming a visual image of "nothing at all": our mind reifies "nothingness" into an object of thought, a *thing*—that is, we make our concept for the total absence of anything into a concept of *something*. "Nothing" is no longer merely a concept denoting the lack of anything—it becomes a reality itself (e.g., a big, black silent abyss, empty of all content) since that is how our discursive mind works. It becomes a negative reality, like a negative number. So too, we cannot realistically imagine that we do not exist: we can, of course, imagine a world in which we were not born, but *we* will be thinking this—whatever we imagine, the thinking subject is always there. Thus, the Cartesian "I think therefore I am" comes back to mess up the process. Our imagining mind cannot be left with true nothingness, nonexistence, and only negation.

Richard Swinburne asserts: "It is extraordinary that there should exist anything at all. Surely the most natural state of affairs is simply nothing: no universe, no God, no nothing." That is, the "most natural" state of affairs would be the empty set. But while that would obviously be the *simplest* state of affairs, it is hard to see how to evaluate whether it is the *"most natural"* state (or the "least arbitrary") or even what exactly that means. In addition, since something can exist, as evidenced by the fact that we are here, the state of nothingness would in fact need an explanation. As Sidney Morgenbesser exclaimed to a group of students arguing about the issue, "If there were nothing, you'd still be complaining!"

Could there in fact have been nothing? Through "ordinary language" analysis we may argue that the claim "There could be nothing" has no subject (since nothing is nothing), and thus the claim is in fact meaningless. Bede Rundle tries to dismiss what he sees as philosophy's central question by arguing that we cannot make sense of the idea that "there might have been nothing." Because of the way that we think, there must always be something. For example, we cannot conceive of a universe coming into being or going out of being: the universe always comes out of something or something is left at the end—we are left with at least the setting from which we ask the question, and so we never have true nothingness. Thus, he argues, there is no mystery why there is something rather than nothing: we cannot actually imagine there being nothing. Ordinary usage of the word "nothing" thus shows that "there could be nothing" is not a genuine, intelligible claim—it can only apply to parts of what exists and not to the whole of reality.

But just because any *idea* of "nothing" that we can possibly form makes it into a "something" does not mean that the idea of nothingness is unintelligible. Certainly, just having a word for it does not make it a something. So too with just *thinking* about nothing: just because it is an object of thought does not mean that it exists otherwise. Similarly, it is impossible to *visualize* true "nothingness"—we are always left with a container, as

Rundle says, and also with someone doing the imagining. By definition, when we try to picture anything—including nothingness—we are always picturing *something*. But it is not clear why we cannot *conceive* the removal of all somethings that leaves nothing, including the big, blank space the things were in and the consciousness imagining it. So too, just because we cannot *imagine*—that is, form a mental image—something does not mean that it cannot exist (contra Rundle), nor does it make the question of why something exists nonsense (contra Wittgenstein). We cannot imagine an infinite number of numbers, but we can handle the concept of "infinity" in mathematics without trouble. We also cannot visualize colorless particles such as electrons without giving them color, but we can conceive them and utilize them in physics—our inability to form literal pictures of them is not grounds to think they do not exist. So too, in cosmology we can conceive of space as an inflating balloon expanding into nothing, but we cannot visualize that *nothing*—we imagine a something that the balloon expands into. As the physicist P. W. Bridgman said, "the structure of nature may eventually be such that our processes of thought do not correspond to it sufficiently to permit us to think about it at all. . . . We are confronted with something truly ineffable."

More generally, there is no reason to believe that reality must comply to what we can visualize or otherwise imagine with our evolved brains. Why should the ability of any evolved creature to *visualize* or *imagine* something be a criterion for what is *real*? Here we can conceive the idea of "coming into existence" and also the opposite process—the removal of all things—even if we cannot create a mental picture of the end without leaving an empty space. But even if beings with our particular brains (or probably any beings) cannot visualize the situation, we should still accept that it might have been the case that nothing ever existed.

Can We Get from Nothing to Something?

Another basic problem is how we could possibly get from *nothing* to *something*. Since the pre-Socratic Thales, many have thought that since something cannot arise from nothing, there must always have been some "something." Indeed, a simple argument can be made that something must have always existed based on that one fundamental premise: "You cannot get something from nothing." That is a premise that is very hard to deny. As William James put it, "From nothing to being there is no logical bridge." If we can get something from x, then x must already have existed in some sense. X cannot be truly *nothing* if it has the capacity or potentiality to create something—something is there.[1] (If something can in fact come from literally nothing without any something causing it, it means that we know nothing fundamental about how reality works.) Thus, if something exists today—and everyone grants that—it could never have come from nothing. Hence, there must always have been something. In short, if there is something now, there could never have been nothing, and reality exists eternally or in some timeless sense.[2] Yet we can still ask why that original "something" exists.

Peter van Inwagen argues why there is something by first imagining an infinite lottery—each possible state of affairs (with each being equally probable), with nonexistence being only one possible state out of an infinite number of possibilities. He then argues that the chance of nonexistence is zero (one divided by infinity). The problem with this argument is that the probability of any other one state of affairs then is also always zero—thus, the probability of our particular world existing is zero, and yet here we are. Indeed, in the infinite lottery under his approach there can be no winner at all. But the real issue here is that there are only two basic options: something versus nothing. Nothingness should not simply be included as one option with all the different somethings (like including zero with the positive numbers—0, 1, 2, 3, 4, . . .). Rather, it is in a different category altogether (like 0 versus the positive numbers 1, 2, 3, 4, . . .). And it is not clear how we can apply probability to that situation.[3] The choice of analogy thus makes all the difference.

Are Values the Answer?

Can an axiological approach explain why anything exists or how to get from nothing to something? The value realized by creating the physical universe may explain why a god would choose to create it—that is, realizing value (goodness, love, or whatever) is the purpose of the universe, or God's goodness compels its expression by making beings to love. Arthur Schopenhauer disagreed. He thought that it would have been better if the world did not exist since no one would then be here to suffer. But even if it is better that God did create a world, this does not explain the existence of the creator god itself and thus does not ultimately explain why there is something rather than nothing—the first reality remains unexplained.

It is also difficult to argue that some value *must be* realized in a physical universe. (And if things of value logically must exist, then no creator god is their source.) It may well be better that something exists rather than nothing, but how does value necessitate it? Why should an ethical or other good *require* or *obligate* that something exists? And *how* could it compel a physical universe to exist? How could any value bring about its own fulfillment by requiring that a universe exist? And if value compels existence, why is there now suffering and evil?

But most basically, why do the values exist in the first place? That ultimate ontic question remains unanswered. Thus, this approach only introduces more mystery. (This approach also assumes some values are objective realities.)

Does Religion Have the Answer?

Contrary to popular opinion, answering the question "Why is there something rather than nothing?" is also impossible in religious terms. God or a nontheistic transcendent reality may explain why the phenomenal universe exists, but its own existence too must have an explanation to get a final answer to the question of why anything exists. That is, we must still ask: why does God exist? Indeed, a creator needs an explanation more than does the created. As Ludwig Wittgenstein said, if the existence of the world is so miraculous that we need to posit God, then God is even more miraculous and not a final explanation but needs an explanation. Gods too cannot arise from nothing. Even if God is uncreated and eternal, we must still ask why he is there. The answer that theologians give is that God is "self-existent" or is his own cause. But how can anything cause itself? Nothing can *do* anything unless it already exists, and so no reality can make itself. And using a Latin label for the concept—"*sui generis*"—does not save it. Only the implicit demand of the philosopher's disease to satisfy our mind by supplying some answer, any answer, to why something exists would lead to such a concept for placating our mind.

"Self-caused" at best can mean only that something is eternal and without a cause—it cannot mean God *caused* his own existence. (Advaita Vedantins consider Brahman to be "unborn [*a-ja*]" rather than self-born, which does not frame the issue of its existence in terms of a cause.) We normally treat a "why" question in terms of where something came from or what caused it, but if something is eternal that approach does not apply.[4] "Causation" and "dependency" are concepts that work for events within the universe but do not apply to reality as a whole. Traditional theistic thinking about "creation" and a "creator god" sets us on the path of thinking of something coming from nothing—that is, an origin rather than eternality. Theists tend to find the idea of an eternal universe incredible—they believe that it must have been created and nothing can just pop into existence—and yet have no trouble with an eternal, uncreated god. But it is not at all clear why if there can be an eternal "self-caused" reality, it cannot be the natural universe. For example, the universe may not be merely the particular "miniverse" that started with our Big Bang but an infinite series of such miniverses—such a "multiverse" would not "pop into existence" any more than an eternal god would. If either the universe or God is eternal, it has no cause at all, not a first cause in the infinite past, as theists tend to think: there is no point when something did not exist, and no origin. Origin-oriented concepts such as "self-caused" and "self-created" only give us a false sense that we understand—the terms are meaningless and only cause our thought to go off track. Even "self-existent" usually involves thinking in terms of a cause—that is, something causing its own existence. (Baruch Spinoza took it to mean a thing the "essence" of which involves "existence.")

But again, even if "self-caused" or "self-existent" means only being eternal and thus without a cause, we still must ask why that reality exists. That is, even if there is no *cause*, we can still seek a *reason* why the eternal reality exists—for example, require a philosophical argument for why something must exist. In short, is there a reason to expect that that eternal something *should* exist? And here the obvious problem is that whatever reason is advanced, it will be an answer from our limited perspective—we will never be in a position within the universe to know if our answer is correct or is simply something that quiets our inquisitive but finite mind. So too, relying on what we take to be "self-evident" is risky: the subjective and historically conditioned element of any such intuition is too great.

It is hard to see how any eternal reality could have an external explanation. Rather, anything eternal is a brute fact unless it can be self-explanatory. But nothing can be self-explanatory any more than it can self-created. In addition, arguing that the universe needs an explanation because it began in time but God does not need an explanation because he is timeless (i.e., existing outside of time) does not get around the problem—we still must ask why God is there. So too, if the natural universe is eternal, we still can ask why it is here. Thus, with an eternal reality we are still left with an unexplained brute fact, not an explanation.

Positing such self-contradictory categories as "self-caused" or "self-explanatory" is only an attempt to address our need to think that we understand. But a brute fact is something we simply have to accept as unexplained. Theists claim that "self-existence" has a logical necessity to it and thus asking why it exists is like asking why a circle is round, but it is a *self-contradiction*. Theists cannot form an idea of "self-creation" any more than they can of a square circle. The theological rejoinder is that "self-existence" must be accepted as a "profound mystery," but gibberish is gibberish. At best, it can mean only that some reality simply exists, not that it is its own cause or its own reason for existing. In short, theists should accept that they do not know why God is there and not bewitch their minds with such meaningless terms as "self-existent."

Thus, we are stuck with a brute fact, and our quest to know why anything exists cannot be completed in this manner—it ends up without an answer but with a mystery. A creator god may well account for why the natural world exists, but it does not account for why it itself exists and thus is not the ultimate answer to why anything exists. Through theology, we always have to end up with something being simply accepted as a brute fact—either an eternal universe or a source.

Does Science Have the Answer?

Science too is no help here: scientists can explain how events happen, but not why there is something here to happen. However, some scientists simply do not get the basic cosmological question at all but try to reduce it to a scientific problem. They reduce the philosophical question "Why is there something rather than nothing?" to the scientific question "How does matter arise from nonmatter?" and believe that they are answering the former by answering the latter.

The idea that the universe emerged as an ordered realm from a prior chaos predates science. In the West, it goes back to the pre-Socratic Anaxagoras. But the Greeks did not argue that an ordered realm emerged from literally nothing—something preexisted. The idea is also common in myths. In the Bible, God does not create (*àsá*) the heavens and the earth but shapes (*bará*) them from a preexisting formless void (Gen. 1:1–2). In India, the *Rig Veda's* famous *Hymn of Creation* (10.129) begins "At the time of the beginning, there was nothing either nonexistent nor existent," but by "nonexistent (*asat*)" the hymn means only what is "unstructured" or "chaotic," not literal nonexistence—there is still present "that One (*tad eka*)" that is beyond the categories of "what is existent" and "what is nonexistent" since these concepts apply only after the creation of the ordered world. And, as the hymn ends: "From what did this creation come to be? Was it is established by itself or not? Surely he who is the overseer of this world in the highest heaven knows—or perhaps does even he not know?"

Today, Stephen Hawking believes he has shown how the universe spontaneously arose out of nothing—that structures within nature explain why anything exists at all—and thus science can prove why anything exists. The universe has no boundaries, and no external conditions are involved. However, he actually explains only why one state of affairs (the manifest universe) must arise from another state of affairs (a certain quantum state). He makes no attempt to explain why that prior state—what Steven Weinberg calls the "quantum stage"—existed or where it came from. If the manifest universe is the result of, say, an unstable quantum fluctuation bubble, Hawking still has to explain why the stuff of the "quantum vacuum" already existed. Thus, in his theory the universe is far from "self-explanatory."

Moreover, there are also *laws* preceding the creation of the manifest universe whose existence remains unexplained. Hawking merely states that because there are certain laws "the universe can and will create itself from nothing"—the basic questions of where these laws come from, why these laws exist and not others, and why any laws have the power to create a material universe are never answered. Nor has he explained why the vacuum is encoded with structures that make the quantum "fluctuation" possible.

An unstable quantum state that can produce the visible universe is not nothing since something can come out of it—anything that is already there and can *do* something is not literally *nothing*. The quantum vacuum is the state of the universe without any stable particles, not nothing. At most, Hawking has shown only that the universe cannot remain stable in an unmanifested state but must become manifest because of certain physical forces—that is, why there is some *thing* rather than *no thing*—but not why there is something already there that could become the manifest universe rather than nothing or why there are laws to make it manifest. There may be a zero sum between the positive and negative energies within the universe, and so no external or additional energy is needed to create the manifested universe, but where did that "stuff" come from? If there is something there that is "unstable" and any "symmetry" must split, there is still something there prior to the present state of the universe. That prior state may be free of the structures ordering the manifest universe and hence not of any scientific interest and thus "nothing" to scientists, but in no sense is it truly *nothing*—its existence too needs an explanation.

Thus, Hawking is discussing only the transition of one state of the universe into another. The ultimate cosmological question of why there is anything to convert into "something" in the first place remains, even if Hawking thinks that philosophy is dead. Switching to a scientifically answerable "how "question does not get around the basic "why" question of what, in Hawking's earlier words, "breathes fire into the equations" and makes a universe for physicists to describe.[5] In the end, Hawking is at a loss to answer the question, "Why does the universe go through all the bother of existing?"[6]

So too, even leaving aside the theories of multiple universes and an eternal universe, the Big Bang does not answer, in Alan Guth's words, where "the stuff that banged" came from. More generally, scientists' interest in prediction and order cannot address the ultimate cosmological question of why anything exists. Any scientific answer may trace the current state of the universe to a prior one, but it will always have to presume that something already existed to change into the current state, and thus scientific analysis cannot explain its existence. There is always an existing medium in which mathematical laws or software is embodied. Nor does science answer why any laws should exist to force the arising of something, even if, as modern-day Pythagoreans such as Max Tegmark see it, mathematics is the generative principle of reality.

Does Philosophy Have the Answer?

In short, science has no answer for why both the stuff of nature and its laws exist. The enigma of why anything exists remains as large as before science. So, does philosophy then have the answer? The philosophers' approach to nothingness discussed above did not prove promising. Still, many philosophers dismiss the question as a linguistic error. Language itself seems inherently to require a something: by saying "There was nothing" or "Nothing existed" (or conversely, "Nothingness cannot exist"), we apparently are committed to claiming that nothing is a something and thus a reality—otherwise, there is no subject to the sentences. That is, we cannot deny nothingness without making it into a thing to discuss and thus implicitly affirming its existence.[7] However, claiming "There was once not anything" or "There could be the lack of anything" gets around such a facile rejection of the problem.

The substantive problem is that we cannot invoke any entity or principle to explain the existence of everything—that would be invoking part of what exists to explain all that exists. Only if it can be shown that some item's existence is *logically necessary*—that is, the claim that that entity or principle might not exist leads to a logical contradiction—can we establish a final explanation without appeal to some further cause or principle, even if this introduces the problem of how an abstract principle could create a phenomenal reality.[8] But this is hard to do. Robert Nozick introduced the concept of "self-subsuming" to get around the problem of "self-causation" or "self-explanation," but this notion still cannot bootstrap beingness itself into existence. Nor can a creator god be shown to be logically necessary: such a god would have to exist in every possible universe, but we can conceive a universe without an outside source of any kind, and so a creator god, let alone the all-powerful, all-loving god of theism, is not necessary in all possible worlds. (What we consider a "possible world" also depends on what we can conceive, and thus again seems to make what we can conceive a criterion for what is real.)

Nor will trying to deduce that something exists by using pure reason without any premises involving something that already exists via an Ontological Argument succeed: we simply cannot establish the existence of something in the world from the analysis of our concepts. A reality with nonmaximal properties would be even harder to establish as necessarily existing. At best the Ontological Argument succeeds in establishing that *if* a perfect being in fact exists, then it must exist. Even in its modern form, in terms of modal logic, we are left in the end with the alternatives "God exists" or "God does not exist," as its one-time defender Alvin Plantinga had to admit. Thus, such reasoning is of no help at all.

Indeed, probably every philosophical argument must fail here. First, there is the Munchausen trilemma, noted in chapter 3: any answer to the question will either lead to an infinite regress of explanations, be a circular explanation, or lead to some assumed but unexplained reality. Second, there is a problem concerning causal chains. Bertrand Russell argued that every state of affairs in an eternal universe always has a prior cause and thus there is an explanation for each state of affairs. We can utilize the infinite number of negative numbers as a model: there is no first number, and yet every number has a predecessor. Theists characterize the universe *in toto* as contingent and thus see the need for a creator god. Such a sustaining source would not be a first cause in the chain but of a different order: the concept "cause" (which was devised for phenomenal events) would not apply to a sustaining source relation to the physical universe, but such a source would be responsible in some sense for the existence of the phenomenal world *in toto*. However, a chain of contingent events does not demand a "necessary being" or any other source, as Russell showed. Nevertheless, even if we have a reason for each event in the chain, we can still ask why the total eternal chain of events exists. Without such an explanation, we are left with a brute fact. And as noted above, a creator would itself need an explanation. Thus, with or without a creator, in the end we remain stuck with a brute fact.

We want to reject the concepts of both self-causation and an infinite regress of causes. This may indicate that we have been looking at the situation improperly from the beginning, but we do not know how else to see it. More broadly, with the way our mind works, we are always looking for a "because" for every "why." Leibniz enshrined this in philosophy as the "principle of sufficient reason": for every event or state of affairs, there is a reason sufficient to explain it. He wanted a final, "ultimate" reason for all contingent events—nothing would be left arbitrary or unexplainable in the end. He believed that the chain of causes had to end with an uncaused first cause—a necessary being (i.e., God) whose existence does not require an explanation because God is not a contingent state of affairs. Thus, Leibniz had to twist the intuition underlying the principle of sufficient reason and end with something allegedly being self-caused. But again, "self-causation" is meaningless.

Thus, resorting to "self-existence" is not the successful conclusion of an argument but an admission that we do not know what we are talking about. To push the principle of sufficient reason beyond what it can rightfully achieve is a clear instance of the philosopher's disease—it is dogmatically demanding that every question must have an answer that satisfies our reason.[9] But why reality must satisfy our demand that there must be a reason for the world simply because we want the universe to be thoroughly comprehensible to us is not obvious. And nevertheless, we are still left in the end with an unexplained brute fact—the mystery of any "uncaused first cause."

The sense of a "necessary being" need not be of logical necessity, but only of metaphysical necessary—that is, a reality whose existence explains the existence of the contingent universe. The necessary being is a creator/sustainer of the contingent realm and thus not the first cause in the causal chain of phenomenal events. But in this case, the creator's existence is as contingent as that of the universe, and we are still left with a mystery. In addition, substituting the mystery of a creator's existence for the mystery of why the natural universe exists does not advance our final understanding one iota—it merely pushes the mystery of existence back one step. This satisfies theists since it pushes the mystery of the natural realm out of the natural realm, but the central mystery of why anything exists remains untouched. If theists accept that God's existence is mystery, then they in fact cannot claim an ultimate explanation for the universe. In short, one mystery cannot explain another.

Furthermore, the choice remains between accepting the natural universe or God as the unexplained explanatory stopping point, and it is more rational to stop with a known reality—the natural universe—especially when positing a further mystery also introduces new "how" mysteries of how creation occurred (if the universe is not eternal) and how the creator/sustainer maintains the existence of the natural universe. (Theists would argue that there are reasons unrelated to this issue to introduce a creator.) Our objective is understanding, not more mysteries, and these metaphysical posits cannot give us any knowledge. Mystery is an admission of not knowing, not an explanation of anything.

The Oddity of the Question

Thus, philosophy also fails to answer the question. In fact, the question, "Why is there something rather than nothing at all?" is actually very odd and probably logically unique. When it comes to answering it, we reach the impasse noted above: any answer we supply—any being, any reality, mind or consciousness, any force, any principle, any scientific law, any value, any event, Schopenhauer's sheer "will of existence" to exist, logical necessity, mathematics, or anything else—is always *something*, and we can always ask why that *something* exists. Even if we could apply the phenomenal concept of "causation" or "origin" to the totality of things, any causal explanation will only introduce a new reality (the cause) to question. Any cause must already exist and thus is part of what is to be explained by means of that cause. As Paul Edwards pointed out, the question "Why is there something?" has a simple logical error: it presupposes an antecedent condition that can explain that "something," but there can be no such antecedent since it too must be subsumed in the "something" that must be explained. Even any answer in terms of a logically necessary reality still does not address why any reality at all was possible to begin with or why reality as set up in such a way that something that could not but exist is a possibility at all. In sum, we simply cannot answer why something exists with a "something" of any nature, but there is no other way to answer the question.

Thus, theism, science, and philosophy are all bound to fail here. They fail most fundamentally because any answer will be in terms of a "something" and we can always ask why that something exists. We want an answer to why "all there is" exists, and this does not permit a reason or cause outside of it. We cannot get from nothing to something without invoking a something whose existence is unexplained, and the alternative of self-explanation does not succeed. Indeed, answering the question may well end up being logically impossible in any terms since we can always ask why that answer exists—we cannot get beyond all that we are trying to explain.

The problem is not merely that our particular evolved brains are unable to deal with such matters: any being inside any universe cannot get outside of all that exists to gain a perspective from which to address the question. We just have to accept that the fact that something exists is an unexplained brute fact and move on. Wittgenstein thought that the riddle of existence does not exist because the question is not legitimate. And many philosophers today argue that it is a pseudo-question since there is no way to form an answer to it. The atheist J.J.C. Smart thought the question "Why does the cosmos exist at all?" is unanswerable and so should be set aside, but nevertheless that anything should exist at all still struck him as a matter of "the deepest awe." Nonetheless, merely because we are not in a position to answer the question does not mean that "Why is there something rather than nothing?" is not a legitimate, well-formed question.

Since we cannot answer the question, why anything exists will remain a permanent mystery for us, and we will just have to accept our lot—that something exists is simply a brute fact for which we have no explanation, causal or otherwise. Maybe there is a "because." Maybe not. The point is that we are not in a position to know. This is not to say that the universe necessarily exists or conversely that it happened by chance or is a random accident or a miracle—we cannot know. In addition, concepts such as "random" or "by chance" cannot apply since these presuppose some kind of *causation* that we would expect from our experience in the natural world, but that is missing for the totality of things. Nor can we call the universe "irrational" or "absurd" simply because we are not able to find a reason for it—that label presupposes that we know that there is in fact no reason for its existence. And if in the final analysis, the universe "just is" with no explanation, then its existence is "nonrational," not "irrational" (i.e., contrary to our reason).

The Wisdom of Queen Victoria

In the end, agnosticism again recommends itself since we are not in a position to answer the question of why anything exists or even to know if there is an answer. All we know for certain is that the mystery of existence will always remain open, however we deal with it: beings within the universe simply are not in a position to know why it exists. Nevertheless, it is difficult to maintain agnosticism and remain open here—even those not under the sway of the philosopher's disease want closure on such a basic question and thus to think that we know.

But if we do make a choice, we are left with having to pick our poison: accepting the existence of the universe as an unexplained brute fact, or positing the existence of a transcendent cause that is itself an unexplained brute fact. That is no better than accepting a cause that is itself a mystery or accepting no cause at all. Perhaps whatever general metaphysics one ascribes to will determine one's choice. But in any case, we end up with something unexplained. We must accept that whichever poison we pick, neither is an explanation providing an ultimate reason, and that in the end we are left with an unresolvable mystery, not understanding.

Thus, this is a genuine mystery that is a permanent part of the human condition—the universe's very existence is simply incomprehensible. Theists may accept that. After all, Job's answer from the whirlwind was "Where were you when I laid the earth's foundation?" (Job 38:4). But the philosophical mind may keep churning away. Isaiah Berlin likened philosophers to children who persist in asking "why?" Inquiring children can be bought off with ice cream, but philosophers cannot—they do not stop until there is a resolution or the acceptance that a mystery is involved. In the *Brihadaranyaka Upanishad* (3.6), the teacher Yajnavalkya is pressed again and again by Gargi over what is the true source of the world, and he finally has to tell her to stop questioning every answer he gives or her head would split open. As Queen Victoria wrote to her granddaughter: "I would earnestly warn you against trying to find out the reason and explanation of everything. . . . To try and find out the reason for everything is very dangerous and leads to nothing but disappointment and dissatisfaction, unsettling your mind and in the end making you miserable." This may be sage advice, but being what we are, we probably will go on searching for a "because" to answer the most fundamental cosmological "why" question even if we know that we can never find one.

Appendix

In the Prologue to his *Why Does the World Exist?* Jim Holt gives a simple philosophical argument for why something must exist:

> Suppose there is nothing. Then:
> (1) There would be no laws, for laws are something.
> (2) If there are no laws, then everything would be permitted.
> (3) If everything were permitted, then nothing would be forbidden.
> (4) So if there were nothing, nothing would be forbidden.
> (5) Thus, nothing is self-forbidding.
> (6) Thus, there must be something.

However, there are three problems with this argument. First, if we begin by supposing that there is nothing, then (2) "everything would be permitted" does not follow: if there is nothing, then there is nothing existing that could do anything, whether permitted or not—that is, if we start with the supposition that there is nothing, then there is nothing to do anything *period*. Second, the sense of "nothing would be forbidden" is different in (3) and (4): in (3) it means "there would be no restrictions on anything occurring"—following from (2)—but in (4) it shifts to something about "nothingness." Thus, (4) cannot follow from (3)—they are in fact unconnected. Third, (4) itself is a problem. Perhaps he means:

> (4') If there were nothing, nothingness itself would be forbidden.

But (4') is obviously wrong: no state of affairs would be forbidden because there is nothing to forbid it—there would simply be nothing. And if (4') is wrong, then (5) does not follow from (4'), and the argument fails. So perhaps he means this:

(4") If there were nothing, then there would be no states of affairs.

In this case, (4") is true and (5) does follow, but (6) does not follow. There would be a state of affairs—the lack of anything (i.e., the null set)—but (6) would follow only if we reify nothing into something: "There is a nothing there." But that would make nothingness into some reality, begging the question (if it made sense at all). Or perhaps Holt means:

(4'") If there were nothing, then no states of affairs are prohibited.

But (5) obviously does not follow from (4'")—indeed, it contradicts it.

I don't see any other options for what "nothing would be forbidden" could mean, and unless some viable option can be found, this argument fails to establish why there must be something, even ignoring the problems with (2) and (3).

Notes

1. Martin Heidegger made a verbal form of the word "nothing"—to "noth." That is, "nothing noths." However, this makes nothing into something—a thing that does something—thereby negating its nothingness. But this does show how our mind works: we cannot help but reify concepts.
2. The converse may also be true: once anything at all exists, there can never be nothing again—we can imagine the process, but nothing can terminate all existence including itself. Indeed, it is odd to think of the universe coming into existing and then going out of existence—as if it exists only for a brief period between two big nothings. But if time is a property only of what changes, we misconceive the situation by thinking that way.
3. This brings up a problem with applying Bayesian statistics to any basic issue: we have to make assumptions. Thus, for example, believers and nonbelievers would make different assumptions that would determine very different probabilities for the existence of God.
4. Seeking a cause to answer any "why" question is encapsulated in the word "because" itself: the word comes from the Middle English "*bi cause*"—"by the cause." The law of the conservation of energy is how we observe things today—it is not itself a natural force that somehow rules out an initial creation of matter/energy.
5. So too with theories such as loop quantum theory: the theory cannot explain why that law itself exists or why the loop is there. Similarly, if we follow the scientific assumption that matter/energy cannot be created or destroyed and thus that the universe is eternal, we can still

ask why that initial supply of matter/energy exists (and why it never changes).

6. Similarly, one should not (as Sean Carroll does) mix up the metaphysical question of whether the workings of nature can proceed without interference from a god with the metaphysical question of whether a god created the natural realm to begin with. Establishing that nature can operate without any transcendent input is irrelevant to the latter question.

7. Platonists assert that numbers and truths necessarily exist: such entities are eternal even if there are no conscious beings to know them or any phenomenal universe to manifest them. Some philosophers argue that there cannot be nothing since if there were no material phenomena there would then at least be the *fact* that there is nothing material or the real *absence* of material reality—thus, there is always *something*. But these philosophical denials of nothingness are irrelevant to the Big Question of why anything that we experience exists, although it does highlight the fact that the question of why *anything* exists is different from the question of why the *physical universe* exists.

8. The notion of "necessarily existing" also introduces the question of why anything that did *not* logically have to exist now exists—that is, why are there contingent realities, or the absence of necessary realities?

9. In addition, if current theories in physics are correct, the decay of a radioactive atom's nucleus is literally *uncaused*. Thus, there are events in the physical world that violate the principle of sufficient reason, and thus applying the principle in metaphysics to the world as a whole becomes very risky. Even if another theory replaces current theories, this still shows that we can conceive of there being contingent events without a cause.

6

Why Is Nature Ordered?

The eternal mystery of the world is its comprehensibility.

—Albert Einstein

When we move from the mystery of why there is something rather than nothing, the next Big Questions are why is there any phenomenal universe at all, and why does it have the general character it has? There appears to be no ultimate answer for why there should be any phenomenal universe—that is, why some principle should be instantiated in a physical form. But obviously something phenomenal now exists, and we can ask why it does and why it has the character it has. For example, why is there matter/energy, and, if there are other substances, why those? And why not others? And why does the universe have the order it has?

If all logically possible universes somehow must be realized in reality, then why ours has the structures and features that it has is not a mystery—some world had to have them. Theists will instead invoke a creator/designer god. There seems to be no way to test these options empirically from within our phenomenal world. Our metaphysical predilections may direct us to jump to a transcendent or a naturalistic answer to close our questioning, but we have no reasoned final explanation, nor do we have any reason to believe that we ever will. Agnostics can accept the universe's structures and features as simply an unexplained brute fact.

Why Any Order at All?

Let's look more closely at one of the mysteries: why is there any order at all? Without order and continuity in the world but only chaos, life could not form, nor could we comprehend nature. And no one can deny that there appears to be an incredibly intricate and complex order to reality.

61

But that the world is ordered at all is no less strange than that it exists. Why if anything exists, is it not just chaos? This question precedes the issue of why the universe has the particular structures and laws it has— it is the question why any phenomenal universe has any structure at all. The existence of a stable order is a presupposition of free will and also scientific testing—otherwise there would be no reason to expect our predictions to be fulfilled. But even a Theory of Everything will not approach the ultimate issue of why the universe is orderly in its operation (or why the order is causal)—no law of nature could explain why there are laws of nature.

So, if there could have been changes without any order, why is there order? Why didn't the "explosion" of the Big Bang bring total chaos? Where did order come from? Why is the universe structured with laws of nature in the first place? Why do laws exist? Did the laws governing nature's evolution exist before the physical universe? Objects do not simply bump into each other—why do higher levels of organization form and apparently have their own causal powers and orders of causation? Why is physics governed by exactingly precise laws? Are laws of nature evolving? Was the physicist Paul Dirac correct in suggesting that natural laws and constants (including the speed of light) may vary over time? If natural forces do change over time, why? If not, why not? Or is there no unique fundamental order, or none that is intelligible to us? If the ordered universe is eternal, order and laws were never created. If Platonists in mathematics are correct, laws exist timelessly regardless of whether there is a phenomenal universe to manifest them and whether there are conscious beings to know them—but we can still ask why they exist and how such principles cause phenomena to be ordered.

Where did this structure come from? Is there an intelligence behind the world? Or can we forego postulating a transcendent architect altogether? Even if being and natural structures both exist eternally, is "order" only something that we impose on reality since our minds seem hardwired to see patterns and agency even when there are none? Virtually all philosophers in the past have believed that reality coheres into a unity and that science shows how the parts fit together in that unity. But was Bertrand Russell correct in his bedrock conviction that the universe is "all spots and jumps, without unity, without continuity, without coherence or orderliness or any of the other properties that governesses love"? Do we make reality more intelligible than it actually is? Indeed, is the entire idea of a "law" of nature merely our invention, just the imposition of our idea of social laws onto nature? Should the idea of "laws" be discarded from science as an antiquated holdover of the idea of God as a law-giver?

Causation

And if there is order, why is the order *causal*? Forget about the problem of how one event exactly "causes" another—why are there laws of certain events and conditions causing certain other events? Or, like Leibniz's monads, are events independent but coordinated and ordered by some principle and we only infer causal connections between them? Since causation does not figure in fundamental physical equations, should we conclude that causation is not in fact a feature of reality? Or is reality genuinely causal? Is there also a fixed determinism of events? If causation is a real part of our everyday world but not the subatomic world, why is that so?[1]

The empiricist David Hume's argument about the nature of causation should also be noted: all we actually experience are isolated individual sense-impressions; we infer that there is a causal connection and order only by habit from the correlations of events that we regularly see together, but we cannot know whether there are actual connections or not. To be certain that there is an unvarying necessary causal conjunction of types of experiences, we would have to demonstrate that nature operates according to unvarying laws, but all we have is our habits, and we cannot extrapolate from them to an objective cause/effect order existing independently of us. Nor do past regularities guarantee that nature will not change and abandon these patterns. Any argument for the objectivity of a causal order inevitably involves circularity. Thus, our reason cannot demonstrate that there is an objective causal order to reality. The same argument applies to any alleged immutable laws of nature. We have no guarantee that our limited sense-impressions reflect reality as it truly is. We can know only our individual sense-impressions. We cannot attain truth about reality independent of them—that remains a mystery.

Why Is There Disorder?

Complexity in the universe seems to grow over time as the structures do their work. But consider the presence of *disorder* in our universe. According to current theories in physics, there are only probabilities at subatomic levels for certain events, not deterministic certainties—such as in the radioactive decay of groups of atomic nuclei: there is no way to predict which particular nucleus will disintegrate. Physicists end up with statistical laws, albeit very precise ones, showing only patterns. Many scientists accept this as the final word on the subject—there is literally no reason why certain events occur. But why is there such randomness in an ordered universe? Some physicists refuse to accept such indeterminacy—as Albert Einstein said, "God does not play dice." They believe that the necessity of using a statistical method shows only that physicists have not yet found the foundational laws of nature, and so they look for deeper deterministic laws. But merely because indeterminacy is "unsatisfying" certainly does not mean reality must conform to our wishes. Why must there be something like a Pythagorean "harmony of the spheres" to reality?

Order and Structure

In the end, order and the presence of structures is as much a mystery as why there is something rather than nothing. The structures of the universe and their origin need explaining just as much as existence itself, as does how structures are imprinted upon the substances they structure. Structures do not emerge from matter but are a separate dimension of reality. Naturalists accept them as simply brute facts incapable of further explanation. As the British emergentist Samuel Alexander put it, the existence of the powers must be accepted with "natural piety." Deists and theists will posit a transcendent god as a law-giver, and their positions cannot be ruled out if invoking a further mystery to explain a mystery is permissible. But are we barred from ever knowing the ultimate explanation? We have no reason to believe that we will ever know with certainty which option is correct or whether there may be other options that we cannot conceive. Beings within the natural order, whatever their cognitive abilities, may be incapable of knowing. If so, why there is order to reality at all will remain an intractable mystery.

Notes

1. One basic question—must any order be causal?—is difficult to address. Even imagining an alternative order for an empirical world is hard for beings within a world such as ours.

7
Reductionism and Emergence

Poets say science takes away from the beauty of the stars—mere globs of gas atoms. Nothing is "mere." I too can see the stars on a desert night, and feel them. But do I see less or more?

—Richard Feynman

If metaphysics is about cutting nature at its joints and establishing the foundational explanatory principles, then central to it is determining what are the true substances and structures of reality at the foundations of things, and this brings up the issue of reductionism. Both reductionists and antireductionists want to explain the world's phenomena with the fewest types of irreducibly real substances and structures—they simply disagree over the number needed. Is there more than one substance to reality (e.g., matter and consciousness), or is all of reality made of only one type of stuff? Is the universe nothing but matter pushing matter in a void? Are human beings nothing but soulless machines, at best existing only to propagate genes? Is the mind nothing but the brain? Is the natural universe all there is, or are there also transcendent realities? In the cases of life, consciousness, and society, do new realities emerge that cannot be reduced to simpler components? How do parts *become* wholes and create new entities? Can wholes act *downwardly* on their own parts? So too, are the structures depicted in physics the only real structures operating in the universe? If so, are all scientific theories and concepts ultimately reducible to those of physics?

What Is a Reduction?

There are eliminationists in metaphysics who deny the very existence of some everyday phenomena (e.g., life or consciousness). But reductionists do not deny the reality of life, minds, and so forth. Rather, they attempt to *explain* such macrophenomena in terms of simpler realities not having the properties to be explained. If the explained phenomena have no causal power, then they are considered merely epiphenomena. A reduction thus gets us away from dependent realities and closer to the independent realities and fundamental causal powers—what is more basic in explanations and thus "more real" in that sense. For example, it is not a reduction to claim that a religious experience cannot occur without a certain neural state of the brain—the reduction is to claim that the experience is *only* that brain state.

An example of a reduction in science is the explanation of the heat of a gas. When we explain why one object is hot by pointing out that it is being heated by another hot object, we only explain why that particular object is hot—we have not explained the *phenomenon of heat* itself. To explain heat itself, we have to invoke something that is itself *not hot*—that is, something to which the concept of "heat" does not apply but which is responsible for heat. For the heat of gas, scientists have advanced such an explanation in terms of the movement of molecules: the molecules themselves are athermal entities, but their movement generates heat. To reductionists, heat is not *caused* by molecular movement but simply *is* nothing but the movement of molecules. The temperature of a gas is reduced to the average kinetic energy of its molecules. It is an aggregate effect like the shape of the mound created by pouring out particles of sand into a pile. Indeed, reductionists reduce all of the thermodynamics of energy and entropy to the kinetic laws of individual particles and their momenta. Thus, there is nothing left to explain about the heat of a gas after this reduction.

An example of a dilemma that inspires reductionism comes from the astrophysicist Arthur Eddington. He presented a paradox: he was actually writing on two tables at once—the *"everyday table"* that we experience (bulky, colored, substantive, comparatively permanent) and the *"scientific table"* (mostly emptiness with numerous electrical charges constantly rushing about furiously). The problem is how to reconcile these two very different realities. Is the table really solid and rigid, or is it mostly empty space? Reductionists have a simple solution: only the "scientific table" is real—there are no composite entities; rather, there are only simple realities without further parts that are arranged by physical forces into entities. That is, there is no everyday table but only subatomic particles "arranged table-wise," and all the everyday phenomena of the table are caused only by those particles. The reality of solidity thus is not denied, but we do not have to include "tables" in our inventory of what is real—a swarm of quarks, or whatever are the real particulars, is all that is really there, and everyday solidity is simply the rigid arrangement of those parts.

Types of Reductionism

Ontic and structural reductionism must be clearly distinguished.[1] Ontic reductionism involves the stuff of the universe, and structural reductionism involves the fields and forces in the universe ordering the interactions of things. To use an analogy, consider this book: the ink and paper are the substance, but the letters, words, and sentences structured by the rules of grammar order the ink. The two dimensions cannot be conflated, and no amount of study of one dimension can give any information about the other. So too, just as grammarians can ignore the ink or any other medium of embodiment, scientists can ignore the ontic stuff of the universe—the "being" of the universe—in which the structures they study are instantiated. Philosophers do not typically distinguish substance and structure and so do not distinguish ontic and structural reductionism—thus they mistakenly believe that a commitment to ontic reductionism also requires a commitment to structural reductionism. So too, looking at the makeup of the universe in terms of "substance" and "properties" without the role of structure is off track.

Ontic reductionists believe that life and consciousness can be explained as exclusively physical phenomena. Ontic dualists affirm a self or mind in addition to the material body. But ontic reductionists may reject structural reductionism and accept that more than only physical structures are at work in nature. For example, naturalists are ontic reductionists—they believe there is only one type of reality and it is open in principle to scientific analysis and so reject any separate life-substance or mind-substance. But naturalists are not necessarily structural reductionists: there is no reason that one cannot be a naturalist and still accept that some types of natural forces are not reducible to physical ones but are open to scientific study. Thus, scientists can affirm the reality of biological structures and still be naturalists. (If ontic and structural reductionism are distinguished, resistance to structural antireductionism may lessen.)

Structural reductionists go further than ontic reductionism: there is only physical structure at work in what is real—everything consists only of the complex interactions of realities having only physical properties.[2] Most structural reductionists may believe that ultimately there are only quantum-level realities and that everything else is only produced from the interaction of quantum structures, thereby unifying all apparently different physical and nonphysical structures. As theoretical physicist Lee Smolin says, "[t]welve particles and four forces are all we need to explain everything in the known world." Thus, all things are only more and more complex combinations of one order of structure. But one can be a scientist without believing that—one can practice science and believe that there are irreducibly biological or psychological structures or multiple types of irreducible physical causes. For example, the mind may be ontologically only the same type of stuff as rocks and trees, but it may have irreducibly nonphysical properties. Even many physicists reject the notion that there are only physical properties, and many reductionists within physics reject the notion that there are only quantum-level structures. Philip Anderson can say that particle physics is "utterly irrelevant" to his work in condensed matter physics. In short, one can endorse ontic reductionism and reject structural or theoretical reductionism and still be a scientist. And according to polls, many American scientists actually reject ontic reductionism: they may treat nature as closed for scientific purposes, but many are theists, deists, or agnostics concerning transcendent realities.

One caricature of reductionists is that they deny the phenomena of the everyday world. Another is that they believe that to determine what actually is real we have to chop up entities into their tiniest parts since only the lowest subatomic particles void of structure exist—all we have to do is look at things' parts in isolation to see all we need to know about the things themselves; we can totally ignore their organization. However, reductionists need not be mechanicalists but can consider the context of a phenomenon as relevant. So too, they must accept that physical structures are an irreducible part of the world. Matter is not inherently attracted to matter: without some form of gravitational structure this would not occur. Thus, there is a difference between a box of loose computer parts and a functioning computer. The box of parts and the working computer are not simply two different arrangements of the parts: materially they are the same, but one can do something the other cannot. Structural reductionists recognize that higher-level phenomena such as solidity are real and not features of subatomic particles—when we step on the floor, it is not like stepping onto a "swarm of flies," as Eddington put it. Nature may be, as Bertrand Russell said, a "vast collection of electric charges in violent motion," but solidity still persists in the everyday world and thus is a genuine feature of reality even if it is not a feature of the atomic and subatomic levels of the world. But these reductionists believe that the subatomic particles *in situ* are all that is needed *to explain* all such higher-level properties: if we ever learn all about the parts *in situ* of any whole, there is nothing more to know about the whole. This is true of persons as well as tables. While ontic reductionists believe that persons are a totally physical phenomenon, they cannot think that persons are unstructured piles of matter, simple aggregates of subatomic parts—structures are at work organizing matter into living, conscious human beings. In this way, amorphous aggregates are distinguished from structured entities: structure gives matter properties other than simply existing. Thus, there is no more to the entity than those atoms ordered by physical structures: atoms in persons have been arranged in such a way that the wholes become conscious.

In sum, for structural reductionists wholes are only the sum their parts *in situ*, but they must accept that structures ordering the interaction of things are a necessary part of the explanatory picture. They do not deny context, but they see all phenomena as completely explainable by their parts *in situ*. They can accept that there is a hierarchy of scales or levels of interactions and complexity beginning with elementary quantum realities up to the everyday world. For example, interactions on the quantum level of a baseball bat and ball may appear to be totally irrelevant to the causal act of a batter hitting a ball, but according to reductionists the structures at work, like the stuff structured, are completely physical, and interactions on each lower level completely determine the next higher level of complexity. Thus, the interaction of the batter, bat, and ball merely requires a very complex description in quantum terms but is possible in principle. Quantum-level physical truths entail all phenomenal truths. In short, reality is nothing more than physical particles and the structures studied by physicists. In the end, there is a simplicity to explaining everything, with no need for multiple types of substances or any nonphysical structures.

Thus, for structural reductionists, all phenomena are only more and more complex layers of interactions of simpler physical parts governed by quantum-level laws or perhaps higher-level physical laws. All explanations in terms of higher-level phenomena are only temporary conveniences—eventually all theories will be in physical terms, and so only physical theories will ultimately remain standing. All will be describable by relatively simple mathematical equations or computer programs. If higher-level theories remain, it is only because of an epistemic problem that we have, not because of the nature of reality: the interactions of lower-level realities that produce the illusion of independent higher-level realities may be too complex for the human brain to analyze, but there is no "emergence" of any new realities in any sense of the word. Many reductionists see unique concepts for higher-level phenomena as indispensable for descriptions of those phenomena those phenomena but only for our convenience—for them, questions of the final ontology can be framed only in physical concepts.

Antireductionism

Antireductionists see reality as more complicated: new principles are operating in the higher levels of phenomena that are not governed by quantum or other level physical laws. Ontic antireductionists claim that there is more than one substance to reality, and structural antireductionists claim that there are biological and psychological structures as well as physical ones organizing nature. Matter does not produce or otherwise generate life or conscious, nor do physical structures—thus, to require an explanation of how matter or physical structures generate life and consciousness (as structural reductionists do) is to view the situation wrongly from the very start. The nonphysical structures create different orders of causal interaction between phenomena, and determinism on one level does not necessarily translate into determinism on another. So too, interlevel causation does not entail a reduction. For example, if quantum level events are one cause of gene mutation, as "quantum biologists" assert, nevertheless biological structures still organize those events' effects. Biological structures dampen the chemical "noise" within a living cell and create order. What is real is not reducible to merely the physical since some properties cannot be explained by the physical properties of their components *in situ*. Antireductive properties are any that cannot be completely explained from the bottom up or as aggregates of the parts and their properties. Wholes are integrated systems with some unique properties that cannot be predicted or explained by even complete accounts of their parts. The parts of such systems are entangled, and so the state of the system cannot be defined simply by listing the state of its parts. Physical structures are not "more real" than other structures, nor do they explain nonphysical structures. (Nor are nonphysical structures any more teleological than physical ones.) Thus, there are higher-level truths that cannot be deduced from lower-level truths. Living and conscious beings have properties and can do things that their parts cannot account for. There is no need for a living substance—such as Henri Bergson's "*élan vital*"—if nature has biological structures (e.g., biotic fields) producing living organisms.[3]

Quantum physics may show that on that scale there are real structures but no real entities (i.e., causal wholes). Nevertheless, structural antireductionists accept different layers of atomic and subatomic particles to be real entities because of their causal powers—atoms can *do* things as a unit that cannot be accounted for simply by their components *in situ* and hence are structurally as much "entities" as their components. Each such organized pattern of activity is an entity in its own right. Lower-level structures merely provide some of the conditions for the new phenomena not found in lower-level entities *in situ*, not create or constitute such phenomena. Some antireductionists consider emergence of new structural realities to be very rare, limited only to life and consciousness or even only to the latter. To others, it is a common event even on the physical level. For example, molecules. John Stuart Mill pointed out that salt crystals are nothing like the sodium and chlorine atoms composing them. And once NaCl molecules are incorporated into a living being, their properties may change again. Wholes depend on their parts for their sustained existence, but the parts' causal capacities become partially dependent upon the whole. The atoms lose their individual properties *in situ*: new features appear in the systems formed by the interactions of the atoms. The wetness of water manifests a property through chemical bonding that the properties of the hydrogen and oxygen atoms *in situ* do not; thus, if we analyze H_2O completely, we will not be able to explain all the phenomenal properties of water in terms of its chemical parts, let alone quarks. The heat of gases may also be an irreducible property—temperature is not like the pressure that is generated by the pounding from the motion of the molecules but is a new type of phenomenon, even if we can correlate changes in temperature with changes in the amount of motion. Some antireductionists begin emergence even lower. For example, a proton is made up of three quarks, but it has properties (e.g., angular momentum) that cannot be found by adding up the properties of quarks. So too, electrons lose their individual identity when they become part of an atom: to understand an atom, we have to look at the properties of the functioning whole system, not those of the components. Overall, as Gilbert Ryle noted, particle physicists in a very real sense do not describe tables and chairs at all.

Thus, if the reductionists' catchphrase is "nothing but," the antireductionists' is "yes, but." Structural antireductionists are not saying that human beings or other phenomena are *materially* more than their physical parts but that nonphysical *structures* operating in them give them properties that can never be found by analyzing their parts even in the context of the wholes. The chemicals underlying DNA do not contain the biological "information" written in DNA—the sequence of molecules is irrelevant to the underlying chemistry and thus is merely "accidental" from the point of view of physics and chemistry. But to antireductionists, DNA is a structural reality in addition to its chemical components.

Thus, higher-level structured wholes are "more than the sum of their parts" and hence are as real as their parts and must be included in our inventory of reality as real entities along with their components. Such phenomena are materially the same as the sum of their parts (i.e., ontic reductionism still applies and there is no need to postulate additional substances), but they are, structurally speaking, separate entities from their material parts. Not all of the wholes' properties are determined by the properties of their parts. In sum, a golden statue must be included in our ontology in addition to the collection of gold molecules arranged in statue form that materially constitute it if it has unique properties as a whole that are not the sum of the properties of its parts *in situ*. If it does not have any unique properties, it is only an aggregate of parts and not a real entity.[4]

Many metametaphysicians think that there is no substantive question about whether the statue exists or is merely a pile of gold molecules arranged as a statue—to ask whether there "really" is a statue in addition to the gold molecules is a misguided unanswerable question. (Presumably, the same applies to "persons" and the physical entities arranged as persons.) But to antireductionists if a structured entity has properties that its parts *in situ* do not, a substantive question of what is real does remain. Distinct causal powers of wholes are especially important. How structures exist and how matter and structure are connected may remain mysteries. But all "spontaneously self-organizing" phenomena on every level have an equal claim to reality, and none are reducible to phenomena on other levels.[5]

Structural antireductionism is usually described as "emergentism." However, basic antireductionism is structurally more modest than emergentism. From the anti-reductionists' point of view, no new reality "emerges" or "emanates" from matter: there need not be an upward power causing higher-level phenomena—the lower levels of structures merely set the stage for higher levels of structures to become operative.[6] No new structures emerge from physical structures, and there is no upward causation of new phenomena from the bases. Thus, according to antireductive naturalists, no new realities sprout miraculously into the universe—only more layers of natural structure are at work in higher-level phenomena such as living and conscious beings. In short, the physical and chemical properties become base-conditions for more natural structures to kick in. In this way, the higher-level phenomena depend on the lower-level phenomena for their appearance, but they are not determined or fixed by the lower-level phenomena or otherwise reducible. The base-conditions are not creative; they are merely necessary preconditions for higher structures to become active. Perhaps the disorder that arises when more and more entities on one level interact is a necessary condition for higher levels of organization to become operational. In any case, there is no need for separate "emergent forces" causing nature to become more and more complex or driving nature upward to make conscious beings: when the bases are assembled properly, higher-level phenomena naturally appear under the operation of nonphysical level structures without anything more. Only emergentists appeal to special upward-driving forces, and only reductionists have the problem of explaining higher-level phenomena as the products of upward causation from lower-level phenomena.

Nor do all antireductionists introduce downward causation, that is, higher phenomena affecting their physical and chemical bases.[7] Emergentists go further and include "top-down" causal power, but antireductionists need not argue that: higher-level phenomena do not emerge out of lower-level phenomena and are not produced by them; rather, higher-level wholes are produced by natural structures and are part of one inclusive causal order; these structures may affect the physical base-conditions, but the higher-level phenomena do not.[8] Wholes do not affect the parts, and no new forces are operating on subatomic levels—quarks and electrons behave the same in inorganic and organic entities. It is not as if wholes that arose later act backward in time to form their own bases. But the components fuse to form the bases for higher-level phenomena.

According to structural antireductionists, two perspectives are needed to understand any phenomenon: both the parts and the wholes must be studied. For antireductionists, there are biotic structures that are as built into the universe as firmly as physical ones such as gravity and electromagnetism, making life as natural and normal as rocks. So too with consciousness. Such nonphysical structures may have existed since the Big Bang, just as did the physical structures that would eventually produce atoms, but they had to wait to become operative until the proper base-conditions arose. Materially, living and conscious beings are only the physical parts making them up, but more levels of natural structure are operating in them. Thus, biologists would not learn more about biological structures by studying quantum physics. Physicists and biologists produce different accounts of a plant because they study different levels of its organization. In this way, no science is more fundamental than any other, even if physicists study the broadest levels that are the base-conditions for all higher-level phenomena. Thus, not all theories in biology are reducible to theories in physics—some may be, but some capture a unique level of properties and activity. In fact, structural antireductionists believe that there are fewer intertheoretic reductions than reductionists suppose—instead, explanatory "gaps" are common. And each level requires some unique concepts to depict its phenomena.

Reductive and Antireductive Ontologies and Explanations

The differences in ontology between reductionists and antireductionists lead to differences in how many types of explanatory theories in science and levels of conceptualizations are needed in the final analysis. Many naturalists follow Willard Quine in believing that we should only accept in our ontology those entities that the best scientific theories of our day require, and thus the number of necessary levels of theories becomes important. Structural antireductionists see multiple levels of organization, each requiring their own explanations and concepts; reductionists see only physics as needed in the end, and thus the number of theories and their ontological commitments will be corresponding smaller.[9]

Many people think that science is inherently reductive in its search for a simplicity to the workings of nature. Scientific algorithms, as John Barrow puts it, condense vast arrays of observational data into compact formulas; and science aims to explain more and more phenomena with fewer and fewer theories. Thus, many believe that all science must push toward a reduction to physics and a final Theory of Everything—the objective of science is to show that simple laws explain extraordinarily complex phenomena that do not possess the symmetries of the underlying laws. (Whether a TOE is in fact a theory of everything or only a theory of *one level of everything* will be discussed in chapter 9.)

However, science involves only *the analysis and explanations of phenomena*. But structural reductionism is not merely a matter of the scientific identification of the physical or chemical bases in a phenomenon—reductionists go a step further and make the metaphysical claim that the reality of a whole is *nothing but its parts and physical structures*. A reduction, in short, reduces the *reality* of a phenomenon to *something else* that it appears to be. In addition, "reduction*ism*" is more than any scientific reductions: antireductionists can readily accept that some apparent realities or theories may be reduced without embracing the "ism" that scientists must march toward reducing all realities and theories—they see limits to how much reduction is possible and see no reason to force a reduction of all structures to physical ones on a metaphysical Procrustean bed. Scientists do try to bring more and more phenomena under the umbrella of one theory, but there may be limits: antireductionists assert that the search for simplicity should not be simplistic and force reductions at all costs merely because the reductionists' metaphysics demands it—that would distort reality. If in the end more levels of structure are accepted by scientists, multiple levels of theory will also have to be accepted, and there is nothing antiscientific about that conclusion—science is fitted to what is real, not to a metaphysics of inclusion that overextends its reach. Antireductionists accept some entities as ontologically real because of their properties as a unit even if the science of the operation of its parts is complete. In sum, scientific analysis itself is neutral to the question of reductionism and antireductionism.

Thus, the issue between reductionists and antireductionists comes down to the basic makeup of the universe: how many substances, entities, and structures exist? It is a question of metaphysics. The reductionists' conviction is that there is a fundamental simplicity in the workings of the universe behind what we experience, both in substance and in structure: all that is needed is matter and however many physical forces there are at work in nature for the universe to evolve into what it is today, even if some randomness is also involved in the history of the course of events. The antireductionists' intuition is that since the physics operating in stones and plants is the same, there must be more at work in plants than just more complex physical interactions: for higher-level phenomena such as life and consciousness, nonphysical structures (and perhaps mental substances) are also needed.[10]

The Mysteries of Reductionism and Emergence

To sum up: even if there is only one substance to the natural world, properties resulting from structures are also real features of that reality. Reality also appears to be a layered hierarchy of levels of phenomena. Structural reductionists do not deny that structured phenomena are real or that there are even multiple levels of properties—rather, they insist that all can by explained by the forces of physics alone. Thorough-going reductionists insist that ultimately only realities on the quantum level (or whatever is the basic field or level of physical structure) have causal power even though describing in quantum terms the convoluted quantum interactions of everyday phenomena is too cumbersome in practice. Structural antireductionists, on the other hand, believe that nonphysical forces are operating in nature and that causal power is not confined to products of physical structures—thus, there are irreducible nonphysical phenomena and multiple levels of irreducible properties. To antireductionists, causal wholes are as real a part of the world as their lower bases. We cannot reduce everything to the physical, let alone quantum, level. More structures are needed to explain all the phenomena of the world, and multiple sciences will remain needed to explain phenomena—quantum physics will never replace, say, biology, even in principle, nor will biology replace a science of mental structures. Scientists simply will not be able to deduce biological or psychological theories from quantum physics plus limiting conditions. A final "disunity of the sciences" will remain standing, not the "unification of the sciences" that logical positivists envisioned.

There are three mysteries to all of this. First, the basic "how" mystery: neither structural reductionists nor antireductionists as of yet can explain how everyday phenomena relate to quantum-level realities. It is a daunting task to explain the complex phenomena of the universe. Reductionists must get "more from less" using only the forces of physics. But they seem unconcerned by the general lack interest by scientists in searching for reductions. Nevertheless, they have only a metaphysical picture of what they assume must be the case—physics has not yet shown how quantum-level events produce, say, the wetness of water or how higher-level phenomena are even possible. Multiple levels within entities must be accounted for. Perhaps unwieldy complexity on one level somehow triggers the arising of a new level of causal interaction that is relatively simple compared to the lower level. But even coming up with testable hypotheses for how higher-level phenomena appear in an orderly manner is difficult. Reductionists may claim that the complexity of interactions is so great that it makes it impossible as a practical matter to specify the details of the reductions, and that the role of randomness prevents a reconstruction of the history of the universe from simple laws. But they will add that this is only our epistemic problem and does not affect the reality of the reductions occurring through physical forces. They may take this problem to be a permanent shield against all criticism—even if some phenomena resist multiple attempts at reduction, this will probably not dent the structural reductionists' commitment to all things being material and that in principle reductions are possible.

On the other side, antireductionists have not found any structures comparable to those in physics to explain life or consciousness or a law of nature governing evolving complexity. All either side has at present are declarations of metaphysics. Because reductionism requires fewer structures does not mean the reductionists' task is simpler—indeed, that makes it harder. But perhaps scientists will discover a way to explain each instance of a higher level of a phenomenon by its lower-level activity alone. Or perhaps they will discover nonphysical structures. But antireductionists need not endorse special structures devoted uniquely to causing emergence.

But the mystery of how higher levels appear may be amenable to scientific resolution. A second mystery is that the appearance of more and more levels of phenomena seems to be *a central feature of reality*. Why is the universe so creative in this way? Even if there are also random events in nature, why is the universe apparently organized into different levels of causal interactions, and why do more and more levels appear? Scientists may be able to explain how higher levels of complexity appear, but why is reality set up to do that? That is, why do higher and higher levels of organization appear at all? Reductionists have to deal with this central feature of reality. Even if scientists could give a quantum-level account of all phenomena, reductionists still must explain why and how reality is organized to produce higher-level phenomena. How do structures exist, and how do they structure the stuff of reality? How do entities unite the causal power of their parts to form new causal wholes and why? (Advocates of hylomorphism invoke special structures that carve out individuals from the sea of matter/energy. At a minimum, this does raise the issue of why reality has individual entities.) Why did our evolving universe generate ever-increasing orders of organization? Why do higher levels have their own laws? Even if large groups of subatomic particles somehow cancel out subatomic properties, why does each level of properties have some unique features? Why do billiard balls and planets behave by new laws? Why aren't higher levels merely disordered products of quantum events? Why didn't the universe remain on the quantum level, and why didn't the complexities of interactions remain of one type? In short, not only how but *why* did the non-quantum world appear?

The structural reductionists' quest to identify the smallest physical parts of reality and the true physical forces and then to explain all of reality in those terms cannot explain the presence of the upward drive in complexity. If nature builds in an upward fashion from physical laws and only entities with lower-level structures, how do these entities happen to become parts that support higher-level phenomena? Why did a pile of interacting inanimate material apparently operating only under physical structures become reproducing and exhibit all the other indices of life? And why did some of the piles become aware of themselves and exhibit the other indices of consciousness? Neo-Darwinian evolution may explain the development of life and consciousness once they arose, but why is reality organized to permit life to appear to begin with? Structural antireductionists accept the full causal reality of different levels of organization. For them, "emergence" is no mystery: more irreducible natural structures simply operate in some things.

Nevertheless, a science of the upward thrust of emergence is needed to explain this, not merely sciences of systems and complexity. The four forces that physicists currently recognized do not appear related to emergence. Each force would only produce more of the same order and if anything would prevent higher levels of order from arising. For example, gravity would only lump more and more matter together and would do nothing toward organizing it, let alone make higher levels appear. Nor would the interaction of all the known physical forces collectively produce higher levels. In short, the basic forces of physics cannot establish how physical connections enable higher levels of organization. As the physicist Paul Davies puts it, the forces of physics merely shuffle existing "information" around, not create new "information." Throwing in a role for random events to explain the history of the universe does not help but only hurts the possibility of explaining the appearance of more and more levels of organization. And when it comes to biology, it is not clear how gene mutation or natural selection alone would lead to greater types of complex organisms. Why is nature set up to permit cells to combine into specialized organs? Is there a "social" dimension to reality provided by structures? (Teleology is not part of basic antireductionism.)

Stephen Hawking once opined: "I think the [21st] century will be the century of complexity. We have already discovered the basic laws that govern matter and understand all the normal situations. We don't know how the laws fit together, and what happens under extreme conditions. But I expect we will find a complete unified theory sometime this century." However, a general theory of complexity has yet to come forth—indeed, the study of the basis of complexity is not showing signs of great advancement. In any case, a science of *emergence* is needed, not merely a science of complexity. A related problem is that a new mathematics may also be needed for a science of emergence—bifurcation theory may be a start, but more is involved in emergence than merely complexity.

A third mystery appears intractable: how can we test between the reductive and antireductive metaphysical alternatives? If we could discover a universe in which, for example, H_2O existed but did not produce the properties of water, we could conclude that higher levels of structure are at work in our universe when hydrogen and oxygen combine in this way. But that test is obviously impossible. Experiments in this world will not help: a scientific finding will not determine if new structures are involved or not since the observed phenomena would look the same either way. If, for example, scientists are able to produce life from a soup of chemicals, the basic dispute would remain: is life produced from only the physical chemicals, or have scientists merely assembled the base-conditions enabling biological structures to become active? Do the chemicals *in situ produce* life or merely *set the stage* for more structures in nature to order the chemicals? Either way, life would appear "spontaneously." This problem exists for whatever scientists establish. (This raises the prospect that scientists may not be able to detect higher structures even if they exist. At least how to test for them would be complicated.) Thus, science may not decide between a reductive and an antireductive explanation. Nor will computer simulations of the interactions of parts help since they will depend on our programming reflecting either reductive or antireductive assumptions—if we write a program that generates emergence from reductive assumptions, we cannot be certain that nature works that way. And this exhausts any way to test between these two schools of metaphysics. The Big Question of what are the fundamental structures and substances operating in the universe appears to be irresolvable, and thus we are left with an unsolvable mystery.

Notes

1. Actually, five types of reductionism and antireductionism should be distinguished: ontic (the number of substances), structural (the number of forces ordering nature), theoretical (the number of necessary types of scientific theories), conceptual, and methodological (see Jones 2013: ch. 1). But for the issue of mystery, the first three types are the most important.

2. The term "materialism" will not be used here since it may mean either one type of ontic reductionism or a combination of both ontic and structural reductionism. In other words, it is not clear whether an ontic physicalist who rejects structural reductionism (and thus accept structures other than those of physics) should be classified as a "materialist" or not.

3. Even in denying vitalism, matter should not be called "lifeless." Unless panpsychists are correct (in which case all matter is conscious in some way), parts of reality are organic and parts are inorganic because of the *structures* operating in them. That is, the stuff of the universe in itself is neutral: whether a whole is physical or both physical and biological (or also psychological) depends on the structures at work, with different properties resulting.

4. How much is the human body worth? The answer varies depending on the level of structure involved. If we look only at the chemicals involved, then the body is mostly water and not worth very much. But if we look at the biological level of organs, then it is worth quite a bit. Structure makes all the difference.

5. "Self-organization" is a misnomer and distorts our picture of what is going on. When theorists speak of a pile of iron filings "spontaneously self-organizing," they do not mean that the filings literally organize themselves—a *structure* (magnetism) is at work ordering them. So too, water does not "spontaneously" freeze magically for no reason—it does so only under specific physical structures and conditions. Similarly, higher-level phenomena appear through natural forces, not "spontaneously." In sum, "self-organization" only means that natural forces alone are at work in a phenomenon.

6. Only the reductionist perspective leads us to think of higher levels being caused by lower levels and thus "emerging" from them. But from an antireductionist perspective, there are merely more structures operating in some phenomena than in others—nothing "emerges" from something else.

7. Reductionists believe that they can handle the social type of downward causation—such as the role of soldier ants in their colonies explaining why their jaws are so specialized for piercing their enemies that they cannot feed themselves. Reductionists see such phenomena as in effect

unconscious genetic engineering determined by complicated physical factors alone.

8. Antireductionists can argue that, say, biological structures shape the chemical parts that form organisms. When we have the idea for something new, we do not proceed by looking around for preexisting things that are laying around—we have the idea of the thing in mind and make the parts that are necessary. In nature, higher structures replace "intelligent design": biological structures create the chemical entities into living cells and more complex entities. In this way, in cases of higher-level causal realities, nature does not build *upward* from preexisting parts (as reductionists believe) but starts with the structures of the wholes and works *downward* to make the parts from the available material. Reductionists must explain how the laws of physics alone make the parts that then combine to form new wholes with new levels of properties.

9. Reductionists are committed to a naturalistic theory of mind in order for it to be reducible. Antireductionists can accept a naturalistic mental structure or an ontic dualism—for example, Henri Bergson's theory of the brain as a reducing valve that lets in only as much of a cosmic "mind at large"as we need to survive; altered states of consciousness may let in more of it.

10. Emergentists have more elaborate ontologies, for instance, an independent soul emerging from consciousness. Samuel Alexander had such a comprehensive metaphysics: matter emerged from space-time; life emerged from complex configurations of matter; consciousness emerged from biological processes; and deity emerged out of consciousness. Even space could be seen as an emergent reality generated as the Big Bang expands, and causation between parts may be a level-effect that only appears above a certain level of phenomena.

8

Does Science Dispel Mystery?

> Theories don't prove nothing, they only give you a place to rest on a spell, when you are tuckered out butting around and around trying to find out something there ain't no way to find out. . . . There's another trouble about theories: there's always a hole in them somewhere sure, if you look close enough.
>
> —Mark Twain (Huck Finn in *Tom Sawyer Abroad*)

The next Big Question is whether scientific theories harbor any genuine mysteries. Science has the reputation of demystifying reality—as with John Keats's claim that Newton "unwove" the rainbow and conquered "all mysteries by rule and line." Indeed, the objective of modern science in the eyes of many (and not just logical positivists) is to eliminate all mystery from reality and to replace it with solid knowledge. According to physicist Niels Bohr, "[s]cience's job is to reduce all mysteries to trivialities." If so, science is a powerful tool against mystery. And its scope is increasing: more scientific knowledge has been achieved in the past few decades than in all pervious history. But is such a view justified?

Basic Science

Science is a way of questioning nature, and this is more noteworthy than the theories held at any particular moment. Fundamental scientific research is about *how things work*. First, scientists attempt to establish lawful patterns of events in the natural world through observations and experiments that are checkable by others. (Much of what even scientists believe in their work-life is taken on faith in previous scientific findings, but at least with the proper training they could in principle duplicate those past findings.) They then use reasoning to posit features in nature that may not be open to direct experience (e.g., fields) that they hypothesize are responsible for the lawful changes in the everyday world. Explanatory theories based on those posits direct observation and the direction of research, thereby affecting what we attempt to know of reality. They also affect what are taken to be facts—for example, the nature of the "sun" and the "planets" in a Ptolemaic versus a heliocentric cosmology.

But there can never be a theory-neutral explanation of phenomena. Empirical testing keeps theories from being groundless speculation, but the human element is always present: we never get a scientific picture of reality that is not answering our questions. As Werner Heisenberg stated, "what we observe is not nature but nature exposed to our method of questioning." Nature constrains our imagination by providing empirical feedback to our questions, but it does not tell us what questions to ask. And, as the ancient Greek Heraclitus noted long ago, "nature loves to hide."

Scientists advance mathematical models of how they think something in nature works. Under antirealist interpretations, science is about only the observed events, and we have no claim to know what we cannot experience. For antirealists, scientific theories are at best merely shorthand devices for connecting observations—it is pointless to debate whether the models are "true" or "real" but only whether they agree with observations. Theories say nothing about what is actually real. So too with such principles as the conservation of energy: these are only mathematical tools and not meant to be descriptions of mechanisms in nature. Some antirealists treat all natural laws as part of our models and thus as human inventions. Empiricists do not deny that real structures are at work in the world; they claim only that we can have no knowledge of them if we cannot experience them and thus we should reject all theories based on unobservables—in short, the unexperienced structures remain a mystery. Thus, under empiricism, all theoretical realities are rejected: all we can know is what we can experience, and no speculation is part of true science. The sparticles of supersymmetry theory and the hidden dimensions of space-time of string theory are paradigms of this today. Instrumentalists such as Stephen Hawking are not concerned with how reality is: different theories present different fundamental elements and concepts, and no theory is "better" or "more real" if all predict equally well. Their motto is "Shut up and calculate!"

But under realist interpretations of theories, scientists identify real parts of the world that explain observed events. To theoretical realists, science is not merely a matter of predicting new observations: it is a matter of discovering, even if only approximately, real structures in nature—an "invisible order" of postulated explanatory realities—and advancing theories as explanations of their mechanisms. Scientific theories may never mirror reality exactly and may always be open to revisions, but to realists they capture some features of reality. (This is a "critical realism" rather than "naive realism.") The problem is that all scientific theories require our speculation. As the physicist John Wheeler put it: "What we call 'reality' consists of an elaborate papier-mâché construction of imagination and theory filled in between a few iron posts of observation." Indeed, even the fixed "iron posts" we observe reflect the questions that we ask nature. Nevertheless, science's claims are testable empirically, and to realists it would be a miracle if predictions are consistently fulfilled without hitting something real in the structure of things. Thus, for realists, theories are not total fictions the way that Mickey Mouse is, but they are human creations that have to be treated as such.

Probably few practicing scientists believe that their theories provide no understanding of nature. However, there are real problems about whether scientific theories give genuine knowledge. Data always underdetermine any theory, and thus there is room for error. All scientists agree that at least in principle all explanations are provisional: each accepted theory is only the best of the then available options—scientists say "It's interesting" or "I'll hold it until a better theory comes along." The classic problem is that correct predictions were taken as confirming Ptolemaic cosmology for over a thousand years. Thus, one's commitment to a theory should remain tentative. Theories today on the edge of research in quantum physics and cosmology present conflicting models of what is real that must eventually be reconciled if we can truly claim to know reality. And if history is any indicator, our science will look very different in a hundred years, if we are not reaching the end of what our technology is capable of aiding us to observe—as more and more exotic phenomena are discovered, today's picture of the fundamental nature of things will be rejected in major ways, and our view of reality will change greatly. (Past books on what would occur in the following ten years in the sciences are interesting for what they get *wrong*—inevitably, the authors' predictions miss new discoveries and lines of research, and their optimism that solutions to the then-current problems are just around the corner is usually misplaced.) Thus, no explanations can ever be considered final or complete.

Simplification and Reality

Reality may in fact not match any abstracted picture that we create. Scientists attempt to explain more and more data with fewer and fewer postulates, thereby bringing more phenomena under the umbrella of one theory. (As discussed, this need not lead to structural or theoretical reductionism.) The quest is for simplicity, but nature is complicated. Even modeling the motion of only three bodies within each other's field of gravity is problematic, even with computers. Thus, scientists speak in terms of ideals and abstractions, like road maps treating the world as flat. We all understand the claim, "There are 3.2 people in the average family" without thinking there can be two-tenths of a person, but we forget that much of science is like that. As the saying goes, "nature has no straight lines." At best, science is like approximating a circle with polygons with more and more straight sides: the actual reality is not reproduced. Are all logically consistent models of the universe "impoverished or simplified" versions of it, as physicist Paul Davies believes?

This brings up the issue of the role of simplicity in scientific theorizing. We assume that, everything else being equal, reality is set up more simply rather than more complexly—if something can be accomplished more easily one way than another, nature will follow the simpler path. (William of Occam justified his "razor" by saying that God would be "vain" if he created something in a way that could have been created more simply.) But why should reality always follow what we consider simpler? Or is applying Occam's razor only the easiest way for us to understand and thus only an all-too-human tool for aiding in the construction of models? Computers, with their massive computing power, are not so confined. A deep unity of structures may be intellectually satisfying, but how do we know that we are not imposing our own desires onto reality? The fullness of reality certainly looks complex and not merely the result of the interactions of a few principles—it is intricate, tangled, and fuzzy, with mathematics applying only to limited aspects of it. The Standard Model in particle physics is certainly less than elegant (although its mathematics is very precise), and the indeterminacy of some subatomic events hurts the case that reality is rational to its core. Or does the simple fact that we cannot express π in terms of the ratio of whole numbers reveal something deep about reality?

Perhaps the universe is not as coherent and unified as we like to think. Alfred North Whitehead's advice is apt: "Seek simplicity and distrust it." Our sense of beauty affects what we consider simple, but why nature should conform to our sense of beauty is not at all clear. Why do we believe, as John Keats put it, "Beauty is truth, truth beauty, —that is all / Ye know on earth, and all ye need to know"? Why should they be connected at all? Consider the contrast between the beauty and simplicity of the surface of a human body versus the messy and complex inner workings of the body. Perhaps the beauty we see in the universe is like that—seeing the universe in terms of beauty may be a gigantic oversimplification. Accurate predictions are not enough to confirm nature's simplicity if we are preselecting only aspects of it to fit. And the presence of possible indeterminacy and the loss of precise predictions in some cases may be pointing to further mysteries about which we have only scratched the surface.

Mathematics

So too with mathematics. Mathematical precision has certainly helped with predictions, but why do we assume that the final picture of what is actually real will be mathematical? Perhaps the "book of nature" is not written in the language of mathematics, as Galileo believed. Bertrand Russell pointed out: "Physics is mathematical not because we know so much about the physical world, but because we know so little; it is only its mathematical properties that we can discover." And why does relatively simple math work so well in helping scientists depict exotic levels of the universe? Eugene Wigner asked about the "unreasonable effectiveness" of mathematics in the natural sciences and found it hard to explain. For example, why does π—the ratio of the circumference of any circle to its diameter—figure in so many physical equations that have nothing to do with circles? More generally, why do physicists so often find that the math they need for some new phenomena has already been devised by mathematicians from considerations that have nothing to do with physical phenomena? Wigner believed the enormous usefulness of mathematics in science had no rational explanation and bordered on the mysterious.

Part of the problem is that we do not know if mathematics is our own invention (conventions we find useful for our models) or part of reality (mathematical objects existing in a nonmaterial realm independently of our thoughts). That is, are mathematical truths just the necessary products of the logic of our symbol systems, or do they reflect something of reality existing independently of our thoughts? Nonrealists advocate the former view and Platonists the latter. But both positions seem wrong: if math were merely a human product, then we should be able to invent simpler and neater symbol systems (e.g., make π a simple rational number), but the idea that our minds are contacting a Platonic realm of fixed and timeless mathematical truths also seems farfetched. Do irrational numbers merely reflect the strict rules of the mathematical language that we invented? Or do numbers, including π and the "imaginary" numbers such as the square root of -1, exist in reality in some way? Problems such as Kurt Gödel's theorems also raise the issue of whether truths in mathematical systems can be complete, consistent, and decidable—why would that be so if math were either our invention or were part of reality?

In any case, mathematics remains a language that we devised by the free use of our minds—so why is it so very helpful in empirical science? If what mathematicians devise are simply the logical implications of the axioms and rules they themselves define, why does math apply to reality? Part of the answer is that we have created mathematics as we have in order to deal with our experiences in the world—math can summarize in short formulas the patterns that we see—and thus our intuitions of what is mathematically true are also shaped by our experiences. Reality corrects some of our intuitions, as with finding Riemannean geometry to be more useful for relativity than Euclidean geometry. But still why does math lead to new insights about reality in realms we cannot directly experience, such as the unpicturable quantum realm? Perhaps there is an implicit circularity: we simply create a language that generates a particular image of nature, and we then take verified empirical predictions as confirmation of the language's objectivity—in the end, we take whatever picture of reality math creates to be the skeleton of reality.

But why does mathematics seem to be the key for understanding all the structures of reality? At present, math is the only basis for believing there are multiple universes or superstrings. But is it safe to rely on math in our speculations? Does reality have a mathematical structure, like some underlying musical harmony? Even if the world is ordered, why should the order be mathematical in structure? Have we simply mathematized reality and thus can see only what our math permits? Even some mathematicians think that the final models of science will be computer programs, not mathematical equations—math was simply a phase scientists went through, and it has done its job and will be passé to the next generation. Indeed, Richard Feynman once remarked: "If all of mathematics disappeared, physics would be set back exactly one week."

Empirical Limits to Knowledge

In addition, the limits of our ability to observe and reason must again be noted. The problem here is not that nature is too complex for us to grasp thoroughly. Rather, the problem is that, for example, we can only sense a fragment of the spectrum of the electromagnetic radiation, and technology can extend our ability to observe only so far: it allows us to extend our sensing to such areas of the spectrum as radio waves, x-rays, and infrared rays. But we cannot be sure what else may be filling the atmosphere.

Moreover, someday further research into the quantum realm and the expanse of the cosmos will come to an end: at some point, we will hit the limits of even technology-enhanced perception. How can we be at all confident that we will have exhausted all that is basic? On the astronomical scale, the universe generated by our Big Bang has at least a hundred billion galaxies each with a hundred billion stars—the celestial phenomena that we can perceive is a proverbial grain of sand in the Sahara. Even in principle we cannot see all of that: unless we can travel faster than light, the vast majority of our cosmos will always be beyond our event horizon and hence unknowable. Add to that the prospect of multiple unobservable universes. Are there basic features of the universe that we are missing and cannot ever find? How does this lack of knowledge impact the completeness of our theories?

On the quantum scale, it is an open question whether physicists will be able to exhaust all the depths so that none are in fact left totally unseen. Scientists may never be able to determine if reality has been fully plumbed—there may be levels of smaller scale that we simply cannot reach with our technology. Perhaps like a fractal (such as the Mandelbrot sets), there is a simple discoverable recursive law working on all levels, even if they go down forever, and no one fundamental physical level to the universe. Or perhaps Freeman Dyson, David Bohm, and others are correct that there are an infinite number of deeper and deeper levels of different structure to reality. Explaining such levels may strain the limits of our imagination. Or perhaps as J.B.S. Haldane suggested: "Not only is the universe stranger than we imagine, it is stranger than we can imagine." That we can comprehend any of the structures outside of the everyday realm at all is in the eyes of many, including Paul Davies, "the greatest scientific miracle of all"—science keeps revealing reality to be more and more complex, and yet scientists still comprehend some order.

Scientists keep pushing back the border of the unknown, but we must remember that what we see is only nature *as we experience it*—all we can hope for is learning the workings of nature that we experience directly or through technology, and we can never be certain that we have reached the basic principles of reality. The limits of technology will one day put an end to any possible empirical checking of new theories that would require access to phenomena outside the range of our then-current technology. Our scientific speculations about exotic realms are guided by our experience of the everyday scale of things, and without an empirical constraint on our theories, our reasoning may go totally off track. Science may not end since there may well always be smaller issues to explore, but the Big Questions in science will then come to an end or be reduced to matters of speculation alone—speculation guided at best by mathematics.

Comprehending Reality

Also consider that reality could have been more mysterious than it is—why isn't it? And when it comes to realities outside of the everyday world, why does science work at all? Why can our minds penetrate, at least to a degree, nature's workings? Minds need not have had the capacity to grasp any depth to reality. Obviously if we are to survive, we must be able to grasp some of the surface of the planet—without some reliable knowledge of our environment, we would not last long. And our brain has evolved as part of nature, and so the forces obeying the laws of nature are at work in it. But this does not explain why our minds can grasp at least something of the underlying structures at work deep in reality (assuming theoretical realism is correct). We have a limited mental capacity, and yet we can discern some underlying structures—perhaps all of them. Where does this mental ability come from? Is the human mind (and hence our reasoning) somehow deeply ingrained into reality? Are we an integral part of the scheme of things? Does our mind reflect "the mind of God"? But if our cognitive capacities are God-given, why are our intuitions about scales of reality far from the everyday level so far off? (It is also important to remember that intuitions, and theories, do not arise out of nowhere: our minds travel along particular ways of looking at things developed from the past history of science.) Indeed, why do we have even optical illusions in the everyday world? Is our capacity to know instead only a fallible product of natural evolution? That is, is our knowledge just a matter of our evolved mental functions rather than anything about our minds innately reflecting the structure of reality? If so, why can we grasp any depths at all?

Also consider a physiological limitation on our knowledge: our senses have developed through evolution for our survival, not for knowledge of all aspects of reality. As noted above, we see only a tiny sliver of the electromagnetic spectrum. If we saw a different range (e.g., bees are sensitive to ultraviolet radiation and the polarization of light), our view of what is real may well have ended up very differently. So too if we relied more on touch and smell, as most animals do. We cannot tell if we are missing major features of reality because of the senses evolution has given us. In addition, there is a related problem: however good our sensory apparatus is, we still only know reality through the sensory stimulation of our brain, and our representations of what is "real" are only our brains' interpretations of those signals. Nature may not be an unknowable Kantian noumenon, but we cannot be certain about how "reality-in-itself" truly is: all we have is our limited sensory interactions with it—nature loves to hide, and much remains veiled.

The Discovery of Mystery

Albert Einstein remarked that there is no mystery in science that does not point to another mystery beyond it. In fundamental research, this has certainly been true so far—in fact, as some puzzles are solved, the presence of greater mysteries has only become clearer. New findings have opened up new horizons that we previously did not even suspect existed.

And, unless reality is truly transparent, at some point we will be up against the limits of what our technological abilities can find out about nature and what we can even conceive about its workings. Perhaps the era of great scientific discoveries is coming to an end. Perhaps fundamental science in a hundred years will not look much different from today. Or perhaps basic science is in only its infancy. Perhaps scientists will find things that we have not yet even conceived. Perhaps important areas of science are only now beginning to be opened. Perhaps the universe is infinitely complex at every level of organization, and there will be fundamental questions to be asked in the future that we do not currently have the conceptual background even to conceive. In any case, once technology has exhausted what we can find, scientists may end only debating alternative explanations, each equally supported by the limited observable phenomena that scientists were able to accumulate. Any more scientific revolutions would then be on only the conceptual side of science, with no new avenues of research being possible to test models. It may be that in the future, human beings or our successors will learn much more of the how-ness of reality. But we have to admit that today we know less about the fundamental how-ness mysteries than we usually like to suppose and that we may never conquer them all.

In fact, scientists' repeated failures to close the openness of reality should make them especially aware of the mysterious quality of reality's structures. Thus, our sense of mystery of the how-ness of reality should be greater now than at any time since the rise of modern science. According to Einstein, "the real nature of things—that we shall never know, never." Max Planck added that "science cannot solve the ultimate mystery of nature. And that is because in the last analysis, we ourselves are part of nature and therefore part of the mystery that we are trying to solve." Even so, he did not think that this stopped science from being "the pursuit of the unknowable"—in fact, he thought that this is its chief attraction. Understandably, we may concentrate on the part of reality that we know, but that our knowledge is surrounded by a sea of mystery cannot be forgotten.

Indeed, perhaps the greatest scientific discovery of the twentieth century was that there is so much that we do not know and that there are limits on our ability to attain more knowledge. The expanse of our ignorance was revealed. Not that this was not noticed before: William James stated "[o]ur science is a drop, our ignorance a sea," and earlier Isaac Newton likened himself to a boy on a beach "finding a smoother pebble or a prettier shell than ordinary, whilst the great ocean of truth lay undiscovered before me." Are we merely finding the smallest niches of nature that are open to our understanding in a vast sea of unknown and unknowable phenomena? Perhaps our minds are able to see only an ordered abstraction of reality. We may be filtering out only a small fragment of reality—the parts that we can order. That is, we can see only what our mind can sense, and this may be only the simplest features of a complex world.

There is no reason to believe that our reason and languages must be able to capture all of reality—it is only the philosopher's disease that would require reality to be thoroughly rational. David Hume rightly asked: "What peculiar privilege has this little agitation of the brain which we call thought, that we must make it the model of the whole universe?" Perhaps one role of the mind is to simplify since we would be too overwhelmed to survive if we received too much information from our environment. If so, what is rational to us about reality is only a very limited slice of it all—scientists may be abstracting out only the easiest parts that we can control but missing many fundamental causal factors at work. For example, theists may claim that there is divine teleological causation at work in nature that scientists cannot detect by their methods. We have no reason to conclude that what we can experience directly or indirectly or can conceive must be all that there is to reality. Much of reality may be darker than "dark matter"—there may well be depths we cannot comprehend or even conceive.

But whatever is the case, this highlights that science is very much a human product and always open to revision. At a minimum, as our island of knowledge grows, so does its shoreline on the unknown—paradoxically, scientific progress also advances our awareness of mystery and its profundity. This does not mean that scientists are not providing us with genuine knowledge of reality—some features discovered through observation and experiment are so well established that they will no doubt be incorporated in one fashion or another into any further refinements of theory. But science provides less certainty than many of us like to think. Even well-established theories are only ideals and abstractions that do not mesh cleanly with reality. Our models of quantum phenomena are ultimately based on ideas arising from our thinking that is embedded in our everyday world, but how reliable can our intuitions be for the exotic realms? And how can we keep ourselves from not seeing what is "real" in terms of our everyday experiences? This makes any quantum-level models very provisional.

It also suggests not that we should deny all theories, but that we should be agnostic about more than just new theories on the edge of research in cosmology and quantum physics. This is not to deny that we are gaining more empirical data—the question is what we know of the basic nature of reality, and this involves the theories of science. Science does progress, but it is not a simple matter of adding new bricks—empirical data—to a preexisting wall. Rather, new theories change the design of the wall and rebuild it from scratch by repackaging the content of the bricks of empirical data in different conceptualizations.

This limits science's power to dispel the mysteries of nature. We will no doubt gain more and more knowledge of how nature works. But we can never be certain that we have arrived at the true fundamental structures of reality and thus at the final explanations of phenomena. Without experiences encompassing all of nature, our understanding will necessarily be limited. But we cannot access all of reality, and because of this limitation we are never in a position to know if our final answers reflect the fundamental order of things. Even if reality is rational through and through and has no ontic mysteries, we may never be able to fathom all of it, and thus we may be stuck with epistemic mysteries. Probably no being inside the universe can explain it all.

In any case, it is an outdated view that scientists will conquer all the mysteries of nature: all humanly possible scientific knowledge will not exhaust all of nature's mysteries or reduce them to trivialities. Science gives us the best and most authoritative knowledge we can have, but the typical exalted view of science gives the illusion that we know more than we do. We are left with uncertainties and probabilities in many matters.

A Two-Pronged Relationship to Mystery

Thus, science has a two-pronged relation to mystery: scientists remove many (and perhaps all) of the "how" mysteries of nature, but we can never be assured that scientists have conquered them all. Our science also exposes the limitation of the knowledge we can gain. Many scientists and philosophers believe that science will dispel all purported "why" mysteries from the world by reducing them all to solvable puzzles. Such thinkers need not dismiss the emotions of awe and wonder at the scales and intricacies of the universe as revealed by science or the humility we ought to express before the majesty of it all even on the everyday scale—in fact, they often wax poetic about how science increases the wonder because, as Richard Feynman reminded us, it is no longer based on ignorance.

Indeed, science can enhance our amazement at the universe, and the failure of theories can enhance our humility before reality. Scientists can unweave the rainbow and a blooming flower by decoding how they arise and yet still express wonder at why the universe is set up to produce such phenomena. But in focusing on the defeasible problems in science, many scientists and philosophers miss the mysteries that lie beyond scientists' capacity to eliminate. So too, scientists can speak of scientific knowledge as only an island in a vast sea of unknown phenomena, but the sea of addressable scientific problems still must be distinguished from grander underlying scientific mysteries. These deeper questions are more fundamental to what we deem to be "reality"—what we consider real changes with shifts in theories, and no final answer to the Big Questions in science may ultimately be defendable.

9

What of Current Mysteries in Physics and Cosmology?

If my view of the future is correct, it means that the world of physics and astronomy is inexhaustible; no matter how far we go into the future, there will always be new things happening, new information coming in, new worlds to explore, a constantly expanding domain of life, consciousness, and memory.

—Freeman Dyson

Consider next the problems at the edge of science today: are they all solvable, or are some genuine mysteries? Not every interesting problem that scientists encounter is a Big Question. Those of profound significance to human beings qualify as philosophical mysteries, but some other problems still qualify as scientific "how" mysteries. There are many such problems. Consider first some in particle physics and cosmology: How did the universe begin (if it did)? How did the universe's present state evolve? How will the universe end (if it will)? Why is the universe made of matter and not just energy? What are the smallest components of matter, and how do they relate to fields of energy? Is space infinite and eternal? Why does the universe have the forces and constants it has? Is the flow of time a component to reality or merely an illusion that our mind creates? Are there other "universes" beyond our possible range of observation? Why does the universe have multiple levels of organization, and how did the higher levels appear? What is the role of randomness in the development of the universe? Or is everything in some sense necessary, so that if the universe evolved again we would end up exactly as we already have? If some of these problems remain standing, they will be classified as philosophical mysteries. Other scientific puzzles may remain scientific mysteries—for example, why some particles have no mass, or why matter has an effect on space. So, do we have reasons to believe today that some of these problems will end up being unanswered or unanswerable and thus will end up being intractable mysteries?

Quantum Physics

Particle physics is one of the greatest achievements in science. A hundred years ago we knew almost nothing of the nature of an atom; now we know its nature and an incredible amount about levels below it. Particle physics' very precise mathematics and experimental results have been established since the 1920s, and the Standard Model of subatomic particles and forces explained in terms of quarks, leptons, and bosons was set in the 1970s. But it is old news that *understanding* particle physics has not advanced since then. When a physicist of the stature of Richard Feynman says, "I think it is safe to say that no one understands quantum mechanics. . . . Nobody knows how it be can like that," we know we are in strange territory. There currently are a number of different ontic interpretations of the mathematics—from the Copenhagen Interpretation favored by antirealists that eschews all attempts to understand how the physics works to a realism involving indeterminacy to realisms involving determinacy (either by each possible experimental outcome being realized in different universes in Hugh Everett and Bryce DeWitt's "many worlds" solution or by David Bohm's inelegant interpretation involving hidden variables and faster than light signals) to Eugene Wigner's interpretation that gives consciousness a role in experiments. So far, all models have produced the same experimental predictions. And no other progress has been made on other grounds for forming a reasoned consensus. It may well be that *all* existing interpretations are wrong.

Many aspects of particle physics are certainly so bizarre as to be an affront to our everyday commonsense—for example, entanglement of particles resulting in connected "nonlocal" effects, or theorizing a possible backward flow of time. But some aspects are presented to the general public as being more mysterious than they really are. For example, the claims "There is no reality in the quantum world," "Nothing exists until observed," and "The Heisenberg Uncertainty Principle shows that physics can no longer provide reliable information about the physical world and that the physical world has lost its claim to objectivity." Those claims are wrong. Even antirealists admit that something exists that causes the observed effects, even though we cannot know anything about it—the mixture of the unseen reality and our measuring procedures produce what is observed, but that is not to deny that that unseen reality exists. That reality exists independently of our observations and is "nothing" only in the mistaken sense that Stephen Hawking says that the world came from "nothing" (as discussed in chapter 5). Nor does the Uncertainty Principle mean that there is no objective knowledge of particles: physicists can gain very precise knowledge of what is really there—they simply cannot measure momentum and location at the same time. The act of observation does affect what is there, but on submicroscopic scales it is not surprising that the light used to measure properties affects what is there. Nor is the "wave/particle duality" usually presented properly: an electron is not both a wave and a particle—it is always observed as a particle. However, groups of particles exhibit some wave properties—that is, wave properties are properties of groups of particles but never the properties of a single particle. What is actually there—the reality-in-itself—is something "we know not what" that can produce either the wave or particle effect when we mix different actions with it in different experimental setups. All that is ever observed are particles, never waves or fields. The only "duality" is that we cannot observe an individual particle and a group of particles at the same time. It is also worth noting that the "wave-function" is only a mathematical construct within quantum theory that shows the probabilities of arrangements of particles—it is not a feature of space controlling those arrangements.

One of the new mysteries in particle physics involves "supersymmetry." This is the assumption that particles of matter may be converted into particles of force and vice versa. Why and how this should happen is a mystery. Is some unknown force responsible for breaking symmetries? There is no empirical evidence yet for such symmetry. There is also the issue of why some particles are massless and why particles in the Standard Model have different masses: why do different particles "feel" the presence of a Higgs particle or field that gives some particles mass differently? The nature of "dark matter" that is not made up of quarks or other parts of visible matter is currently a mystery, as is the nature of the "dark energy" that is hypothesized to explain the accelerating rate of the universe's expansion. Thus, what we can observe may constitute less than 5 percent of the mass of our universe. And to what degree theories about these matters will be testable is an issue.

Relativity

The bizarre effects described in the theory of relativity are well known—the twin paradox, the contraction of length of objects moving near the speed of light, the absence of a universal "now" (and consequently of simultaneity), and so forth. The loss of simultaneity wreaks havoc with the notion of causation and thus with the very idea of "natural laws." Scientists question whether time exists. Is matter continuous or digital—is it, to use Bertrand Russell's metaphor, a bowl of jelly or a bucket of shot? And why? Space is no longer seen as a big empty box but as the reality out of which matter arises, and yet matter can bend space. Thus, matter loses its status as the primary category for what is physically real to a space-time field. Is matter just an excited state of space-time—the surface fluctuations on an ocean of energy? But to see matter metaphorically as "condensed energy" or "condensed space-time" only pushes the mystery of beingness back one step to "what is space-time?" It also adds the mystery of how matter arises from it. That space itself, and not merely its contents, is expanding is a mystery: the galaxies are not expanding "into" space but are being carried along as space itself expands—space is not expanding *into* anything and yet is somehow still getting larger. And recent theorizing about "atoms of space-time" with literally nothing in between tightly meshed atoms only adds to this model the mystery of nothingness in between particles of space.

Both general relativity and the Standard Model in particle physics are extremely well confirmed—most recently in relativity by reportedly finding the gravity waves that Einstein predicted. They also are complete enough that they leave few puzzles pointing in the direction of where possible new theories may lie. But this leads to a big problem: the two fundamental and well-confirmed theories are *incompatible*. The physics of the very large and the very small simply conflict. Relativity is deterministic, while particle physics appears indeterministic. More basically, gravity requires a continuity that particle physics cannot provide. Thus, there is something basically wrong in our theory of things—we cannot conceive that both theories can be correct. We believe that one or both theories must be revised, but attempts to reconcile them (such as "quantum gravity") have failed for decades. Nor has any attempt to reconcile them in terms of the emergence of space-time out of quantum realities been attempted. No one wants to accept that there is no reconciliation, but the lack of headway may indicate that we have not yet reached the fundamental laws in one or both fields.

Theories of Everything

This brings up attempts to find a single theory for all the known physical forces—that is, devising a "Theory of Everything." If devised, we would end up with an equation that would fit on a T-shirt that encompasses all of basic physics, or at least the shortest possible computer program whose output is the laws of our universe. It would show that our universe could not be ordered otherwise than it is—it would give a necessity to all that is since there would be no contingent posits, and we would have a certainty and completeness that many crave. It would show that the laws of our universe are not arbitrary. It would answer Einstein's question: God had no choice in creating the world as it is. But a "Theory of Everything" embraces all phenomena only if *reductionism* is correct: only if reality is organized reductively would a physical TOE be the foundation of all chains of explanations—if reality is organized antireductively, then a TOE would be only a "Theory of *One Level* of Everything." Alternatively, if antireductionism is true, a TOE would have to incorporate all biological and psychological structures. In the end, all structures would be different manifestations of one underlying structure.

Also consider what a TOE must explain. A true TOE must explain why there is both visible and dark matter and energy, why there are six types of quarks and not more or less, why there are the number of different particles there are and why they have their particular masses and properties, the strengths of different physical constants, and so forth.[1] Why did four forces disentangle from the primal force—why these and not others? Why weren't matter and antimatter created in equal amount (and so destroy each other)? Why, as Paul Davies asks, are there a set of laws that drove the featureless gases of the Big Bang toward life and consciousness? Why is the universe set up to gain more and more levels of complexity? How do different levels of organization appear? Why didn't the universe remain simpler—for instance, having nothing more complex than quarks? Indeed, why was the universe so unstable that it could not remain in its initial state of symmetry? Why wasn't the universe governed by something like Newtonian laws rather than relativity and quantum laws? In sum, why does the universe have all the fundamental features it has and not others, and why is the universe as creative and complex as it is? In addition, there are the questions of the initial conditions of the Big Bang, why the stuff of our universe was set up to "bang," why inflation can happen, and what happened before the Big Bang? Indeed, why is there any space-time at all? Answering these questions is obviously a tall order, but nothing less constitutes a truly total explanation. And this is not to mention the philosophical issues of why anything exists for the TOE to operate on, why there is order in nature, and why any TOE exists at all. The contingent events of history would not have to be explained, but no fundamental scientific laws and constants could be left as unexplained brute facts for a theory actually to be a "Theory of *Everything*."

Theories of superstrings—one-dimensional lines of energy that wiggle in different ways—are one candidate for a TOE. They unify general relativity and quantum physics in a consistent way. They also would bring order to the current hodgepodge of subatomic particles.

One version—Edward Witten's M-theory—predicts the existence of particles carrying gravitational forces. However, this theory has problems: it requires more than half a dozen more dimensions to the universe that are not "unfurled," and there are a mind-boggling number of alternative types of universes in the model (at least 10^{500}). More importantly, it runs up against a major roadblock: it is not yet empirically checkable—it does make predictions, but ones that cannot be tested with the energies available with our current accelerators. It does encompass all the discoveries that preceded it, but it is based on no more than the mathematics of the theory of our universe's initial inflation and its own elegance. Thirty-five years ago, Richard Feynman quipped that superstring theorists do not make predictions but excuses, and the same is still true today. "M-theory" has become "Mystery-theory."

Alternatives to string theory that might be testable today are being proposed. So too the recent discovery of dark matter and dark energy—if they in fact exist and are not merely epicycles of theory—raises the question of whether we are in a position to believe that we know all the basic features of our universe. When scientists claim that dark matter and dark energy constitute more than 95 percent of the mass of our universe, one has to wonder whether anything else of such a magnitude has been missed. The same for undiscovered items on the smallest scale: scientists at the Large Hadron Collider in Switzerland recently reported possible traces of a new particle that does not fit in the Standard Model. Evidence of a fifth physical force (possibly connected to dark matter) has also just been reported. Computer simulations of a universe without the weak nuclear force have also worked fine, suggesting that we do not really know what the true fundamental forces of the universe are. In addition, mathematicians may not have yet devised the proper math to summarize the patterns that are being observed.

Thus, today we may not be anywhere near ready to devise a true TOE, and it is arrogant to think otherwise—indeed, all of the current relevant theories may be in a relatively primitive state. Perhaps a conceptual revolution unifying general relativity and particle physics would so alter how we see things that any TOE proposed now would then look silly. Nor can we be confident that there are no forces on the smallest and largest scales that simply lie beyond our capacities to know. Even if we could reach the level of superstrings with some new accelerator, we can never be confident that there is no further level explaining them. So too, we cannot rule out that there may be a rational structure to all of the cosmos that is simply permanently mysterious to beings such as ourselves.

There is also the entire issue of how science could show that there is only one consistent set of physical laws. Perhaps there are many possible TOEs that could produce viable universes, and this raises the issue of why our particular TOE is embodied in our universe—perhaps a creator god would still have had a choice even if there is a TOE. Any necessity to a TOE would be lost. For Steven Weinberg, the possibility that the world could have been operated by another TOE is an "irreducible mystery" that cannot be eliminated. Thus, our TOE would require an explanation for why it was instantiated in reality: something would be needed to explain why that equation is in force and not another. A multiverse theory would be one explanation: if each "miniverse" has its own TOE and is causally unrelated to the other miniverses, one with our features is only to be expected. But in that case, the laws of our miniverse are accidental and not universal. Moreover, no law can explain itself—gravity cannot explain why the universe is set up to allow gravity to operate in the first place. Nothing can be self-explanatory—it is either explained by something else or is simply an unexplained brute fact.

Or perhaps no TOE is possible. There may be no one fundamental underlying order but only local ones. Perhaps there are some arbitrary constants or laws in our universe. Perhaps the idea of unified cosmos—a "uni-verse"—is, as Bertrand Russell suggested, only a relic of pre-Copernican astronomy. Perhaps, as Freeman Dyson hopes, the world of physics and astronomy is inexhaustible, infinite in all directions, and that a TOE is an illusion: just as Gödel's theorems show that axioms in mathematics leave unanswered questions, so too no set of axioms in physics produces answers to everything—otherwise, "the Creator had been uncharacteristically lacking in imagination." Certainly, Stephen Hawking's declaration in 1980 that the goal of theoretical physics might be achieved by the end of the twentieth century did not pan out.

In any case, enthusiasm for TOEs has greatly waned in the last twenty-five years.

Cosmology

Also consider the old and new mysteries in cosmology. One bit of old news is the "fine tuning" controversy. Various physical constants seem perfectly suited to an amazing degree for producing life (even if there turns out to be comparatively little life in the universe).[2] It looks as if conscious beings are built into the universe. As Freeman Dyson said: "I do not feel like an alien in this universe. The more I examine the universe and study the details of its architecture, the more evidence I find that the universe must in a sense have known that we were coming." And it is hard to accept this as simply a brute fact—most of us feel that it demands an explanation. So far there have been three responses. First, many scientists say that, despite appearances, "fine tuning" is an illusion, just an effect of the early inflation of the universe—the variables are interconnected and by this interconnection necessarily produce a stable universe with many features, only one of which is life. Others offer one of two deeper explanations: either a designer god set things up for conscious beings to appear, or a multiverse theory explains it. In a multiverse scenario, as long as there are a sufficient number of miniverses, and the laws and constants vary from one miniverse to another, then of course a world like ours should exist— many may be without laws or otherwise sterile, but some producing life would occur. But many theists fervently resist any multiverse scenario since it would be an alternative explanation to God: a creator god could, of course, create a multiverse as easily as one miniverse, but the order of our world could no longer be used as evidence of a god. To Richard Swinburne, it is the "height of irrationality" to posit trillions of other worlds simply to explain the features of our one world. But multiple miniverses were not posited to explain fine tuning. They are the consequence of other generally accepted theories—in particular, the idea of the inflation of our world, an idea well supported by both observational data and established theories. That multiple miniverses would explain the apparent fine tuning is only a bonus.[3]

In fact, multiverse models are becoming increasingly popular among scientists. The idea of an eternal multiverse was first hypothesized by Alexander Vilenkin in 1983. Various models have been inferred from various theories in physics and cosmology. Many agree with Paul Davies that some form of multiverse theory is "probably an unavoidable consequence of modern physics and cosmology." The idea of countless worlds arising and dissolving goes back to the pre-Socratic Greek Anaximander's idea of the Boundless (*aperion*), but the contemporary theories result only from spinning out the consequences of the math of other theories (such as superstring models) and are currently only theoretically testable. They add a whole new dimension to the question of whether the cosmos is infinite and eternal since other miniverses would not merely be hidden dimensions of our own miniverse. These theories expand the universe in a way not comparable to any theories in the past—that the stars are far from our solar system, that there are other galaxies, and that our universe is expanding. Each miniverse is distinct from ours, and the "mother universe" or even each miniverse may be propagating new miniverses forever, each possibly with its own set of laws and constants. Finding evidence of, in effect, other entire universes would have an existential impact on us second only to finding intelligent life on other planets.

Philosophers David Lewis and Robert Nozick go to the extreme of advancing an all-worlds hypothesis: every logically conceivable world exists. But any of the models would not only explain why our miniverse has the structure to produce life, we no longer have to ask what an eternal creator god was doing prior to 13 to 14 billion years ago before our Big Bang occurred. It also introduces the issue of whether the universe is eternal and offers different options for the ultimate fate of our miniverse. If what occurred prior to the Big Bang is cut off by the heat of the Big Bang, science is precluded from empirically addressing what may have come before or the nature of any other miniverses or of the multiverse of all the miniverses and their source (the "mother universe"). In addition, we could never tell how many miniverses remain undetectable or what their laws are. So too, the whole question of the origin of the entire cluster of miniverses becomes unanswerable. Physics and cosmology become at best only sciences of our local observable miniverse, not truly universal of all of reality. We would have an explanation for why our miniverse is the way it is, but only as a random result of a far larger incomprehensible universe. Mysteries within our miniverse may be dampened, but the mystery of the total universe only vastly increases.

But again, the drawback to multiverse models is testing for the presence of other miniverses unconnected to our own. To John Wheeler, Hugh Everett's "many worlds" solution to problems in particle physics has to be rejected because "its infinitely many unobservable worlds make a heavy load of metaphysical baggage." Observations may actually be possible to detect a past collision of our miniverse with another miniverse, but critics contend that until such evidence is found the entire multiverse scenario is only a matter of metaphysical speculation—elegant metaphysics that is guided by mathematics, but metaphysics nonetheless.

What Is the Nature of Science Today?

The general lack of testability and observational support in multiverse and string theories has generated a dispute among physicists about the nature of science itself. Some physicists such as Sean Carroll claim that "empirical checking" is now an outdated notion (at least for these Big Questions in physics and cosmology). They want to change the rules of science: in "post-empirical science," what matters is elegance, consistency, and the mathematics of a model. As Helge Kragh puts it, this would be an "epistemic shift," a redefinition of science, not by philosophers but by a minority of active scientists. Leonard Susskind labels advocates of Karl Popper's falsification requirement "the Popperazi" for trying to impose unrealistic and irrelevant methodological restrictions on science.

Disparagers of this view respond that this redefinition spells the end of science in these fields: when we abandon checking, what we have is no more than speculative metaphysics, not scientific theories at all. (Of course, experimental physicists, as opposed to theoretical physicists, have always had a great disdain for philosophizing.) If a theory makes no checkable predictions, it is worse than useless from a scientific point of view—it leads to just concocting fairy tales. Such speculation reflects the age-old human need to have creation stories, but ideas that predict nothing produce no testable claims and no fruitful research—they are not science but no different than theology or astrology. Advocates of the standard view readily admit that all theories begin with speculation, but they see no reason to end the demand that at some point observable consequences are required for a theory to be science—the speculation must become empirically useful at some point down the road. For them, to drop the need for some empirically confirmable or refutable claims would be the end of science. As Einstein said in the first half of the twentieth century, "Time and again the passion for understanding has led to the illusion that man is able to comprehend the objective world rationally by pure thought without any empirical foundations—in short, by metaphysics." He added (and Kant would agree): "Concepts are simply empty when they stop being firmly linked to experience."

Advocates of the new view of science point out that problems with these theories have persisted for decades with little progress: competing theories interpreting quantum physics have remained intact since the 1930s; the Standard Model has only gotten more and more complex since the 1970s; and theories such as cosmic inflation and superstrings have been around since the 1970s with little or no advancement. This stagnation is sufficient, they argue, to redefine science: the new theories may be one step beyond empirical science, but they are not unbridled speculation or groundless fairy tales, as critics assert—it is not "anything goes." Mathematics develops along with science, and perhaps developments in math can take the lead here. (That we do not know the nature of math adds to the problem. Advocates of the new physics would have to be Platonists: math must structure reality and not merely be our invention to summarize data if it is to be the basis of a new speculative science.)

But critics still insist that this makes "particle physics" into "particle aesthetics" and theories become grounded only in our sense of beauty and our untrustworthy intuitions of what is real—we cannot call a theory "science" unless it takes the risk of making some confirmable or disconfirmable predictions.

Must a theory predict novel phenomena, or can it merely make sense of existing data and still be called "scientific"? Can a theory remain testable only "in principle" indefinitely and still be called "scientific"? Can such a speculative theory be the basis for further research? Or is "scientific research" reduced to speculation alone? Do the new "post-empiricists" simply want to keep the honorific name "science" rather than admit that they are doing metaphysics? How will this dispute be resolved? Certainly, philosophers cannot dictate to scientists how to practice their craft. Perhaps this is a case where physicist Max Planck is correct: "a scientific truth does not triumph by convincing its opponents and making them see the light, but rather because its opponents eventually die, and a new generation grows up that is familiar with it."

However, whether we label these edges of science "science" or "metaphysics" is not important: if the theories never become checkable, it would mean either way that science is hitting a wall. How do we know a theory is true and not just a groundless overextension of a theory into metaphysical illusion, no matter how elegant it is? How could a theory accepted solely on grounds of elegance be the basis for further speculation? In old-fashioned "empirical science," elegance and consistency are part of the set of criteria utilized for selecting one theory from among the available (but empirically equal) options, but they never become the sole grounds for acceptance when testing is impossible. And remember that Ptolemaic cosmology and Newtonian physics were once considered the most elegant options.

Is the End of Theoretical Science at Hand?

This points to another issue: are we approaching an era when the only "revolutions" on the Big Questions in particle physics and cosmology will be on the conceptual side, with multiple theories all explaining all of the available data? Could scientists reconceptualize nature around another root-metaphor (e.g., the universe as the output of a computer program) with other idealized conditions in a way that not only does not need certain hypothesized entities (e.g., dark matter or black holes) but also rejects what are now considered basic laws such as the law of conservation of energy or the invariance of the speed of light? (And there is a cottage industry of scientists who reject the Big Bang, the expansion of the universe, relativity, or the Higgs particle.) This in turn leads to such issues as whether there is a genuine question of whether space-time is flat or curved: do we mathematize nature, and could we come up with another mathematics for the geometry of space-time? If computer programs come to dominate physics, will we see space and particles as digital? Does such a prospect render the whole question of the "real" nature of reality moot, as antirealists argue? Or would the end of "empirical science" mean the end of antirealism in philosophy of science since science would no longer be able to make predictions? Are laws not "objectively real" but just the way we currently happen to describe things? Are they, as Victor Stenger puts it, "simply restrictions on the ways physicists may draw the models they use to represent the behavior of matter"? Arthur Eddington thought that the laws of nature were subjectively chosen by us: they are the rules for recurrent patterns that scientists observe, but the footprint we find in nature is only our own. If any of this is so, what does this say about science in general?

We always like to believe that we are living at the dawn of a new era, but if testable alternatives to the currently untestable theories are not devisable today, any new research on these Big Questions may have to lie dormant until sufficient technology is developed, if ever. If not, these questions in physics and cosmology may come to an end, not because the quest to find final answers has been completed, but because there are limits to what we can know about these matters. Interest in these Big Questions may fade away, as with past efforts to confront them in creation myths. A sense of ennui may engulf them as new scientists turn to what they find to be more productive areas of study. Many scientists may become as depressed as Sheldon Cooper was on *The Big Bang Theory* when he realized that the field he had devoted his professional life to— string theory—was untestable and that in his mid-thirties he would have to start over in another area.

Facing the Mysteries Today

In any case, today the science of these Big Questions seems to have hit an impasse. Since relativity and particle physics cannot be reconciled at present, we have no reason to believe that fundamental physics is approaching finality. Perhaps all of today's models are in fact only poor approximations of future ones and will have to be discarded. And as the historian Daniel Boorstin noted: "The greatest obstacle to discovery is not ignorance, but the illusion of knowledge." Old ways of thinking may interfere with devising new ways of conceiving things. We have to rely on intuitions, and our intuitions are shaped by our everyday world, and these may very well not only be useless when dealing with the more exotic realms but warp our thinking—especially when they are no longer guided by new research data. But human beings being what we are, we may be satisfied by our guesses. All this means that asking the right questions in our situation may prove to be even harder than finding any answers.

But as discussed, we must face that at some point particle physicists will have theorized the smallest components or the most basic fields that human beings are capable of exploring empirically or even conceiving, and that will be the final frontier in this field. But whether this means that scientists will then have reached the most fundamental physical level of organization to reality is still an open question: Are there levels of scale beyond our reach or beyond our comprehension even through mathematics? Are there also other fundamental forces at work on these levels that we cannot know? Indeed, we may in fact be vastly ignorant of the true workings of nature. Current particle physics may be like Ptolemaic cosmology—great on predictions, but fundamentally wrong on theory. At the least, the problem of modeling what is further and further from the everyday realm will only get worse—any reality that physicists strike will no doubt remain highly counterintuitive.

So too with the opposite scale of things: we may have only an inkling of the true nature of the universe as a whole—it may remain fundamentally incomprehensible. Many agree with astronomer John Barrow's conclusion that the astronomer's desire to understand the structure of the universe is doomed—we can merely scratch the surface of what is out there. "All the great questions about the nature of the Universe—from its beginning to its end—turn out to be unanswerable. There is a fundamental divide between the part of the Universe we can observe and the entire, possibly infinite, whole." We can expect, he adds, the universe to be endlessly diverse both throughout space and historically—it is most unlikely to be even roughly the same everywhere. We most likely "inhabit a little island of temperate tranquility amid a vast sea of cosmic complexity, forever beyond our power to observe." So too, we should "regard with a Copernican suspicion any idea that our human mental powers should be adequate to handle an understanding of Nature at its ultimate level."

In such circumstances, accepting mystery and remaining agnostic about the theories is mandatory. Indeed, it may be most reasonable to withhold even tentative assent to any of the untestable theories. In addition, we have to accept the prospect that scientists may never be able to answer the big "why" and "how" questions here. However, we are a species that wants answers to these questions, and so we may continue to speculate—these questions affect us existentially in a way most questions in science do not. But we have good reason to believe that we will reach the limits of our knowledge in these areas and no good reason to believe that nature is transparent in all its scales to beings like us. Thus, there are matters that are permanently unknowable. We will have to accept with humility some physical and cosmological realities simply as brute facts incapable of further explanation.

Notes

1. A change in one theory can wipe out problems in other theories. Here, adopting a multiverse hypothesis makes the stubborn problem of why elementary particles have the particular masses they have simply vanish: each miniverse may have its own set of values for the elementary particles—there is a randomness and arbitrariness to such values in any given miniverse, and no further explanation is needed for the values in ours. Thus, physicists may have been struggling over what is really a nonproblem, and no TOE needs to explain such values. Of course, we do not know how future theorizing may change the whole landscape of physics.

2. "Fine tuning" can be expanded to include other things. For example, if water contracted when frozen like most liquids do, the oceans would have much more ice, and life as we know it probably would not exist. Or would life have adapted to this and taken another route around this problem? Why are quarks and leptons related to each other in simple ratio? Why do electrons and protons have the same electric charge value?

3. How Occam's razor applies here depends on your point of view: ontologically, a multiverse is obviously immensely larger, but it is actually simpler from a theoretical point of view—it is simpler for a theory to posit the entire range of logically possible miniverses than only one since for there to be only one miniverse, a new ad hoc rule would have to be added to the theory explaining why only one of the possibilities is realized (e.g., perhaps our universe is the only miniverse because it is the best for producing diversity from limited natural laws, and some unknown force destroyed all other miniverse).

10

What of Current Mysteries in Biology?

I cannot think of a single field in biology or medicine in which we can claim genuine understanding, and it seems to me the more we learn about living creatures, especially ourselves, the stranger life becomes. . . . The only solid piece of scientific truth about which I feel totally confident is that we are profoundly ignorant about nature.

—Lewis Thomas

Biology today has its own set of "why" and "how" Big Questions. What exactly is life? And how did it begin? How, in particular, did human beings arise? Are human beings nothing more than evolved, gene-driven organisms? How does life fit into the physicists' picture of reality? Why do cells die and atoms don't? Why do genes and amoebas self-replicate and inorganic material does not? Is the earth itself a planet-sized interconnected ecosystem or even a whole that can be likened to a single life-form, as Gaia theorists argue? Why is reality set up to produce and sustain life and conscious beings? Is there a teleology to life—that is, does life appear accidentally and evolve unguided, or are there natural or transcendent principles at work guiding its course?

What Is Life?

Consider first what exactly "life" is. A living entity is not inert matter or a soul embodied in inert matter. What exactly distinguishes a living person from a dead body? If a deceased person is just a machine with a broken part, why doesn't repairing that part bring the person back to life? This is harder to define than one might think. Scientists are not in agreement on what constitutes "living," but the processes of self-reproduction (things making copies of themselves out of inorganic material), self-repair, growth, and an autonomy not exhibited by inanimate objects are central to life. Biologists debate whether macromolecules or viruses are "alive." Crystals can "seed" other material to make more crystals, but nothing characteristic of life ever appears.[1]

Despite the problem of definition, life appears as a distinct level of complex phenomena, and how nature made this monumental leap is *the* basic mystery underlying biology. Scientists do not know how life began. Neo-Darwinian theory does not purport to explain how life arose, but only to explain changes once it arose. And finding a natural explanation for the origin of life has proven harder than once expected. In 1953, Stanley Miller discovered that the "building blocks of life"—certain organic compounds such as amino acids—could be synthesized by sending an electrical charge through a soup of methane, hydrogen, ammonia, and water. However, few strides have been made since then beyond creating some self-replicating amino acid molecules, and doubts have been raised whether the experiment duplicated early earth conditions. But even if scientists can generate life in a laboratory, this does not mean that they have duplicated how nature did it any more than the airplanes that we build duplicate how nature made birds. Nevertheless, naturalists are confident that a purely natural explanation of life will be forthcoming.

All sorts of conditions had to appear for life to arise, requiring millions of years of preparation through the evolution of the earth and atmosphere. Most scientists agree that the original DNA or RNA template for life was so complex that it could not have appeared by pure chance— natural forces had to play a role in restricting the events surrounding how it came into existence. But life on earth still appears so miraculous that Francis Crick suggested that it began by being seeded from space. (Of course, this only pushes the question of the ultimate origin of life back one step to how the life of the seeds arose.) Certain chemical bases are needed, but what exactly the necessary bases are may not be known until we find life in different forms on other planets. For example, is carbon necessary, or are non-carbon-based life-forms (e.g., based on silicon and methane) possible? The complexity of any form of life on earth has also proven to be a problem. A cell is more complex than any inanimate entity of the same size. Even the simplest one-cell animal is so complex that how it arose perplexes everyone. The astrophysicist Fred Hoyle likened believing that the first cell originated by chance to believing that a tornado ripping through a junkyard full of airplane parts could produce a Boeing 747.

The Evolution of Life

The historical question of the emergence of life may never be answered, but however life was established, the next problem is what Charles Darwin considered the "mystery of mysteries"—the evolution of distinct species. All life on earth—animals, plants, fungi—appears to have evolved over the last three billion years or so from the same DNA. Thus, all living things on earth are related. That is firmly established, but the *explanation* of how evolution has occurred has given rise to disputes. Charles Darwin and Alfred Russel Wallace proposed a natural mechanism for the changes ("natural selection"): members of a species that have survival-related genetic advantages over other members in their environment tend to thrive and to produce more offspring that survive; with enough genetic changes, a new species branches off.[2] This idea was combined with modern genetics by 1950: changes occur randomly in the genes (e.g., radiation may alter a gene), and these are then passed on in a lawful manner to the offspring through inheritance. Thus, both randomness and laws are involved in generating new species.[3]

But nothing in neo-Darwinism explains the general trends toward greater diversity and greater complexity. Even if complexity enhances survivability, nothing about natural selection or gene mutation, any more than the underlying chemistry, would predict or explain the very possibility of a continuous increase in diversity and complexity. Why would changes in the environment cause beings to acquire greater and greater complexity? Even if adapting to changes in the environment is responsible for the appearance of new species, why do new *degrees of complexity* develop? How could natural selection, random mutation, and the transmission of genetic changes alone produce greater types of complexity rather than simply more of the same type of complexity? Natural selection may effectively weed out the unfit, but how does it create something genuinely new?[4] Even if an accumulation of small changes over long periods of time can create an entirely new species, why is there a drive to create new species at all? Even if the drive is for new species that are better adapted to their environment, why is nature set up to permit, not just diversity, but more and more levels of complex organisms with specialized parts? In sum, why did novelty originate?

Most generally, why didn't life remain on the one-cell level? Why would single-celled organisms begin to fuse together, as it were? Why did cells begin to have specialized functions? Why did complex, specialized organs evolve? Wouldn't one-celled animals that can survive in very harsh extreme conditions be more easily adaptable to changes in the environment? Growth in size and complexity without structure should lead to instability and collapse. Are as yet unknown forces at work organizing life-forms? Or consider this: do some natural structures explain why we share 99 percent of our DNA with our cousins the chimpanzees and yet are so different? Other species exhibit consciousness and altruistic social behavior—why are human beings and our consciousness so much more powerful? Do our ancestors' evolutionary needs alone explain why our cortex is now so much more complex than that of other animals? Do we differ only in degree, or is something more at work? The Human Genome Project proved disappointing—mapping the genome led to more mysteries about heredity than answers.

Nature apparently has programmed within it not only an urge for organisms to thrive through adaption, but also for life to gain greater complexity. Why are chemicals "designed" (for lack of a better word) first to assemble into living organisms and then the organisms "designed" to become parts that assemble into more complex organisms? Anti-reductionists argue that biotic structures as basic as those in physics must be at work in the origin and evolution of life. Some rules must be programmed into reality to generate novelty—the universe seems set on getting more and more complex and leading to life and consciousness. As Paul Davies says: "This systematic advance in organized complexity is so striking it has the appearance of a law of nature." Such a "complexity law" would involve exclusively natural forces, not an active transcendent designer—biotic principles can be as natural as physical ones. They would be "designing life" without a transcendent designer and without any further goal or the future orientation of "final causes." A biotic structure, however, is basically non-Darwinian since it limits the role for randomness in the course of evolution. Antireductionists accept that natural selection plays a role in evolution, but they think that neo-Darwinism does not provide the full picture and that some new theory of evolution incorporating natural selection, genetic mutation, and biotic principles will one day be forthcoming when scientists know more about the workings of life. This may mean that a true revolution is needed in biology. If Darwin was the Newton of biology, we may still be waiting for its Einstein to explain the emergence of more and more complex organs and species.

Stalwart reductionist defenders of neo-Darwinism such as Richard Dawkins will have nothing of this. Many biologists, such as Edward O. Wilson, are reductionists who anticipate the demise of their science as biology becomes explained by chemistry and ultimately physics. Why naturalists should be committed to only physical principles is not clear, but structural reductionists oppose any biotic structures. They think that natural selection and random mutation operating at a genetic level are the only mechanisms at work in evolution, and thus neo-Darwinism explains the history of life. They believe that Darwin solved all the great mysteries of life—as Dawkins says, all that is left is for biologists to fill in the details and for chemists and physicists to reduce biology to chemistry and then to physics. A few simple physical laws will ultimately explain it all. For example, John Conway's computer "Game of Life" showed how complexity can arise from only a few simple rules and time. Indeed, that DNA is determined by the laws of chemistry and physics is, according to Francis Crick, the "central dogma" of modern biology. (His former colleague James Watson thought in 1984 that biology still had "at least fifty more interesting years" in it.) All we have to do is discover the basic physical laws at work—the actual history of life on earth is a history of contingent events and thus is, as the chemist and reductionist Peter Atkins says, "scientifically unimportant" since scientists only identify and explain the laws and forces at work in nature.

Reductive and Antireductive Views of Life

The Big Question here is how ingrained into the universe life really is. The biological level of reality seems to be as natural as atoms and molecules. Reductionists believe that life arose only as an accidental product of physical forces and random events—the inanimate is "more real," and life on earth is just a fortuitous fluke of nature. But to antireductionists, biological and mental levels of reality are features of the universe on an equal footing with the physical: plants and animals are as much built into the overall structure of reality as atoms and molecules. Thus, we are a normal feature of the universe and not a freak occurrence. To reductionists, however, life should be rare in the universe: life will occur "spontaneously" under the right physical conditions, but random events are necessary for these conditions to appear, and so the right conditions occur only by chance. Complex beings crossing the threshold to self-consciousness would be an even rarer accident. But for antireductionists, the mere presence of conscious beings on earth provides enough evidence to show that life is as firmly implanted in reality as material objects. Thus, if antireductionism is correct, life should be fairly common throughout the universe since some life- and consciousness-generating structures as fundamental as physical and chemical structures are ingrained throughout the universe, along with their base-conditions. Indeed, to some antireductionists, the universe is not only "bio-friendly"—life is central to the universe's design, since without conscious beings, the universe would be a silent, colorless, meaningless affair.

But how can we test between the reductionist and antireductionist alternatives? Finding that life is common in our galaxy would be a point for antireductionism. Physicists and astronomers tend to think that life will be common in the universe because they predict that there will be millions of bio-friendly planets in the galaxy. (That our solar system is comparatively young suggests that the odds are against intelligent life on earth being the first occurrence in our galaxy if intelligent life is common.) But biologists are more aware of the history of contingent events leading to life and side more with reductionists: they predict that life may be very rare in our galaxy—if life on earth is any indication, it takes a lot of work for any conscious life to appear, and our level of consciousness is obviously even rarer. Some biologists suggest that life may even be unique to our planet.

But a basic mystery remains: do the laws of chemistry alone explain the appearance of life, or does chemical bonding merely set up the necessary base-conditions for natural biotic structures to kick in and produce life? Chemical bonding is completely closed on its own level, and nothing in it suggests that this could lead to anything new in terms of higher levels of phenomena. Complete knowledge of the chemical structure of living entities does not help us understand why some wholes are living and some not. Chemistry simply does not appear to account for the origin of the existence of a biological level of "information." Reductionists must explain by the mechanics of bonding or other physical or chemical processes how molecules obeying only chemical laws could become arranged into entities that maintain and reproduce themselves. But on the other hand, how can we test for antireductive biotic structures? How could we isolate an ordering principle in action?

Consider gene mutation. It appears to be random.[5] Reductionists deny that any guiding laws are involved in gene mutation—it is in fact truly random. That evolution is not pretty but inefficient and wasteful is enough for them to conclude that no guidance is involved in how life evolves: nature is indifferent to what comes next. Antireductive naturalists believe that biotic structures such as a biogenic field cause the course of mutation and the preservation of genes to flow in the direction of more complexity and higher levels of organization, including conscious beings. More complex forms then arise from earlier forms. Thus, they believe that the dice of evolution are loaded: some as yet unknown structures "select" among random mutations those needed for complex forms of life and preserves them. It would like a machine in which rules of grammar control a random flow of letters so that only when words and sentences are formed do strings of letters survive, while other strings fall aside, and thus over long stretches of time different texts eventually arise.

But how can we determine if mutation is in fact truly random or is guided by some biotic law? What test would rule out biotic structures or test for purpose? Short of finding trademark notices on genes from God, nothing that scientists could find would be decisive (and naturalists would still question whether such notices came from powerful but perfectly natural alien beings). Whatever scientists find would look random to those holding that theory, and the big picture of evolution would look guided to those holding that theory. If there is no way to detect guidance empirically, this issue will never be resolvable by science. Science does not require random mutation, but biologists will treat evolution *as if* it is truly random if guiding principles cannot be demonstrated by science. The fact of evolution, as opposed to the neo-Darwinian *theory* of the causes, is neutral to the issue of guided versus unguided mutation, as the National Academy of Science acknowledges. But if evolution is in fact guided, then science is currently not only incomplete but in fact wrong. And philosophers cannot rule out the possibility of biotic laws a priori.

So too, if scientists ever succeed in cooking up life from a prebiotic molecular broth, this would not resolve the issue of whether there are biotic structures at work or not: we would still not know whether physical forces are producing life or whether scientists merely have assembled the necessary base-conditions for the biotic structures to become operational. Reductionists claim that life arises without nonphysical causes from a collection of interacting physical parts: once simple chemicals reach a certain level of complexity, the chemicals undergo a transition no more mysterious than liquid water becoming solid ice. The chemicals "assemble themselves" under physical structures alone. But antireductionists would still insist that more structures had become involved in the "self-organization" of materials.

Intractable Mysteries Remain

Thus, both "why" and "how" mysteries persist surrounding both the origin and the development of life, even if scientists find the natural conditions that cause life to arise from chemicals. Moreover, whether the universe is set up reductively or antireductively, why is it set up in such a way that life is even a possibility, and why is the trend toward diversity and higher levels of complexity so prominent? Neither reductive nor antireductive metaphysics changes the fact that, as Karl Popper said, life represents something utterly new in the universe. Even if only a few simple natural rules account for the origin and development of life, we can still ask why these rules exist. In sum, why did even microbes emerge, and why did higher levels of biological complexity evolve? (Of course, in a multiverse model in which all logical possibilities occur, this needs no explanation beyond why life is a logical possibility at all.)

All in all, we know less about the basics of yet another familiar phenomenon—life—than we normally suppose. And in the end perhaps biology should be more central in our overall understanding of the universe than the more abstract sciences of physics and chemistry. That is, a better understanding of the nature of the universe may come by starting with the full flowering of nature, including both life and conscious beings, as central to the scheme of reality rather than focusing on their physical bases. After all, physics is the science with the most assumptions about what can be ignored from the fullness of reality, thus leading to the greatest abstraction from nature. Only the reductionists' intuition that physical structures are older and thus "more real" than life and consciousness leads us to think in terms of life "emerging" from physically ordered matter. Nor should naturalists be certain that life is nothing but configurations of "dead" matter. Reality is not less than living: nature is not inanimate or free of sensory properties—life and conscious beings are at least equally part of what is real, and perhaps more central to nature's overall structure.

Notes

1. If human beings reach the "singularity" where we merge with machines, or if our creations surpass us in an Age of Artificial Intelligence, a new set of Big Questions concerning life and human beings will arise.
2. Which came first, the chicken or the egg? If neo-Darwinism is correct, the egg came first: it was laid by a creature that was not a chicken, but the egg had a mutated gene that caused a new species—the chicken—to be born from it.
3. Disputes have arisen over the ultimate unit of selection—genes, individual beings, or groups. Various theories have been advanced—the selfish gene, inclusive fitness, evolutionary and developmental biology, unique genes—with no consensus emerging to date. Even a form of Lamarckism has returned in epigenetics.
4. Antibiotics are seen as producing new resistant bacteria, that is, the bacteria mutate in reaction to the antibiotics and new resistant strains result. But that may not be what happens: it may be that antibiotics kill off certain strains of bacteria and leave the field to the already existing resistant strains, thus letting the latter multiple without competition. If so, the antibiotics are not a source of novelty—they only kill off the competition.
5. "Random" does not necessarily mean *uncaused or indeterminate* but only our inability to predict an outcome—the outcome of a roll of a die is random, but this does not mean it is physically undetermined. In evolution, "random" means that natural events such as mutation are *not guided* by the adaptive needs of organisms or by a designer god. So too, physical events that affect the course of evolution, such as the meteorite that wiped out the dinosaurs, are not physically uncaused, but they are random from a biological point of view.

11

What Am I?

If we're destroyed, the knowledge is dead . . .We're nothing more than
dust jackets for books . . . so many pages to a person. . . .

—Ray Bradbury

Next consider something even more familiar than life in general: you
know you exist, but what exactly are you? For a philosophical examination, we should start by accepting that our bodies consist of the refuse
of a past supernova and that we are products of evolution here on earth,
not by claiming to be special divine creatures placed here by a god. But are
we only evolved animals? Or are we merely a chemical machine, and if not,
how do we differ?[1] Can this "I" be reduced merely to tissues? Antireductive naturalists may add psychological structures to our makeup, but we
would still be a purely natural reality. Even if we cannot exist independently
of the body, is there anything more to us? Or is there an immaterial component to us that might exist independently of our body? May we continue in
some form after death? Are we in fact embodied transcendent beings? Can
science determine if we are only evolved entities for propagating genes or
a chemical machine? Should we follow the school of personalism and take
"the person" as the irreducible primary ontic category—that is, all reality
is a society of persons, and personhood is the fundamental explanatory
principle? Or is personhood at least one irreducible category of reality?

If human beings are a *social* animal, then another class of Big Questions
arises: Are there social structures to reality? Is there one "human kind," or
do persons vary from culture to culture and era to era? Should we follow
George Herbert Mead's antireductive social approach in which the person
is composed of both a "me" (a "self" defined by social roles and the attitudes of others) and an "I" (by which the individual responds to the social
"me")? Are there social realities (communities, nations, and so forth)?
Does any account of any individual human require a social dimension? At
least for human beings, are societies in fact more real than individuals?

Or are reductionists correct that there are no social entities at all but only individuals? Was former British Prime Minister Margaret Thatcher correct when she said, "There is no such thing as society. There are individual men and women and their families"? (But, of course, a "family" is a social unit.) Is there one best type of society? Where does the authority of laws come from? How do we know what is right? If we are social creatures, how does love figure into our lives?

The Self

In philosophy, these questions coalesce around the issue of whether there is a "self"—that is, an individual real entity having some relation to the body. We have a sense of continuing personal identity and a core of agency to our actions that do not seem to be material—it seems to be a simple, singular reality. We seem to own our actions, experiences, and feelings. This sense of "I" is experienced as different (if not distinct) from our body. This "I" cannot be localized anywhere within the brain, or indeed anywhere in space and time. It is more than the thoughts, feelings, and sensations that we have at any given moment: it is allegedly a reality underlying all of our mental and bodily functions that persists throughout all our changing mental and physical events—the self is the bearer of our states of consciousness and the subject of those states. It gives a unity or identity to the total content of our inner life.

But is there such a unified reality? The traditional answer in most cultures is an ontic dualism of a material body and a "soul," "self," "spirit," or other substance that exists independently of the body. However, problems related to the effect of damage to the brain on consciousness and the difficulty in figuring out how an immaterial mind could make the material body move leads most philosophers to reject the idea of a self as a "ghost in a machine." Indeed, apart from what occurs in the body and brain, we would have no idea that there is a "soul" or "spirit"—we do not know what it is in itself or what it does without a body. Nevertheless, most people believe that there is some entity that thinks their thoughts and experiences their experiences. Such a subject can exist without self-conscious reflection. Most agree with René Descartes's "I think therefore I am": I may not be awake and in control of our thoughts—I may be dreaming, I may be a brain in a vat, I may be being deceived by an evil demon—but for any of these scenarios to occur I still must exist. Thus, the mere fact that I am conscious proves that I exist.

However, naturalists question whether there is such a reality independent of our body. To naturalists, any talk of disembodied persons or realities without some physical vehicle for memories or continuity is absurd. To speak of a disembodied life is meaningless. The human mind develops by interactions between the brain with other body parts and the world. Thus, the nature of our mind is not a pure, disembodied consciousness: it is tied to what we *do*—that is essential to being a human person, and thus a disembodied person is impossible. We are part of nature and tied to our environment.

Francis Crick sums up the ontic/structural reductionists' view of a person:

> "You," your joys and your sorrows, your memories and your ambitions, your sense of personal identity and free will, are in fact no more than the behavior of a vast assembly of nerve cells and their associated molecules. As Lewis Carroll's Alice might have phrased: "You're nothing but a pack of neurons."

To these reductionists, a person is only a natural product of the universe resulting from combining organic material—a physical body undergoing causally connected changes in physical states. There is no "self" but only a hierarchy of sublevels of different activities in our brain. Some philosophers argue that the sense of a "self" is merely a creation of our language: because we have terms that we use for convenience—"I," "me," "mine"— we mistakenly believe that some reality must correspond to them, and so we posit an entity, the "self." But the "self" or "person" is not a reality, and as we advance in our understanding we will see that. Daniel Dennett argues that the brain generates "self-consciousness" and the illusory sense of "I" (the unified center of mental activity) through a process of editing all the mental activity going on throughout the brain. This posited source of the narrations occurring in the mind is an entirely fictional product of the brain and not a causal reality in any sense. The sense of a "person" is merely a story that our brain tells itself.

Derek Parfit's Humean "bundle of connected perceptions" theory is an example of the eliminationism that is popular among naturalists today: all the experiences of a "person"—memories, sense-experiences, emotions, pains, a sense of identity, and so forth—exist but can be described without an actual "person" or "self" existing. That is, we can give a complete description of our inner reality without invoking the idea of a "person"— we consist of a body and a series of interconnected physical and mental events, but our ultimate ontology contains no category "person." Such eliminationists may also accept that the psychological components are not reducible to physical ones.

According to those naturalists who are structural antireductionists, human beings on earth may not have been predestined to exist or be the goal of evolution, but because of natural nonphysical structures the appearance of conscious beings somewhere in the universe is as expected as stars and planets. The physical is a necessary part of what it is to be a person, but it is not all of it: there is an irreducibly psychological character to persons—a mental level of organization to matter—that is not captured in a reductive ontology. Antireductive naturalists reject any dualism of substances: there is no separate substance called a "self" that could survive death. But they accept the reality of persons and believe that the concept of a "person" is incoherent if we subscribe to the reductive physicalists' program: mental phenomena have causal power, and a "person" is a complex of physical and psychological components that has causal power as a unit and thus cannot be reduced to a collection of those components. Hence, persons are irreducible realities—wholes with causal powers—that must be included in our inventory of what is real. In sum, antireductionists accept mental phenomena as irreducibly real and include "personhood" as a fundamental category of reality that cannot be eliminated ontologically or conceptually.

Many antireductionists such as Robert Nozick and Mary Midgley speak of reductionism not only as a philosophical blunder but as a *moral failing*: in reducing persons to something nonpersonal, it *devalues* people. If a rock or machine breaks or ceases to exist, there is no moral problem, but not so if a person or animal is a reality worthy of moral concern. Reductionists reply that they do not deny the phenomena constituting "persons" and "animals" and that we must treat persons and animals differently from rocks because we can *suffer*, and that must be taken into account when we decide how to act. But this still does not fully value human beings. Under antireductionism, our humanness is fully affirmed: conscious beings are not only real but part of the fundamental blueprint of reality and not accidental. To biologist Stuart Kauffman, this worldview beyond reductionism is one "in which we are members of a universe of ceaseless creativity in which life, agency, meaning, value, consciousness, and the full richness of human action have emerged."

Indian Alternatives

Many mystics affirm the fundamental reality of consciousness but deny the reality of the ego, that is, a real "person" within the phenomenal world. According to Advaita Vedanta, our everyday sense of a "person" is an illusion: the one and only reality is a pure, self-existent consciousness, called either "Brahman" or "*atman*." This eternal and unchanging consciousness constitutes all phenomena—all of what we classify as "subjective" and all of what we classify as "objective."[2] Thus, the being of a "person" and of all of the phenomenal world is Brahman, and the illusion is to imagine and experience the person as a separate reality in a plural world of real objects (*maya*) that we fabricate out of what is in fact only one (Brahman). The true reality is called the "self (*atman*)," but it is not an individual person (*jiva*)—that "person" is no more than a character in a dream that mistakes the dream to be a reality distinct from Brahman. This view is the opposite of solipsism since no individual exists, only the one undifferentiated consciousness. Thus, translating "*atman*" as "self" is misleading: Brahman has no connotations of personal selfhood. Instead, the only reality is a nonpersonal consciousness with no real objects of consciousness: the ontic substance (*atman*) of everything, including a person, is only that consciousness. This consciousness is not based in matter, nor is there any matter for it to interact with. And there is no pluralism of individual consciousnesses.

Descartes took the one "unshakable and unchallengeable reality" to be the individual self experienced in self-consciousness. He conceptualized the situation this way: "If *I* doubt *I* exist when *I* think, then the existence of an *I* is affirmed by that very fact." But Advaita Vedantins take the very same experience to be immediate awareness of the one reality (Brahman) constituting ourselves and all that we take to be objective realities. Thus, consciousness transcends the "dream" realm: no individual "self-consciousness" is involved in our awareness of our ontic substance (*atman*). Advaitins thereby see the situation in terms of a nonpersonal transcendent consciousness alone. But all either Descartes or Advaitins can be certain of is that *consciousness* is occurring when we think—we cannot be certain that a distinct individual "person" is involved. Thus, even if we can be sure that consciousness exists, we cannot be sure of its nature or its relation to a person based on this experience alone.

The Samkhya school of India presents a classic dualism of matter and consciousness. Yet Samkhyas see things quite differently than we do in the West: they separate an inactive, pure consciousness completely from all matter, and they take perceptions, a sense of "I," and the other mental activities that we take to be nonphysical actually to be *material*. They identify a center of pure consciousness as our true self (*purusha*) and distinguish it completely from the equally real physical world (*prakriti*) that also includes all other mental activity.[3] The universe contains a multiplicity of such real selves. Thus, unlike in Advaita, there is no one reality. Each individual self is a separate eternal and unchanging conscious unit that witnesses or illuminates thoughts and the other material content of the mind, but it exists independently of such content and continues to be aware in the absence of any content—it is like a searchlight that is on even when no objects are being illuminated. This consciousness is unmoving and yet affects matter, like (to use their simile) a magnet controlling iron filings. Thus, each true self is free of all content and intentionality and continues in a disembodied state after the death of one who is enlightened.

Most Buddhists take a different tack: they do not treat consciousness as fundamental. Instead, "persons" are only aggregates of nonpersonal realities. In this pluralistic ontology, persons (*pudgalas*) consist of five components, one physical (its form) and four mental (sensation, conceptualization, dispositions, and perception). The whole is not ultimately real or a unity. No reality emerges from the parts: the "person" is not treated as a causal whole but only as "conventionally real." Each "person" is a temporary aggregate of parts, like (to use their simile) a chariot that has its parts replaced over time. Each component of a "person," like all the components of phenomenal reality, is impermanent and conditioned by other components. Consciousness is not an eternal and unchanging transcendent reality as in Advaita and Samkhya that "persons" are identical to; it is temporary and contingent, existing only during conscious episodes of a person. So too, there is no underlying, permanent "self" experienced in the phenomenal world in addition to the parts—all that is real in the world are only streams of constantly changing mental and physical components that we label "persons" for convenience. (A karmic residue of our unenlightened desire-driven actions in one life persists and is reembodied in a next one.) In short, there are "selfless persons": there are thoughts without a "thinker," and pains without a distinct "self" feeling them—there are only temporary bundles of impermanent components succeeding each other in a continual flux. Conventionally, we can still speak of "persons," but from the correct ontic perspective no such entities exist. However, the reality of a working chariot is not denied—all that is denied is that there is some separate, permanent, unchanging entity called a "chariot" in addition to the parts that exists independently from those parts. And the same applies to "persons." Persons exist in a way that Mickey Mouse does not since there is a stream of impermanent parts that we label "persons" for convenience, but ultimately the talk of "persons" is also a fiction and not part of the true inventory of things.

The Reduction of the Self

But as noted above, the effect of the body on our mental functioning convinces most philosophers to reject a dualism of mind and body: evidence from the effect of illness to split-brain patients suggests that the mind is not independent of the brain.[4] The latter also raises problems for the sense of unity to our subjectivity. Thus, for naturalists, everything connected to a "self" is connected to the body: everything that science reveals suggests that we are no more than mortal animals, and our sense of "self" is too tightly tied to a body to permit an immortal soul. When death occurs, all that happens is that the body breaks down and the brain stops functioning—we cannot say that the "self" ceases since there was no "self" to begin with.

Ontic dualists, however, reject such a reduction. They believe that some substance—a soul or spirit—existing independently of the body survives and may also have preceded any embodiment in the natural universe. Thus, death is an illusion because the individual survives in some form—either a coherent personal identity or at least personal traits continue on. Some naturalists assert a sort of cosmic law of the conservation of what is real: in a person cannot die but must continue—not just the parts of the body, but mental features—even if the individual no longer exists. Some emergentists argue that God or natural psychological structures supplement biotic and physical structures to generate a new reality—a soul—that then has a reality independent of physical nature and thus can survive its current embodiment.

Mystery Remains

Is there any way science can determine if one of these options is correct? There may be good reasons to embrace naturalism, but it is hard to see how science itself could disprove something alleged immaterial and transcendent: science can give a potentially complete account of the "hardware" of the body, but it is neutral on whether any "software" of a person is also involved. In short, science cannot demonstrate that we are only machines. Nor does any other resolution seem possible without resorting to sheer metaphysical speculation. Near-death experiences and out-of-body experiences are prima facie evidence for the reality of a mental entity existing independently of the body. But naturalists dismiss near-death experiences, explaining them away as due to oxygen deficiency (although other instances of that deficiency do not give rise to such experiences) or as merely something the brain evolved to make dying more peaceful and thus easier (although why that effect should arise at all or be passed along to offspring to help in survival is far from obvious). If the drug ketamine can give rise to out-of-body experiences, is it producing only a hallucination, or is it disrupting the connection of the "soul" with the body? Some naturalists argue that these experiences indicate only that brain activity takes longer to cease upon death than our sensory technology can indicate. Overall, researchers are split on the issue. Thus, we must conclude that, even if it is reasonable to believe that anything real survives death, what happens to a person at death remains a mystery today.

Indeed, the Big Question of a "self" is surrounded by mystery. To Kant, the true self is as much an unknowable noumenal reality as anything else. Descartes argued that we know the existence of the self with absolute certainty and that this is the cornerstone of all of our knowledge, but many philosophers now argue that the self does not exist at all. Mystics have other views. Paradoxically, there is something so very obvious to us—that we exist—and yet we do not know our basic ontic nature at all. Views range from a soul existing independently of the body to human beings being merely evolved animals whose idea of a unified "self" is an illusion. On the one extreme, we are so certain of our existence that some people actually defend solipsism. On the other extreme, perhaps "personhood" or "a self" is only a cultural creation that we ourselves fabricate only from the grammar of our language about a "person" and there is no real entity distinct from the rest of reality. We do not know how to answer questions about its nature—we literally do not know what we are talking about here.

The mystery here may be epistemic rather than ontic: there may simply be something about how our brain evolved that keeps us from knowing the nature of a "self." But it is nonetheless a genuine mystery—one that probably will persist forever. Even if we learn more about how the brain works, the problems persist. That our subjectivity is always a subject and never a phenomenal object of perception only complicates trying to address the mystery. We press up against the limits of our ability to know in a way more like when we confront the beingness of reality than when we approach scientific problems. All we know is that the universe somehow has created a way of knowing itself through us—what the nature of that reality is we do not know.

Notes

1 An interesting question is whether the natural evolution of human beings has ended. Our gene pool is now too large to accommodate large-scale changes easily. Can the scope of genetic engineering affect the future of humanity or only affect a few individuals?

2. This is not, however, an idealistic reduction of all reality to *mind* in the modern Western sense: for Advaitins, the mind and its content (except consciousness itself) that Westerners consider "mental" are as illusory as what we consider "objective, physical" entities.

3. In traditional Indian psychology, the thinking mind (*manas*) is not the self or a soul but merely a sixth sense, with the brain as its sense-organ and ideas as its sense-objects.

4. Ontic dualists can respond that this merely shows that the brain is a receiver of a soul: when the receiver is damaged, the reception is damaged—the coherence of the signal is undamaged, but the signal is badly received, as with radio waves and a damaged radio. The condition of the body at death would also be irrelevant to what occurs to a soul after death.

12

What Is Consciousness?

> How it is that anything so remarkable as a state of consciousness comes
> about as a result of initiating nerve tissue, is just as unaccountable as
> the appearance of the Djin, when Aladdin rubbed his lamp.
>
> —Julian Huxley

It is hard to overemphasize the importance of our type of consciousness. Unlike the consciousness of animals, we can transcend ourselves,
thereby making it easier to think about things that are not immediately
before us. Our consciousness makes us more aware of the universe and
ourselves, and this makes us more fully alive in our world. It is the source
of our ability to create language, culture, and science—and enables us to
foresee our own death.

But understanding the nature of consciousness could not be more
difficult. It is always a subject and cannot be made into an object—
paradoxically, it is never known as an object, but we can be aware
that we are conscious at any time. That is, intentional consciousness
is always consciousness *of* something, but consciousness itself is never
that something: we can be aware that we are conscious, but it is always
a matter of being aware of some object, not awareness of consciousness itself. So too, nothing is more obvious to us than the fact that
most of us can make our body move at will. But how exactly does this
happen? What is the difference between thinking about picking up a
pen and actually initiating the process of picking it up? How does the
"mind" get the "body" to do something? What is the difference between
a wink and an involuntary blink if they are physiologically the same?
Despite all the advances in neuroscience concerning the activities of
the brain, we still know no more about this most basic aspect of being
alive than did the ancient Greeks: we are simply at a loss to explain
how consciousness or our "will" brings about an action.

To many naturalists, the mind is the last surviving mystery. Do brain events cause mental events, or do mental events cause brain events, or is there some entirely other relationship? Or is our mind actually nothing but our brain? Are consciousness, perceptions, intentions, feelings, the will, and desires irreducible features of reality? Are they merely powerless epiphenomena, or indeed entirely nonexistent, or does the mind have causal power? Is "consciousness" a total illusion? Are we in the end nothing more than mindless piles of matter?

This issue divides philosophers like no other. Many doubt that their opponents really believe what they are saying. But most speak with a confidence that would make theologians blush. In fact, they cannot even agree on what "consciousness" is. But they concur that the mind is indeed complex. It is not just sense-perceptions, emotions, reasoning, and imagination. There is a sense of here and now, the kinesthetic awareness of the body, and also a unified "self-awareness." Perhaps there are more exotic properties such as parapsychological powers or a Jungian collective unconscious. There is certainly more to the mind than we are aware of by introspection: there are subconscious processes. Cognitive scientists now find that much of our thought and motivation occurs subconsciously. For example, we all have had the experience of ideas that "just came to me." What exactly distinguishes subconscious mental activity from conscious ones? Do all of these activities converge into one unified "mind," or are there multiple unconnected mental functions?

Even if we take a common-sense "I know it when I see it" approach—that is, consciousness is any state of awareness occurring when we are not unconscious—how do we begin to analyze it? The mind feels embodied; it seems related to the body, and not just the brain. Bodily actions often feel almost a part of the thinking process. Nevertheless, accepting a dualism of mind and body is understandable since our inner life feels different from any sensed inanimate external object. But most philosophers today believe that René Descartes got us off on the wrong track by framing the issues in terms of a dualism of substances—a material body and an immaterial "thinking substance." How can an immaterial substance cause a physical event, when by definition it does not have any physical energy to bring about a change in the physical? How can the two substances interact? How could an immaterial substance intervene in the body without violating the principle of the causal closure of the natural world and the law of the conservation of energy if "mental energy" could somehow be injected into matter? Approaching the subject with such a dualism, we are left with a mystery that seems unresolvable.

Reductive Naturalism

To naturalists who are also structural reductionists, science requires that we are merely physiochemical machines and the events that we think are mental are actually nothing but inanimate physical events ordered by physical structures alone. Sensing is just a physical event involving sense organs—it is no more "mental" than a camera taking a photograph—and thinking is just a physical event involving the brain, even though they *feel* different than an object while the events are occurring. Thus, consciousness and all mental states are reduced without remainder to states, properties, or processes of the brain or are useless epiphenomena. Consciousness is at best an illusion generated by the brain: the brain only makes it look as if there is something nonphysical involved. Thus, the vexing question of "what is consciousness anyway?" is eliminated. To reductionists, consciousness is just brain activity under another name. But eliminationists go further and simply deny the existence of the mind. To Daniel Dennett, we are no more conscious than a TV set that is on. So too, characters on the TV screen appear conscious but are not, and the same illusion applies to us. The brain merely records our prior physical actions and plays them back, thus giving our brain more and more new material to react to as we age. Mindless zombies are not different from us because *we are zombies*.[1]

However, reductionists have a problem: why are there mental states? Even if consciousness is an illusion, how can it be there at all? How is it possible? If the mind is simply a state of matter, why does consciousness accompany physical events? In addition, how are mental states "realized" by some physical state? The problem is not merely that at present we do not know the mechanisms that give rise to consciousness—rather, we cannot imagine how any mechanisms *could* give rise to it. Reductionists like Patricia Churchland readily admit that today we cannot imagine how consciousness could be a physical process, but they see this as only a psychological limitation on our part and that science will eventually explain how consciousness is merely physical. But the very idea that something exists outside of the physical is to reductionists, in the words of J.J.C. Smart, "frankly unbelievable"—"I just can't believe it." Like him, they cannot accept that physics can explain everything except consciousness. When we finally engineer robots that can do everything that we can do, the illusion that consciousness is real will go the way of a vitalistic substance in biology. Today philosophical therapy to overcome our deep-seated intuition of consciousness being real must suffice.

Antireductive Naturalism

However, naturalists who embrace structural antireductionism see the situation very differently. They deny ontic dualism, but they treat the mind as causal and thus real. It is hard to see our feeling pain as causing C-fibers to fire, but there is no reason to think that all mental properties must be like pain. Instead, the mind is a natural product and part of the one causal network in nature. (Antireductionists also do not have the problem with the placebo effect and its inverse that reductionists have.) To John Searle, just as the stomach produces digestive acids, so the brain "secretes" the mind. But this does not mean that physical structures must be the source of the mind—instead, nonphysical structures are at work that make the brain the base for consciousness and other mental activity. But the mind does not violate the principles of the causal closure of nature and conservation of physical energy since no immaterial "mental energy" is injected into the natural realm. Rather, how computer software guides the flow of physical events in the computer's hardware is more analogous: the electronic flow in integrated circuits conforms to the laws of physics, but the flow is also directed by the commands in the programs as operated by a user without violating the law of conservation of energy. Similarly here: the causal completeness of the physical is preserved—there are no gaps in physical events in which the mind works—and there is no overdetermination of causes since the mental does not interfere with physical operations; rather, mental information merely guides the flow of energy, and the physical account of events would thus be complete on its own level.[2] Nor is mental causation a matter of downward causation since the mind is not a product of matter. There are no separate mental events existing independently of matter but only separate biological and mental structures operating in matter and ordering it. In sum, every event on the level of the body would have a set of natural causes, some of which are mental—demanding that the causes all be physical is only a matter of reductive metaphysics.

To structural antireductive naturalists, there is no mind apart from matter. But even though consciousness cannot exist without a brain, this does not mean that they are identical or that consciousness is merely physical. Rather, the physical and biological levels of organization are only the bases that must be present for mental phenomena to appear. But the mind does not "emerge" out of the physical: it is simply the result of another level of structures ordering matter that is on a par with the physical and biological levels. But psychological structures become active only when the proper base-conditions are properly assembled. Such structuring is an objective part of nature's structure even if we experience its results only subjectively. It is not the creativity of the physical level of organization that generates mental realities—it is not as if some currently unknown property of, say, electromagnetism produces consciousness—but the creativity of other aspects of the universe.

The physiologist Benjamin Libet proposes a "conscious mental field"—but a field that, unlike a magnetic field, can act upon its base (the brain). Some naturalists endorse the "neutral monism" espoused by Bertrand Russell and C.D. Broad: nature consists of only one substance, and that substance is neither physical nor mental but can be organized by structures differently. To David Chalmers, consciousness is a fundamental feature of nature—it is as irreducible as such physical properties as electrical charge. Others are also willing to consider a panpsychism in which all matter has consciousness or a potential for consciousness ("proto-consciousness") as an inherent basic property, just as matter has physical properties, although this introduces the problem of how the consciousness properties aggregate or are structurally combined to produce conscious beings. (Critics argue that such panpsychism is counterintuitive, but then again, so then again so is the reduction of mind to matter.)

First-Person Experiences

Central to antireductionism is the difference between the physical and *subjectivity*—that is, all our first-person experiences of thoughts, sense-perceptions, emotions, pains, and so forth. Subjectivity always has a private inner dimension that any corresponding neurological correlates cannot have. Our awareness of ourselves as subjects and agents is distinct from our awareness of ourselves as physical objects. Scientists may well be able to reduce some mental functions to the mechanical operation of physiological states, but this subjectivity cannot be reduced. Indeed, it cannot be studied at all by examining the electrochemical activity of the brain—science is limited to what can be produced for inspection by others, and subjectivity is not an objective, observable phenomenon. Thus, we cannot reduce the first-person ontology of consciousness to a third-person objective one. No third-person account can capture first-person experiences. We know ourselves and our consciousness immediately, not through any accumulation of third-person descriptions. In sum, first-person experiences are an irreducible field of reality all their own. Thus, the reductionists' method of explaining any *x* in terms of non-*x* will not work here precisely because what is to be explained is not something with physical properties, and physical properties can only explain other physical properties.

Thomas Nagel stresses part of this subjectivity: the irreducibility of our *perspectives* to any framework that admits only the physical. A point of view or what it is "like to be" something cannot be grasped by even an exhaustive physical analysis of the brain. It is something that we can imagine only from the inside. We can ask what it is like to be *a bat* because they presumably are conscious and thus have an "inner life," but it makes no sense to ask what it is like to be *a chair* since it has no inner life. This subjectivity is real and cannot be reduced to something else: we could know all there is to know about a bat's brain, but it would not tell us what it like to be a bat. There simply is more than one dimension to the world, and the gap between the two is unbridgeable. A point of view cannot be constructed out of components that do not have a point of view; such a process would be logically, not merely empirically, impossible—even God could not create conscious beings by piecing together a lot of particles having nothing but physical properties. Subjective events have a "view from the inside"—perspectivity, intentionality, and experientiality—that objective events do not and that cannot be grasped from the "outside." In John Searle's words, any attempt to reduce intentionality to something nonmental will always fail precisely because it leaves out intentionality.

Also central to our mental life are the *felt aspects* of our phenomenal experiences—the greenness we sense when we look at grass, the hotness of touching a hot surface, and so forth. These are strictly subjective elements, as opposed to the physical input or resulting behavior. Such qualia are in a totally separate category of reality from physical causes and results, and thus they are not reducible to them. As Albert Einstein once said, science cannot explain the taste of soup.

Reductionists realize that they have a major difficulty with the presence of qualia in a physical world. Even if qualia play no causal role in our actions, they are still there, and without a physiological reduction their existence is incompatible with physicalism. Jaegwon Kim had to modify his position to "physicalism, or something near enough" because why qualia arise from neural substrates remains a mystery—he simply can see no way to fit them into a reductive physicalist system. Some reductionists just awkwardly brush these phenomena aside and, in Francis Crick's words, "hope for the best." Others, such as Daniel Dennett, blithely deny the obvious—our inner experiences—and simply eliminate them as completely unreal since to affirm them, they believe, would be unscientific. It seems "intuitively clear" (at least to reductionists) that the mind and the brain are one. Reductionists redefine subjective terms in physical terms— such as "pain" as the physical damage or our resulting behavior—but this does not change the nature of experience. As John Searle says, it is merely playing with the words, not making a new empirical discovery about the world. Reductionists have not analyzed the mind and found it to be the brain, like analyzing water and finding it to be H_2O—they merely declare it to be the brain because their metaphysics demands it.

Antireductionists see the reductionists' ploy as a flat-out refusal to face reality. They insist that we must accept that there are in fact features of reality that are not reducible *even in principle* to physical features. The sensation of color is as real and as much a part of the world as light waves and the sensed physical objects. It is a feature that requires the mental level of organization to appear, but it is no less real for being so. Thus, a neuroscientist who sees the world only in black and white is missing something about reality: when she finally sees in color, something new is learned, and thus her knowledge of the mind was previously incomplete, even if she had complete knowledge of how perception works. No new knowledge-claims may be forthcoming and no new evidence for old ones, but she now knows more of reality. Reductionists reply that qualia are not the result of seeing something new in the world but are only properties of the experiencer: as color blindness shows, colors are only inner representations that the brain creates to help us distinguish things in the world.

Is Consciousness Reducible?

The "easy" problems of consciousness are explaining the brain mechanisms for such phenomena as memory, sense-perception, and information processing and storage, although these are proving harder than once thought. For example, sensation may be readily explainable in terms of sensory stimulation of nerves, neural signals, and computational mechanisms. But the "hard problem" is why the physical workings of the brain are accompanied by any subjective experience at all—that is, why do subjectivity and qualia accompany neural events? In short, how do we explain *consciousness itself*? It is not merely a different scale of physical events that can be reduced to another physical level. Can it be explained in terms of memory and our language ability? It is especially puzzling in those cases where it is not needed—for example, computers can simulate thinking and robots can behave like us and perform some of our activities without any accompanying subjectivity.[3] We may assign a derivative status to the images produced in sensory experiences, but we cannot do so with consciousness itself: it is not the *appearance* of some underlying reality but *is* the reality in question.[4] Our "subjective" experience is as much a part of reality as what is experienced—the subjectivity involved in seeing the Mona Lisa is as real and irreducible as the canvas and paint.

We have as yet no idea why consciousness exists or how it is connected to the brain, although scientists are coming to understand the neural mechanisms accompanying it. But can science conquer the hard problem of how and why consciousness appears? How do neural firings give rise to subjectivity? Why is consciousness connected to neurons and not blood cells? Why do systems of neurons form and grow, thereby permitting more types of consciousness? And most surprising, why does anything new at all appear from nonconscious elements, let alone something so unexpected as consciousness? Moving the locus of the arising of consciousness to computation on a quantum level does not help with the basic gap of matter and subjectivity. Consciousness and matter seem so contradictory as to be irreconcilable. (Hence the appeal of ontic dualism.) Scientists may be able to explain all chemical properties as products of electromagnetic forces acting on electrons and ions, but now try to do that for consciousness. In short, why is consciousness even possible? The mystery surrounding consciousness will remain until we gain a clear idea of how anything in the brain *could* cause conscious states. But it is not obvious how any increase in our understanding of the mechanisms at work in the brain or the functions of other mental activity will shed light on how or why consciousness accompanies some physical events or anything about its nature. Nor does introspection help: we only "see" the mental phenomena, not how they can be related to the brain.

Indeed, antireductionists argue that consciousness itself will never be explainable in terms of physics or any third-person science, no matter how thorough our knowledge of the structural and dynamic properties of physical processes may become. No account of the mechanics of sensing color or hormonal explanation of a person's condition can account for the person's experiences themselves. The laws of physics cannot in principle encompass consciousness: it is impossible to deduce from the laws of physics that a certain complex whole is aware of its own existence. The unbridgeable gap between consciousness and the physical mechanisms supporting it is as much logical as empirical since the natures of the two are totally distinct. We lack any idea for why the neural firings in the brain could give rise in experiencers to a *felt aspect* of the event. Even treating consciousness as merely a biological phenomenon would not account for its uniqueness—it differs from, say, stomach acid in being totally subjective and not objective.

Some antireductive naturalists such as Thomas Nagel think that, although at present a solution to the mind/body problem is literally unimaginable, it is possible that in the future some explanation of consciousness may be forthcoming. Others would agree with Freeman Dyson: "Mind and intelligence are woven into the fabric of our universe in a way that altogether surpasses our understanding." Indeed, the "mysterians" such as Colin McGinn and Steven Pinker think there are good reasons to believe that no explanation will ever be forthcoming. McGinn suggests that the way we are constructed cuts us off from ever knowing what it is in the brain that is responsible for consciousness: our brain has evolved to navigate us through our physical environment and not to reflect upon itself, and thus we will never know very much about consciousness. Thus, how a system of insentient neurons generates subjective awareness will remain insolvable in principle: we need a new type of category that links the mental and physical, but we cannot think in categories other than the mental and the physical. How could we step back from our situation and come up with the missing way of thinking? It is a limitation of our cognitive abilities, like not being able to visualize four dimensions in mathematics. We have evolved to look outward for survival and not inward, and so we do not have a cognitive apparatus to observe conscious states *qua* conscious states. The senses are geared to represent things in the world with spatially defined properties, and it is precisely because consciousness lacks these spatial properties that we are incapable of resolving the mind/body problem. We cannot link nonspatial consciousness to the spatial brain and so are not in a position to figure out the right questions to ask.

Thus, there are, McGinn believes, physiological causes for the limitations in our ability to understand subjectivity and how consciousness arises: it is a question that falls outside the "cognitive space" of beings like us and thus will remain a mystery for us. (In fact, McGinn believes that most philosophical issues will remain mysteries because of our physiological limitations.) Consciousness is merely another natural product, and nothing is really magical about how the brain generates it—we will never be able to fathom the process because of cognitive limitations, but it remains a purely natural fact, and its appearance is not different from that of any other higher-level natural phenomenon. Just because we do not understand it is no reason to start invoking souls or a god. In short, the mystery lies within us, not nature, and thus is epistemic, not ontic.

The Reductionists' Dilemma

Reductionists can readily agree with this last point. Eliminationists eliminate consciousness altogether as illusory (and thus deny there is a gap or hard problem), while reductionists admit that they do not have a clue as to how consciousness arises but still insist that it must be physical because reductionism is true. But for antireductionists this mystery cannot be brushed aside with simply a declaration that the mind must be material because science cannot deal with the immaterial. They believe that even if we knew every last physical detail about the universe such information would not lead us to postulate the presence of conscious experience. Reductionists cannot just smile and pretend it is not a problem. Indeed, the rationality of holding reductionism today is very much in question—it is based on what we do not know.

In fact, structural reductionism is so counterintuitive here that it needs a very strong argument before we can accept it: the reductionists' accounts of the mind totally miss the central features of what is to be explained—*subjective experience*. This feature is so clearly part of our experience that it seems to be a fundamental feature of nature. Even if consciousness were a mere fluke of nature, as reductionists contend, why is it there and how could it appear? That is, the basic mystery for reductionists is how and why consciousness and other mental phenomena appear at all if they are not real and have no causal power. Even if consciousness is only a product of evolution, developed in conjunction with the body, it is hard to see why it would have evolved or survived if it had no value.[5] As Karl Popper put it, from a Darwinian point of view it is hard to see how an utterly useless consciousness should have appeared at all. Why would nature generate and preserve causally useless epiphenomena or illusions? So too, the accompanying consciousness must give us some advantage for adaptation and thriving (e.g., by creating mental pictures for us to work with).

Reductionists have the monumental task of explaining how consciousness could have evolved from quarks and why consciousness is even a possibility in a material world. Antireductionists at least have no problem affirming the obvious—that consciousness exists. And reducing subjectivity to some objective reality simply misses its very nature completely. It may be open to explanation, but it cannot be explained away by denying it merely by fiat. To Thomas Nagel, reductionism here is self-refuting: it denies the very data that it meant to explain—Daniel Dennett's book *Consciousness Explained* is actually *Consciousness Ignored*. As the Galen Strawson says, the eliminationists' denial of the reality of their own consciousness "is the strangest thing that has ever happened in the whole history of human thought, not just the whole history of philosophy."

If this is so, one must explain the reductionists' reluctance to accept consciousness as real. Their basic intuition is that the physical—both matter and physical structures—existed for billions of years on earth before life and consciousness appeared, and hence it must be "more real." But simply because it took time for nature to assemble the base-conditions of consciousness does not mean that consciousness is any less real than its bases or must be a physical rather than a nonphysical natural property. Indeed, the presence of consciousness adds a new dimension to the question of why there is a nonconscious universe at all.

Science and Consciousness

Naturalists believe that science in principle gives a complete picture of reality. And reductionists contend that only their brand of naturalism comports with science: they start with the premise that science deals only with the physical and can in principle give a complete picture of reality; thus, if consciousness does not fit in the picture, it cannot be real. But merely because scientists must approach all phenomena from the "outside" does not mean that no reality has an "inside."[6] To practice science certainly does not require that—scientists *qua* scientists need not deny there is more to reality than what they study. Merely because first-person phenomena cannot be studied by third-person scientific methods in no way means that scientists have *proven* them to be nonexistent. In addition, the idea that the mind is a systems-feature of the human body with causal powers shows that the alleged inconsistency of mind and science only comes from the reductionists' metaphysics: the completeness of physical causes is incompatible with any real mental causes, but the causal closure of the natural realm is not—rather, it may be that the mind in fact produces one type of natural cause in one total natural causal order even if the mind is subjective. Nor would the mind's action in this scenario violate the law of the conservation of energy even if how it works is not yet understood. Thus, the reductionists' truncated view of a person results from their metaphysics alone—it is not required by science. An antireductive naturalism is "close enough" to science in light of what we know today to be the more rational choice.

Structural reductionism rests on the claim that the physical bases are both necessary and sufficient for the appearance of the mental and thus explain them, but without scientific evidence for this, it is merely a bald metaphysical assertion. However, science only shows that the physical is a necessary condition for the appearance of mental phenomena in us—it cannot show that the physical is both necessary and *sufficient* for causing it. That is, if we affect or remove the physical level upon which a mental property depends, then the mind also will be affected or terminated, but this cannot show that matter and physical structures are the only factors in the appearance of the mental—it may be that physical and biological base-conditions are only *necessary* for psychological structures to kick in. In fact, even if we could make computers or the internet conscious, antireductionists could still argue that all that was demonstrated is that mental structures can operate in a different set of base-conditions to make consciousness appear, not that consciousness is reducible to those physical material and conditions.

In addition, the current approach in neuroscience will not be able to resolve the reductionist/antireductionist dispute even if scientists attain a complete mapping of the brain. Our knowledge of the brain has increased dramatically over the last two decades, but neuroscientists are only discovering *correlations* of physical and mental states—they cannot prove a brain/mind identity or epiphenomenalism or establish bodily causation of the mental. In themselves, correlations of mental and brain events give us no reason to claim that the mind is dependent on the brain or identical to it—antireductionists and dualists have no problem accepting such correlations. Indeed, nothing is explained merely by correlating consciousness with physical phenomena. In fact, doing so introduces a new puzzle to be solved: reductionists must explain how physical structures produce the type of mental phenomena that appear, and antireductionists must explain how nonphysical structures require specific base-conditions to become operational. Questions such as whether the flow of adrenalin causes anger or vice versa or have some other relation remain more metaphysical in nature.

Today most neuroscientists may adopt reductionism, but they cannot argue that science proves it. Neuroscientists can practice their science *as if* reductionism is true because their findings are neutral to the metaphysical issues. In addition, even if they ever achieve a complete understanding of the brain's wiring, *how* subjectivity appears remains unanswered. Moreover, even if we ever establish correlations between neural processes and all mental events, *why* a new layer of nature—consciousness—should accompany some mental phenomena is still left unanswered. What empirical finding could even suggest that subjective experience would accompany physical facts? No neurophysical theory may be able to explain why consciousness accompanies mental functions. That is, science cannot explain why reality is set up to permit that possibility at all.

Furthermore, we may never know whether conscious beings are an almost impossible miracle in the universe or a common occurrence. It may be that consciousness is a fundamental feature of reality programmed into the universe, that is, the universe has written into its forces and laws a way of knowing itself. Or maybe not. As Bertrand Russell said, we simply have no idea of life's relation to the universe: it may be the final climax, an accidental and unimportant by-product, or just a disease affecting matter in its old age.

The Essential Mystery of Consciousness

Thus, the Big Question of consciousness leaves us with yet another unanswered basic mystery surrounding something that we are intimately familiar with. Somehow we became little outcroppings of nature by which the universe became aware of itself, but the *why* and the *how* remain central mysteries. Science cannot help because we cannot get distance from consciousness to analyze it objectively. If the possibility of a reduction "in principle" is the reductionists' fallback position for when all else fails, then the untestability of subjectivity and the question of whether the brain generates consciousness or is only the base-condition for the appearance of consciousness is the antireductionists' counterpart. But how subjective consciousness appears and why it is part of the natural world at all remain mysteries for both metaphysics. These mysteries seem intractable, despite the reductionists' creed that these are problems only to be solved by science. Our descendants may develop an intelligence that makes ours look like an ant's, but the basic problem may well remain for any being with a brain structured like ours—if so, consciousness will remain an unexplained brute fact.

We seem here to be again at the limits of our cognitive capacities. But it is possible that we have created a false mystery by misconceiving the situation: by conceptualizing our state by separating "mind" and "body" into two non-overlapping categories, we may well be blocking ourselves from any solution—this way of conceptualizing ourselves does seem to make it impossible to get the two categories back together again and thus forecloses any explanation. The best that philosophers can do in these circumstances is to come up with a better conceptualization than a relation of "mind" to "body." Antireductionists are attempting this, but they have to invoke nonphysical structures for which there is currently no scientific evidence.

Notes

1. Substance dualism is not entirely dead, but today it is advocated chiefly by the religious who want something to survive death and who invoke God as the cause of consciousness. They argue that the mind is independent of the body and somehow initiates which neurons will fire in the brain. But how a particular soul is tied to a particular body, what it is about the nature of mind and matter that permits this interaction, and how the interaction occurs are not explained but remain a mystery. Nevertheless, today some ontic reductionists (such as William Lycan) admit that, while their reductionist stance is rational, they do not proportion their belief to the evidence: arguments for both reductionism and dualism fail to be compelling, and reductionists should admit that the standard objections to dualism are not very convincing.
2. While analogies of the brain to a computer are popular today, scientists are finding the brain to be more complex than any current computer and to operate differently. In a hundred years, another technology may well be the model for the brain.

3. That computers can simulate our thought does not mean they are conscious any more than the fact that they can simulate digesting food means they eat. What computers do is transform one set of symbols into another by an algorithm. Making computers such as IBM's Watson that analyze massive amounts of data does not impinge the issue of whether computers have consciousness. John Searle's "Chinese Room" thought-experiment makes a strong argument that computers as currently constituted will never be able to *think*: understanding is not merely a matter of manipulating symbols—no increase in computing power will duplicate consciousness. The critics' best reply is that a new type of computer is needed, one that we have not yet conceived, after we learn how the brain actually works. So too, robots would have to duplicate how we perceive and intuit before the issue of consciousness arises. However, even if the simulation is good enough to pass the Turing test, we would still have to ask if a computer or android is only *simulating* human reactions or is actually *conscious*. After all, an android could perfectly simulate what it is like to feel pain when its arm is jabbed with a pin (e.g., saying "ouch" loudly, grimacing, and jerking its arm away), but without nerves it would be hard to conclude that it is actually *feels* pain.

4. This impacts the question of reality in another way. There is no color without us: the greenness of grass is not independent of our neural system—it is a matter of the interaction between us, lightwaves, and the grass. But reality is not *colorless or devoid of other sense-qualities*. Calling colors "subjective" or "only in the mind" is misleading—they are as much a part of reality as anything else we sense. Nature is not, in Alfred North Whitehead's characterization, "a dull affair, soundless, senseless, colourless"—the world is not colorless any more than objects in a closed drawer are invisible just because they are not being sensed right now. Calling objects invisible, is, to use George Santayana's example, like calling a drum silent because we hear the sound waves and not the drum. Seeing color is a complex phenomenon: it requires physical objects, the generation of lightwaves, and beings capable of transforming the signals into color. Nature had the capacity for color and created all that was necessary for the generation of color, including color-sensitive subjects, even if it took time for the conditions to develop.

5. Antireductionists need not deny a role for evolution in the development of levels of consciousness. For example, why didn't dinosaurs, which survived for a hundred million years, develop our level of consciousness? Simply because they did not need any greater level of consciousness to survive in their environment. Hominids had more challenges to survive, and that led to a need for greater consciousness, and through evolution a set of base-conditions accommodating greater consciousness arose.

6. The new "mind-reading" technology actually reads only brain activity, not consciousness.

13
Do We Have Free Will?

The conundrum of free will and destiny has always kept me dangling.
　　　　　　　　　　　　　　　　　　　　　—William Shatner

Since we have a physical component, most of us agree that some mental control over the body is necessary if the mind is at all real. Indeed, this ability is the most important of the mind's functions, if it exists. And if the mind does not have such power, a person could not have true free will—we would not have the genuine power to choose how to act but would instead be completely controlled by nonconscious physical events in our body.[1] But does the mind have causal powers, or is free will an illusion? How could freedom be even possible in a material being? Are what appear to be free acts really done by the body without our control and determined solely by a chain of physical and biological forces operating in our body? If we have the personal control of free will, we have genuine choice and agency to at least some degree, and our choices would then have to be taken into account for any complete explanation of our actions. (The classical formulation of free will in terms of "could have done otherwise" ends up causing more problems than clarification.)

So do we have free will or not?

The Reductionists' Denial of Free Will

Naturalists who are also structural reductionists reduce the mind to the nonconscious brain, and eliminationists eliminate the mind—either way, free will is eliminated altogether. Thus, mental phenomena are seen as at best powerless epiphenomena. An immaterial mind, even if it existed, could have no causal power. To use Thomas Huxley's image, a mind could no more cause actions than a train's steam whistle could cause the train to move. To accept more would be to deny that there can be a complete physical description of physical events. Moreover, a sufficient physical cause precludes the need for any other cause. Physical phenomena are the actual causes at work when we mistakenly think the mind is causing an event. Moreover, free will could not possibly arise even in principle in a deterministic world. Thus, we have no more free will than any other animal, including those animals that we think have consciousness. If determinism is true for all events in our universe, then there is no free will or random events: from the beginning of time (if time has a beginning) it was fixed that I would be typing this sentence right now on this planet and that you would be reading it whenever it is that you read it, and nothing could change these events from occurring. As Sean Carroll puts it, given the quantum state of elementary particles of a person and the environment, the future is fixed by the laws of physics—any true free will would violate everything we know about the laws of nature. If there are some random events at the quantum level or above, the history of the universe would be different, but there is no reason to believe that such randomness could somehow create free will.

To reductionists, only the brain acts, with its nonconscious actions based on only our accumulated past experiences, our abilities, and our environment—no mental decisions are involved. Those experiences fix what occurs next through the determinism of events governing nature. Even if our brain, acting like a computer, can distinguish different reasons and follow what the chain of past experiences dictates to be the best, no free decisions occur. The brain does not "decide"—there is no agent or choice but only mechanical operations. All events are really physical, and all physical events are determined completely by previous and concurrent physical events. The appearances of personal agency and free will is no more real than the appearance that a thermostat freely adjusts the room temperature. Only because we do not know what will happen next do our actions appear to be freely chosen—our brain does not (and perhaps cannot) predict the next outcome of the complex phenomena operating in us. But we are not the author of our actions: nonconscious matter is in control. A string of inanimate events in the brain that we think we initiate by free will are caused merely by neurological events. Actions happen to us, and the feeling of a conscious "will" is only an illusion generated by the brain thereby creating in us a sense of ownership of our actions. (Why evolution created the illusion of ownership is not clear since actions in a deterministic world would occur the same way without a sense of agency or ownership.) It is only because we, unlike everything else in the world, are conscious that we have this illusion.

Since Thomas Hobbes, "compatibilists" within the reductionist camp have tried to put a smiley face on determinism: as long as one is not restrained by outside forces or an inner compulsion caused by mental disorder, there are no compelled actions, and one is thus autonomous and free. Compatibilists think this the only "free will" we have. One is morally responsible for one's actions as long as one acts only from one's inner desires that are not caused by a brain disorder. So too, habits or dispositions conditioned by previous actions may determine an action.

Compatibilism is the most popular position in philosophy today, but many philosophers object that there is nothing "free" about our actions in compatibilist "free will." Compatibilists have formulated several defenses to try to make the position convincing, but none are very strong: what they mean by "free will" simply is not what is normally meant—we are still left with a purely deterministic chain of physical events. For compatibilists, we are still only a biochemical puppet, and when Sam Harris says "a puppet is free as long as he loves his strings," opponents would respond that he is only playing with words. How does the unconstrained or unhindered operation of a deterministic brain form "free will" in any sense? And if all acts are determined, it is not clear why the absence of any internal and external constraints makes a relevant difference—it is just another type of determination. It may make a significant difference legally but not philosophically: a person's actions are still totally fixed by nonconscious events—"unconstrained" only means that normal bodily mechanisms determine our actions, not that any free will is involved.

Affirming Free Will

In opposition are the "libertarians" of the philosophical (not political) kind who claim that mental states have at least some causal power over the body. This permits the possibility of true free will: we can choose our course of action—the course is not fixed by physical events. Structural antireductionists can offer an explanation for this: nature has psychological structures that are real and on par with the physical and biological structures that set up minds with causal powers, personal choice, and control. Because mental phenomena have their own causal consequences, they are a nonnegotiable feature of reality and not reducible to products of the physical or biological structures. Making a choice is different from a physical action: it has an "inside" that mechanical actions do not. Mental phenomena are dependent on the physical (both matter and the physical level of organization) as the base-conditions for their appearance, but they are equally real in their own right and can exercise causal power over the body.

To structural antireductionists, the mind causally enters into events (as discussed in chapter 12). This is no more problematic than any other level of causation—it is simply another level of normal structure, and thus of ordinary causation, that nature has produced. Prior to the appearance of beings with self-awareness or a self-reflective mind in the evolution of the cosmos, a determinism may have prevailed (although uncaused events on the subatomic level would present an issue). But once the base-conditions for mental phenomena are fully assembled, such a mind arises, and psychological-level structures operate in implementing our beliefs and values, emotions, intentions, and so forth into actions. Indeed, how free will could evolve in a world that is deterministic before the appearance of self-conscious life if consciousness is not the result of a separate level of organization is not clear.

Thus, the antireductionists' account accepts the autonomy and agency of a person, genuine choice, and mental causation as components of the overall causal system affecting our actions. Collectively, this permits the possibility of free will. If so, our behavior results from intentionality and agency, and these cannot be accounted for solely by the causal role played by physical forces. We then have at least some degree of choice in our actions, and a complete explanation of our actions would require reference to our choices as causes, not just to the physiological conditions of the event. Under this approach, there also is no causal overdetermination since physical events are not the complete causal account of the course of events. A complete account of the course of brain activity requires a role for beliefs and decisions, even if events are closed on a neural level.[2] The mysteries surrounding mental causation are merely a subset of the general mystery of how any level of organization operates in nature. (But that the mental level is involved and is not determined by the physical level does not *guarantee* that there is free will: a more encompassing determinism including determination of events in the mind may still prevail. Mental structures must enable a freedom of choice for free will to prevail.)

Determinism versus Causation

To address whether we have free will or are determined, we must first distinguish *causation* from *determinism*—free will requires the former but is incompatible with the latter. If our actions were totally chaotic, we would not have the control permitting acts of will, but causal order permits control by enabling us to predict the outcome of our actions: if actions X and consequences Y in the past routinely occurred together, then we can confidently predict that if we do X, then Y will probably follow. Determinism, however, goes beyond causation: it entails a fixed chain of causes: A (along with some surrounding conditions) causes B, B in turn causes C, C in turn causes D, and so forth. For reductionists, all the causes are physical. In determinism, all events and properties are completely fixed by past causes: if we know all the causes and conditions, once a chain of events starts we can predict its determined end. Thus, causation is only about isolated lawful conditionals, while determinism is about the antecedents of those conditionals and how they lead to a fixed chain of consequences from an initial action. (Calling an isolated action "determined" is slippery: it can mean simply "caused" without loading in all the metaphysics of determinism.) With genuine free will, one can control some of the antecedents in causal chains, picking the antecedents as we go along. Thus, we can affirm the lawfulness of actions and consequences necessary for choice and affirm that every human event has a cause and yet still reject determinism.

Unfortunately, philosophers usually do not distinguish causation and determinism. Instead, they equate the two and thus see the rejection of determinism as having only one alternative: *chaos*—a randomness of physically uncaused events, like that theorized to be happening on the subatomic level of organization. But with the distinction of causal order from determinism, one can reject determinism and still affirm the order of causation: the alternative to determinism is not necessarily *indeterminism* but may be the middle ground of *causation* that permits predictive control. Thus, with causation the resulting actions of a human agent are not random but selected by our decisions and carried out by voluntary actions.

This distinction also permits dismissing a standard refutation of free will. The argument goes: either determinism is true or it is not; if it is true, then all our actions are fixed by prior states, and thus there is no free will; if it is false, then there is only subatomic-like randomness, and so we have no way to control our actions and no way to guide their results through predictions, and thus once again there is no free will. In sum, there is either an unstoppable, uninterrupted chain of physical events and so no free will, or there is no predictable outcome and so no meaningful free choice can be exercised. But if we can predict the short-term outcome of our actions at least to a degree through our knowledge of recurring causal patterns and can also control our actions at least to a degree, then there is a third option—causal control without determinism—and free will is possible.[3] In sum, free will does not entail randomness but requires control, and causal lawfulness without determinism provides such control.[4]

This distinction also renews the possibility of an "agent causation" in which a person can exercise free will in his or her actions without any determinism. Peter van Inwagen believes that free will remains a mystery even if there is agent causation because free will and determinism both obviously exist but are incompatible. But if causation and determinism are differentiated, this particular mystery disappears: there is in fact no determination of human actions, and we can cause actions in an ordered way. Every event still has a cause and is lawful, but mental causes can be in its chain of causes of human actions and so for our actions there is no determinism of inanimate causes. Causal order prevents randomness by giving persons the predictive control needed to exercise free will, and we then supply a cause in the chain of actions. But the question then is: How does the decision of how to act *arise*? Is there still a gap in the causal chain? Are the decisions determined by something other than physical events? Does some causeless event still occur? Does a thought how to choose just magically appear from our subconscious—just "pop into the mind"?[5] And are subconscious events determined by physical events alone? This may remain a mystery, but libertarians accept that in some way a person enters the picture as a cause by freely choosing how to act.[6]

Science and Free Will

Thus, the stark contrast: under determinism our actions are a fixed chain of physical events, while under libertarianism we can control at least some causes by selection. Can we ascertain if the events in our brain are deterministic or permit causal control? Neuroscience may be a way. Benjamin Libet conducted experiments in the 1980s that showed that apparently freely chosen acts were in fact initiated by the brain a fraction of a second before the conscious decision to act occurred. These experiments have since been replicated and expanded by others. Determinists have jumped on these results as proving that free will does not exist and that in fact the conscious mind plays no role in the chain of our events—indeed, for them this is the last step necessary for science to remove all aspects of mind from science.

But neuroscientists have not been so quick to reach that conclusion. They have suggested other explanations for the results. For example: that the "readiness potential" (which occurs in the sensory motor-cortex) that these experiments actually measure is unrelated to the decision making (which occurs in the parietal lobe); that the readiness potential actually begins to build up before the choice has to be made in anticipation of having to make a choice when the participants in the experiments are told that they will have to make a decision, and thus it is unlikely to be related to the actual decision of choosing which way to act—that is, the urge to move is unrelated to the decision itself; that it simply takes more time for the conscious mind to register its actions in the brain; that the participants could not report the timing of their acts of will accurately; or that these results apply only to snap judgments rather than complex thought-out decisions that require reasoning, planning, and choosing and thus take much longer. They also note that the predictions are correct only about 60 percent of the time—which is clearly better than a 50/50 guess but not anywhere near certainty. Libet himself still believes in a "robust free will": he affirms that the conscious mind has veto power over the unconscious originating events—the conscious free will not does initiate acts, but our conscious ability to veto has a control function. Nor, he claims, is there any evidence or even a proposed experimental design that definitively or convincingly demonstrates a physical determinism of human action. In fact, he thinks there is prima facie evidence that conscious mental processes can control some brain processes.

Thus, neuroscience to date has not decided the issue. And there does not appear to be any other empirical way to reach a resolution. We are once again left with metaphysics and mysteries. The determinists' mystery is why we have the illusion of free will since it cannot be of evolutionary value—the illusion would cause us to believe that we could act freely, but if all actions are determined there is no point in the brain creating that illusion. The libertarians' mystery is how mental action occurs. Libertarians can readily accept some points made by determinists: that there are a myriad of nonconscious events in the body in any human action; that all our actions are preceded by nonconscious causes and conditions, biases, and influences; that we are much more conditioned by our genetic and social background than most of us realize; and that subconscious processes dictate the options given to the conscious mind. But these points do not mean that our conscious mind cannot then exercise free will control over what is presented to it—they mean only that what options we have are more limited than we usually accept. That is, we cannot control the cards that are dealt us, but we have some freedom in how we play them.

Thus, current neuroscience does not refute free will, and if current theories in physics are correct, not all of reality is deterministic. Subatomic indeterminacy is currently considered ontic—a feature of reality and not merely the result of our cognitive limitations. So science has not answered the Big Question of free will yet, nor is it obvious that it will ever be able to answer it since a test for it is hard to devise. And there is a simple explanation for why there has not been any progress on the matter in philosophy: once again we apparently lack the cognitive apparatus to answer a vital question due to our physiological limitations in how we have evolved, just as we are incapable of answering the Big Question of consciousness.

Free Will and Agnosticism

Given the state of science on this issue, should we remain agnostic about free will? One might conclude that considering what is at stake about our view of what we are that we ought to affirm the obvious despite its problems—that the mind has causal power—over a determinism of brain events. In addition, there is a clash of metaphysics based on conflicting intuitions (free will versus reality being deterministic), and the intuition about determinism has already been damaged by particle physics. Thus, common sense says to affirm a free will. (William James saw the question as a quarrel of unverifiable metaphysics, not science, and chose to reject the pessimism of determinism.) In light of our experiences, we can continue to believe in it even if we cannot explain it. We only have to give up the philosophical demand of an explanation of how free will would work before we decide to affirm it, which is only a consequence of the philosopher's disease.

But there is an odd twist here: we cannot help but presume to have free will even if we did not want to. It is hard, if not impossible, to give up a sense of the mind's control and simply let our body do whatever it was conditioned to date to do—we feel we are choosing and acting. (This leads pragmatists following C.S. Peirce to conclude that it makes no difference if we have free will or not since it does not affect our disposition to act.) To put the point ironically: we have no choice but to believe we have a choice. Even determinists admit that we must act *as if* free will is real. And fatalists still must seem to themselves to choose actions because they do not know in advance which actions are predetermined or the result of fate—if you fell off a boat into the ocean, you would still try to save yourself, no matter what you think about fate and determinism. And there is a further twist: how can one *pretend* not to be determined without having the actual mental causal power and free will to do that? It is hard to see how those who deny free will could convince themselves into pretending to have free will. It is one thing to feel controlled by physical causes and to consider free will as an illusion as one goes through life—like the illusion of a straw looking bent in a glass of water that we still see even though we know better—but how does one believe that we are puppets on a string and *pretend* to have free will? And again, if we have that ability to pretend, how can we not have genuine power? In this way, the very ability to pretend that we have free will becomes an argument for the existence of free will.

Thus, at worst we should be agnostic about whether there is genuine free will—it is an open empirical question that we simply cannot answer at present or perhaps ever. And those who remain agnostic about free will on philosophical grounds can go on acting exactly as they must in any case.

Notes

1. Lack of control over our actions would also raise the issue of whether we are morally responsible for our actions. Criminal punishment would be only a type of conditioning—a way to adjust the pool of experiences from which the brain derives our next action.

2. The events in the brain may still follow a strictly physical order of causation. (The analogy to the mind as software to the brain's hardware was noted in the last chapter.) When we walk, our actions are constrained by the law of gravity—indeed, our actions must conform with all physical laws—but gravity does not determine where we walk. So too, if free will is genuine, the course of the neural activity is not determined by the physical laws that govern the activity of the neurons in the brain: the laws governing neural activity no more determine our choices than gravity and the physical laws governing our bodily movements determine what direction we choose to walk in. If free will is real, persons are free even if their brains are not—it is the person who makes decisions freely, not the brain. The brain would still affect the way we operate, but it does not explain all of how we think, desire, and choose.

3. If reality is organized into levels of causation, indeterminacy on the subatomic level is irrelevant to decisions on the everyday level. In any case, science has not shown that subatomic randomness affects a predictable causal order of the everyday world—billiard balls still behave like billiard balls despite what is going on at their quantum level. It also raises the possibility that causation is a power produced only on higher levels.

4. Another standard problem is that if there is an omnipotent god, his omnipotence and our free will are not compatible: if we have free will, then there is something even a god could not control and thus he is not all-powerful; conversely, if God has all the power, we have no control of events. God's perfect knowledge would also be incompatible with our free will: if God knew from the beginning of time what I am going to have for breakfast tomorrow, do I have any free will in the matter now? If God knows now that I am going to have pancakes, that fact is now set and there is nothing I can do about it. One might respond that he knows only what I am going to freely choose tomorrow. But there is still a problem: one can only *know* what is *true*; thus, if God now knows what I am going to have, it must be so now, and thus I now have no freedom to do otherwise tomorrow morning. Some theologians try to get around these problems by making the ad hoc assumption that God somehow withdraws his omnipotence and omniscience in the case of human action.

5. An illustration of this occurred while I was writing this chapter. One Saturday morning I was planning on getting pizza for lunch. Then "out of the blue," the idea of getting a falafel came to me. At that moment, I was not

thinking about lunch or where to go for lunch—the thought "just came to me," and no conscious decision making or act of will was involved. (I went for the falafel. The question is whether I had the free will to veto that impulse.)

6. Whether this requires a commitment to the metaphysical concept of personhood—a unified agent or center of action—or whether one can accept all the personal properties and capacities without such a commitment remains an issue.

14
Does God Exist?

On the one hand, nothing seems more certain that faith or more compelling than religious experience. On the other hand, nothing seems less certain than any one particular system, for to any one system there are so many vital and serious alternatives.

—Ninian Smart

A prominent Big Question is whether realities such as gods and a soul exist that transcend the natural realm of space and time. Do we have good reasons to believe that such realities exist, and, if we do, can we know anything of their nature? Let's limit the question to whether the personal god of Western theism exists and what its nature is.

The Classic Arguments

First consider the classic arguments for the existence of God.[1] The Ontological Argument attempts to prove the existence of a being "greater than which nothing can be conceived" simply by analyzing the concept. But most philosophers agree that we cannot get the existence of something merely by analyzing our concepts for it, although identifying exactly where the Argument fails has proven surprisingly difficult. At best, all that can be established is that *if* God exists, then that reality by definition must be "greater than which nothing can be conceived" and must of necessity exist. (Charles Hartshorne argued that if God *possibly* exists, then he exists necessarily.) In addition, that we could not conceive a further reality is irrelevant: reality is not in any way restricted by what human beings can or cannot conceive or by what is consistent in any of our conceptual systems—our ability to conceive simply has no bearing on the issue of what is real or what can exist. Changing the Ontological Argument to make God a "logically necessary" being—that is, a being that must exist in every conceivable world—does not help: even if the idea is coherent (which most philosophers doubt), we are still left with the unanswered question of why those worlds could be there to begin with (i.e., why something rather than nothing exists) and thus with no ultimate proof of God —God becomes just another being within what exists.

Probably the most popular argument for the existence of God is the Cosmological Argument.[2] It is used to explain why the world exists: starting with the principle of sufficient reason, we can argue that everything (or at least every contingent thing) requires an explanation, and the chain of explanations must logically end with a reality that does not need or there would be an infinite regress of causes; so there must be a self-explanatory and self-existent first cause, and that is God. But while this may explain the existence of a created universe, this does not explain the existence of God: even if God is eternal, we can still ask why he is there. In addition, as discussed in chapter 5, the concepts of "self-existent" and "self-created" are simply incoherent. Moreover, if there can be an eternal, uncaused, self-existent reality, it is not obvious why it cannot be the natural universe itself. Certainly, the ancient Greeks, Indians, and Chinese had no problem with the idea of a creatorless eternal universe. (Baruch Spinoza also accepted that God was "greater than which nothing can be conceived," but he equated God with nature or substance, not a transcendent reality.) Our particular miniverse may well have a beginning and an ending, but an eternal flow of miniverses is not impossible. If one argues that the universe cannot be the source since the universe is constantly changing, then one must explain how God is changeless and yet he creates, answers prayers, and so forth since any action involves change.[3] Claiming that "self-existence" is simply "a profound mystery" does not help since our account of reality would still end up with a mystery. So too, we could accept the claim only if we knew what the claim meant. It would be no different than if I were to type a line of gobbledygook and say, "Don't try to understand it—it is a profound mystery!" Nor can we invoke a bigger mystery to explain a lesser one (the phenomenal world's existence)—our overall understanding does not increase at all by such a move. Theists think in terms of a creator, but God only introduces an entirely new order of existence that must be explained and new "how" mysteries of how it creates and sustains the universe.[4]

The only alternative to being uncaused that we can conceive is an infinite chain of causes. And as noted in chapter 5, it is not obvious why there cannot be an eternal, infinite chain of contingent causes: each cause would have a cause, and there would be no first cause in the ancient past— no "necessary being" is needed to start the chain. Nevertheless, we can ask why that chain of causes exists in the first place. If theists say that God creates and sustains the chain, we still must ask what creates and sustains God? Even if the concept of being "self-grounded" is coherent, why God is there still requires an answer. If "self-grounded" is not coherent, then there must be some other reality that sustains God, and that reality needs a sustainer, and so on and so on—in the modern version of an old image, the flat earth rests on the backs of four elephants that stand on the back of a turtle and after that "it's turtles all the way down!"[5] That too is a mystery that we cannot comprehend. But naturalists, for whom all that exists is space-time and its contents, see no reason to postulate even the elephants—the universe is all there is. This may seem "intellectually unsatisfying" to theists, but to naturalists it is only the theistic point of view of *creation* that leads to a need for a creator and sustainer—that is, asking *where something came from*—when nothing empirical suggests a need for a transcendent source of the beingness of things. To naturalists, we are not in a position to know why the universe is here, and only the philosopher's disease compels us to demand an ultimate explanation.

In sum, we are stuck with mystery with either answer. Theists prefer to adopt a concept that they concede makes no sense rather than accept a creator god as an unexplainable brute fact—they happily agree with Alfred North Whitehead that "God is the ultimate limitation, and his existence is the ultimate irrationality." Naturalists have no problem with an infinite past with a beginningless chain of causes, although why the chain should be there at all is still a mystery. Theists kick the mystery out of the natural realm and into a transcendent one, but naturalists see no reason to leave the natural world by introducing a new layer of reality that has its own "why" mystery and that creates new "how" mysteries—we still end up with no more understanding but now with greater mysteries. We can pick our poison or accept that we have no answer and accept the universe as a brute fact. There is no reason to suspect that beings with our mentality can answer these questions, and naturalists see fabricating some ultimate explanation just to fulfill a demand by our limited mind as illegitimate. But the important point is that no matter what we do, we end with a mystery. We have again reached limitations on what we can know.

Thus, the Cosmological Arguments fails to end mysteries. The Teleological Argument has a parallel difficulty. The argument is that we can infer the existence of a transcendent designer from both the order and the complexity that we see in the world. However, who designed the designer? "Self-designing" makes no more sense than "self-creating." And if "self-designing" is intelligible, why can't the natural universe self-design itself? Whether God is alleged to be only a little more complex than the complex creation he created or to be infinitely more complex, the source of that complexity is still unexplained. We think that a designer must be at least as complex as what is designed, but if the complexity of our universe requires a designer, then so does the complexity of the designer who designed this universe, and that leads to another infinite chain.[6] That God is supposedly a reality that is personal in nature cannot make God self-designing—a person is complex, and we can ask the source of that complexity. Indeed, how can we get any complex realities from a simpler reality? However, if the designer need not be as complex as what it created but can be simpler, then why can't a set of simpler nonconscious natural laws embedded in the universe be the source of the designing? If these rules need a designer, we are back to the infinite chain of complex designers. Because of their beliefs, theists may think in terms of agents and purpose, but naturalists see no reason to do that—the convoluted course of evolution shows how complex phenomena can arise from simple natural processes—and they dismiss the theists' intuitions as merely vestiges of children seeing agents everywhere. But either way, order and complexity does not receive an ultimate explanation—neither nature nor a creator/designer is self-explanatory. And so we are once again left with an unanswerable mystery.

Another popular claim is that morality requires the existence of God. In fact, Jean Paul Sartre claimed that the starting point of existentialism is Fyodor Dostoyevsky's statement "If God did not exist, everything would be possible." That is, there is no objective standard of morality without God—nothing would be morally wrong. However, philosophers have argued that morality is autonomous from religion ever since Plato first posed the problem in the *Euthyphro*: "Do the gods approve the holy because it is *holy*, or is it holy because the gods *approve* it?" In theistic and moral terms: "Does God command acts because they are *moral*, or are they moral because God *commands* them?" Either way, theists have a problem: if God commands acts because they are moral, then there must be a standard of morality independent of God's power and control; on the other hand, if the acts are moral merely because God commands them, then whatever God commands must by definition be deemed moral. Under the first horn of the dilemma, God is not the source of morality, and thus God is not omnipotent and not sovereign in all matters; that is, there is something—morality—that exists independently of God and is beyond his control; thus, God has not created everything and is not omnipotent in the universe but, if moral, is constrained by something more substantive than the formalities of logic. Even if God is a *loving* god who is necessarily moral and thus incapable of commanding an immoral act, this still leaves morality independent of God's control. But under the second horn, theists must hold that if God commanded the gratuitous torture of babies, then it would be morally good to torture babies. But few people would say that such torture is immoral only "because God says so" and would be moral if God said so—God could make it a *religious* requirement by decree but not a *moral* one. Some theists do maintain that God controls morality—in fact, some maintain that God controls mathematical truths. But this would make ethical precepts simply a matter of might makes right, and most of us think that morality has more substance than that. Morality is a matter of concern for others' welfare for their own sake, and this cannot be mandated by God: God may ordain concern for others, but obeying for that reason then becomes a matter of prudent self-interest (to gain heaven or avoid hell) rather than a genuine moral motivation (i.e., acting out of concern for others). Thus, if morality has a demand upon us, it does not establish the existence of God—its source is still a mystery.

Natural Suffering

A problem related to both the Moral and Teleological Arguments is natural suffering, that is, the suffering beings endure simply by being alive in a material universe—for example, babies who are born with severe birth defects, who never live free of excruciating pain, and who die young. Even if we accept that human evil is the result of human free will and that God had moral reasons to grant us free will, the problem of natural evil remains despite creation supposedly being good (Genesis 1:25). Some philosophers such as Alvin Plantinga are not troubled by this philosophical problem: they point out that there is no *logical contradiction* between suffering and an omnipotent, omniscient, and omnibenevolent god: theists can always simply assert that God has his reasons for permitting natural suffering that we cannot know because of our cognitive limitations, and suffering then is no longer incompatible with such a god.[7] Finite beings can never see the big picture and thus cannot be certain that some greater good is not being achieved by what looks like horrendous evil. In short, for all we know, God may have his reasons for what looks to us to be gratuitous suffering. But this appeal to ignorance begins to ring hollow if we have no idea why God would permit so much apparently gratuitous suffering. Indeed, that refrain makes belief in God logically reconcilable with any amount of suffering, no matter how horrendous it is—after all, if there is a hell, it was designed by God, and according to traditional doctrines, the vast majority of humans go there to be tortured eternally by some of God's creatures.[8]

In sum, claiming "God may have his reasons that we cannot know" is absolutely irrefutable, but no amount of suffering would be counter-evidence against the existence of God, and thus it is not a satisfactory explanation of suffering. Granted, if this universe was created for our "soul-making," to use John Keats's term, then there should be hardships and suffering: the world should be challenging—as Yogi Berra said: "If this world was perfect, it wouldn't be." Thus, some evil may be necessary to create a greater good. However, Plantinga's tack gives up trying to find a sufficient reason for suffering and rests content with it being merely logically possible that God might have a justification. This relies only on faith and hope: our ignorance shields God from criticism—all counter-evidence is dismissed as "a mystery known only to God"—and theists no longer have to defend their belief in God from any amount of suffering. Nevertheless, an appeal to mystery is never itself a positive argument *for* anything: it is an admission of how little of the nature of God and his plan is known. Also, if God's values are a mystery, then they may be utterly unlike our own, and we then cannot reasonably apply the attributes "good" or "moral" to him without knowing more of his nature. Nor could theists be certain that he is worthy of worship. Thus, an appeal to ignorance here only raises the question of the rationality of believing there is an all-loving god.

In fact, one has to ask: does the world look like it is the creation of an all-loving, all-knowing, all-powerful god? Naturalists see the amount of natural suffering in our harsh and cruel world as irrefutable proof against such a god. As the philosopher of biology David Hull notes, evolution is cruel, haphazard, "rife with happenstance, contingency, incredible waste, death, pain, and horror"—all evidencing, not a loving god who cares about his creatures, but the careless indifference of an almost diabolical god. In our universe, life is not precious—even life feeds upon itself. Couldn't an omnipotent god have made all animals vegetarians? That would have greatly reduced suffering of animals. So too, cancer has recently been discovered to have been in hominids for over a million years.

All in all, the traditional hymn about God's goodness "All Things Bright and Beautiful" must be counterbalanced with Monty Python's revision—"All Things Dull and Ugly." Arguing that at least we will be compensated in the next life for suffering does not make it any less evil but is only an admission that we do not understand why there is so much suffering. At a minimum, most people would agree that it is far from obvious that such a being created our world. As Alfred Lord Tennyson wrote: "God is love, transcendent and all-pervading! We do not get *this* faith from Nature or the world. If we look at Nature alone, full of perfection and imperfection, she tells that God is disease, murder, and rapine." In such circumstances, it in fact is hard to argue from any feature of the world to the existence of a moral creator.[9] Nor is it clear that we are the final conscious beings to evolve: perhaps a creator has plans for another species that will follow us, or perhaps nature will show no more care for us than for the many other humanoid branches that have gone extinct.[10]

Religious Experiences

Perhaps religious experiences are more promising evidence of God. After all, most people appeal to their experiences or religion's impact on their lives to justify being religious, not philosophical arguments. But there is a major problem with the appeal to religious experiences and revelations: religious beliefs from around the world and throughout history genuinely conflict, and no neutral way to adjudicate between them to determine which one, if any, is valid is apparent.[11] Even if one set of beliefs is superior to the others, how do we establish by experiences what is best and what is not? Revelations notoriously conflict, with no neutral way to decide between them. So too, those mystics who have types of mystical experiences that allegedly involve transcendent realities cannot themselves tell if their knowledge-claims are correct when other equally well-experienced mystics make conflicting claims. If so, transcendent realities may be apprehended by mystics but not comprehended by our conceptualizing mind.

In addition, religious experiences have the problem that scientific explanations of the events occurring in the brain during these experiences may be the complete explanation of such experiences—that is, there may be no more to these experiences than internal brain events. The scientific explanations themselves do not prove such a naturalistic reduction: all cognitive experiences have some basis in the brain, and the religious can thus accept that any scientific account of religious experiences in terms of brain events is compatible with them being cognitive—after all, an experience of God must have some mechanism in the brain to permit it to occur. But the very real possibility that such experiences may be no more than subjective brain events greatly harms the claim that religious experiences are evidence of any transcendent reality—religious experiences may in fact be exhaustively explainable as natural events having no cognitive significance. How can we tell if a religious experience is cognitive if it is phenomenologically the same whether it contacts a transcendent reality or not? And even if the experiences are cognitive, are mystical experiences at best only experiences of our own consciousness or of the beingness of the natural world? Or may the feeling of joy or love given in many religious experiences come not from God, but only from more mundane natural causes such as from feeling connected either to other people or to the natural realm, or simply from the mind during mystical experiences being empty of all its typical noisy clutter? Or is a sense of love merely being read in because the experiencer is already immersed in his or her religious tradition's teaching of love?

But even if we reject all such natural explanations and take the experiences as at least indicating that some transcendent reality exists, does what we can know by experience, even when combined with reasoning, get us to a full theistic god that responds to human needs, or, say, only to a nonpersonal deistic reality that creates and then leaves the universe alone, or only to a transcendent nonpersonal consciousness that we participate in? Indeed, why should a transcendent creator be experienceable? If our mind is totally natural, why should we expect any contact or participation in what transcends this realm? Even if one interpretation of a given type of mystical experience is correct, most understandings must be *wrong*, and this undercuts the *reliability* in general of all such experiences for establishing any substantive cognitive claim. Mystical experiences, like psychedelic drug experiences, may open up more levels of our own consciousness and thus affect how we see reality, but can they be the basis for cognitive claims about reality beyond the mind? Mystics may have the only human access to noumenal reality when the mind is empty of all differentiated content, but what is its nature? We may decide that it is reasonable to conclude that mystical experiences are in general generated by a healthy brain and not by a pathological condition and thus that mystics have experienced some reality that we do not normally experience. Nevertheless, the conflict of understandings among mystics from around the world shows that even mystics themselves cannot answer the question of the nature of what is experienced in introvertive mystical experiences. That question is answered outside introvertive experiences in our baseline "dualistic" subject/object state of mind. The reality that mystics experience may be the depth of their own mind, a mind transcending the universe, a deistic source of this world, or a personal being—or it may simply be the ordinary mind that gives a sense of calm or euphoria or connectedness when spinning its wheels while it has no real content to engage that mystics later mistakenly take to be cognitive of a greater reality.

Overall, there are too many questions about religious experiences for us to have any confidence in relying on them as a solid basis for believing that we know transcendent realities exist or to know anything about their nature.

Theology and Mystery

Theists may well find that collectively all of these matters can be best understood under a theistic assumption, but even most theists would agree that the case is not compelling. At best, the arguments lead only to it being rational to hold one's own religious faith and to accept that those of other religious faiths are equally well grounded in experiences. "Inferences to the best explanation" always rely on intuitions that opponents do not share. Naturalists, of course, are totally unconvinced of the need to posit any type of transcendent realities in order to better understand the natural realm. (But it should be noted that not all naturalists end up being nonreligious: today there are now "religious naturalists" who deny any transcendent realities and reduce theism to merely matters of ethics by reductively reinterpreting Biblical claims in naturalistic terms—in particular, "God" becomes in the words of Ralph Burhoe, "the ultimate necessities of laws and boundary conditions imposed by nature.") Many others argue that at best the arguments only get us to an intellectual postulate like a deistic Aristotlean "prime mover" (who got the eternal universe moving) to round out a metaphysical system. Theism is not better grounded experientially, and its speculation is just that—speculation. And as Charles Darwin asked, why should we believe the ravings of a "monkey mind," especially when they are not tied to scientific checking? Indeed, many naturalists dismiss this as *irrational* since it goes beyond what science can check.

This can lead to the *via negativa*: renouncing attributing any positive phenomenal attributes to God—all that human beings can do is declare what God is not. In the words of Thomas Aquinas: "Now we cannot know what God is, but only what He is not; we must therefore consider the ways in which God does not exist rather than the ways in which He does." However, our inability to know God's nature either through reasoning or indisputable experiences leads to basic mysteries. But this is only to be expected: if scientific phenomena outside the range of everyday experiences lead to mysteries, we can only expect that an alleged reality transcending the natural realm would be, almost by definition, mysterious. Certainly, to claim to know the "mind of God" seems extravagant. And accepting that we do not know is not an excuse to believe anything—theists cannot fill in the blank with any doctrine they like but must accept that we they do not know.

But this leaves theists in a conundrum: if God is an unfathomable, ineffable mystery utterly unlike anything from the temporal realm, then no understanding of God is any better than any other—indeed, all understandings of God in worldly terms are wrong. But theists also want to assert that they can know something of God's nature—for example, they can know with confidence that he is not the nonpersonal Brahman of Advaita Vedanta but is a conscious personal being who is moral and all love and the source of our being, for otherwise he would not be worthy of trust or worship and could not answer prayers. But this means that he is not utterly unlike anything temporal.

In addition, once it is accepted that God is a total mystery, what reason would there be to believe that he exists? Even mystics who emphasize more the incomprehensibility of God want to align their lives with reality as it truly is, and this requires beliefs about what reality truly is. But mystical nonpersonal conceptions such as Meister Eckhart's "Godhead" or Paul Tillich taking being itself as the "God beyond God" have not proven to be religious satisfying. So too, theists cannot rest with accepting God as a deistic reality that created the universe and supplied its laws and then sat back and was no longer active in this world. Moreover, if God made us "in his image," the human person should be a model for him. Nevertheless, anthropomorphism has been recognized as a danger ever since the ancient Greek Xenophanes asserted that if oxen, horses, and lions could draw, their gods would look like oxen, horses, and lions. However, since theists believe that God is a conscious person, how can they curtail engaging in deeper anthropomorphism since they have to model any ideas of the nature of transcendent realties on what we are familiar with?

In sum, theists accept that God is a mystery but not a complete mystery: they assert both mystery and some closure of mystery through their tradition's revelations or other means, although again revelations conflict and there is no neutral way to determine which, if any, are true. Theists' speculation is not totally groundless since it is based on experiences giving a sense of transcendental realities, but it still goes beyond what the experiences justify, and members of other traditions (including naturalism) can reasonably reject it. Thus, theists do not depict God as completely unknown, but they must defend their tradition's revelations, if challenged, on grounds other than these revelations and religious experiences.

Religious mysteries become aspects of what is known, not an indication of what is completely unknown. To mystics, a transcendent reality is experienced as "bright and dazzling," not obscure—their experiences illuminate a depth to a transcendent reality even if they baffle the conceptualizing mind. But the otherness of any transcendent reality still presents a problem: to most believers, God is unique and hence beyond all temporal categories, and therefore nothing truly accurate can be said of him. Thus, applying terms from our familiar realm leads to paradoxes. Probably the best theists can say is, as William Alston put it, talk of God is not "strictly true," but it is "close enough to the strict truth" to be useable in the religious life. Nevertheless, the tension between affirming God's otherness and the need for some familiar conception for a religious life remains. Theists will have to engage in speculation based on what a person is in this world, but they also have to realize the limitation of doing this when they are talking about a transcendent reality. Because of our limitations within the phenomenal world, human beings cannot rely on our intuitions of what a transcendent reality must be like. Our intuitions lead, as Kant pointed out, to antinomies concerning the phenomenal world, and matters are only more obscure concerning alleged transcendent realities.

Once the otherness of God from all human conceptualizations is accepted, the mystery of God should receive more emphasis. Pluralists in comparative theology who see multiple paths equally leading to salvation see more mystery and ineffability to transcendent realities and to what the afterlife is like. But those who believe that their own religion is the exclusive vehicle for salvation tend to de-emphasize mystery. Overall, there is very little mention of mystery today in Christian liturgy and worship. In the modern era, there has been, in William Placher's phrase, a "domestication of transcendence": transcendent realities are no longer seen as "wholly other" but as comprehensible—God is now taken to be an object remote from the phenomenal world but still comprehensible in terms meant for phenomenal objects. The demand for "clear and distinct" ideas of God made him wholly encompassed by our reason. Placher wants to reclaim the mystery of God, but he recognized that to admit that God is "transcendent in a more radical sense" would be admitting that "in important ways we do not know what we mean when we talk about God." (But only a theologian could add that language about God "enables us to say something true while not understanding what is means.")

Today theologians at best preface remarks by affirming the mystery of God but still plow ahead by affirming attributes to God—like tribal cultures that affirm a high sky god but base their religious life on more approachable gods and lesser divine beings. Thus, theologians may affirm mystery in theory, but in practice they defuse mystery and end up with an anthropomorphized version of God. Perhaps totally new conceptualizations of God are needed today, but all will be limited by being metaphoric extensions of terms that were invented for phenomenal realities. That being so, one would think that theologians would exhibit more humility before a transcendent reality and be tentative in their speculation. But if Alston is correct, contemporary Anglo-American analytic philosophers of religion exhibit "a considerable degree of confidence" in their ability to determine the nature of God. For example, many theologians believe that God takes "great pleasure" in watching his creation evolve. Richard Swinburne apparently knows that God is "very anxious" that human understanding of him should develop through experience, effort, and cooperation.

Theists assert that to reduce God to only our conceptions of him would create an idol, but this has not stopped theologians from engaging in the paradoxical task of, in David Burrell's words, of trying to "know the unknowable God." The point of theology today is to close off mystery, not to face the fact that it is a mystery or to increase our sense of mystery or to generate religious experiences. Ironically, it is naturalists who emphasize more the mysteries of reality, and it is theologians who want more closure. Here it is the theologians who suffer from the philosopher's disease. But as Peter Byrne has found, the history of Christian theology has not exhibited an accumulation of insights into the nature or actions of God. Rather, there have been only changing conceptions as knowledge in other fields changes—for example, process theology arising in the twentieth century in response to quantum physics. So too, mystical experiences no longer add any new knowledge but are only repetitions of the same experiences that have occurred for many centuries. (Mystical and other religious experiences are an embarrassment to many theologians since alleging actual *experiences* of a transcendent reality is even more out of step with their naturalist friends than merely asserting the metaphysical claim that a transcendent reality exists.) Nor can God be engaged the way that scientists study nature since by definition there can be no empirically checkable tests on alleged transcendent realities. Thus, not only is there is no good reason to believe that we are gaining more knowledge of God, there is reason to doubt that we have any certain or absolute knowledge here at all.

Agnosticism

In such circumstances, agnosticism both about God's existence and his attributes is not only acceptable but is more reasonable than asserting belief or disbelief. In fact, Thomas Huxley invented the term for precisely this situation, and it should be the default position in philosophy today (although surveys show that the majority of philosophers are atheists).[12] Agnosticism is not an atheism that accepts that the concept "God" is coherent, and so concedes the logical possibility of the existence of a theistic god, but sees the preponderance of evidence (especially natural suffering) as indicating that no transcendent realities exist. Nor is it indifference to the issue or the doubt of skepticism, although agnostics tend to adopt a nonreligious way of life. Rather, it is the admission that we are *not in a position to determine* the truth or falsity of the claim that transcendent realties exist: because of our situation in the world, no arguments for or against theism are seen as compelling. Even if some doctrines about God are correct, we are not in a position to determine which ones they are. The limitations of our cognitive abilities strike again.

But note that one can accept philosophical agnosticism and yet still be committed to practicing a particular religious or antireligious way of life. One cannot be both highly skeptical about the existence of God and committed to a theistic way of life. (So too, one can be an "agnostic Buddhist" as Stephen Batchelor claims to be, but not a "skeptical Buddhist," by practicing the Buddhist bodhisattva way of life and being agnostic about a cycle of rebirths.) Theists and atheists may have different degrees of confidence in their beliefs: probably few theists or atheists are 100 percent certain about their beliefs, but few adopt agnosticism about not being in a position to know the answer—they still believe but without certainty. However, one can be both agnostic about our being able to establish the existence of God and still believe in him. (If an agnostic bets that God does exist, he or she cannot condemn on philosophical grounds another person who bets differently.) For example, it is not inconsistent or an instance of false consciousness to claim, "I am not sure that we will ever be in a position to prove or disprove God's existence or know his nature, but I believe that there are some good reasons to believe that he exists, and I believe that my theistic way of life is an appropriate response to his existence." Thus, theists can affirm a creative mystery at the heart of things while acknowledging that our position in the world precludes establishing it.

Notes

1. Probably few in the West in the Middle Ages genuinely doubted the existence of God. The classic arguments were not advanced to refute atheism but only to show that not only revelation but reason too could show that God exists.

2. It is good to remember that the religious are not usually religious because of beliefs: religion is a matter of the ultimate nature and meaning of things, but it is not a matter of accepting certain metaphysical arguments. Theists do not advance God as an explanatory posit. Faith is a way of life, and the faithful are typically uninterested in arguments about beliefs entailed by their way of life. (This can go to extremes: the only adamant atheist I know, someone who enthusiastically enjoys arguing that there can be no god or life after death, is a practicing Catholic. He goes to church and confession regularly, and he and his wife are raising their children as Catholics. He enjoys the social life of his church and the pageantry of the rituals, and when I ask him how he could be a practicing Catholic and not believe in the existence of God, life after death, or that Jesus is the son of God, he just looks at me funny and says, "What does that have to do with anything?") So too, many accept their own versions of doctrines and are not interested in any mysteries surrounding transcendent realities. It is Blaise Pascal's overwhelming "God of Abraham, Isaac, and Jacob," not the truncated and domesticated theoretical entity that is the "god of philosophers and scholars," that is the common basis of belief and worship. (Not that these are different realities—rather, it is

two ways of looking at the same alleged transcendent entity.) As David Holley says, religious talk of God is not so much an explanation of what seems puzzling as a way of expressing an apparent apprehension of a deeper meaning disclosed in experiences in general and that stories of revelations are the key that unlocks awareness of the deeper meaning. The justification of belief is a matter for philosophers, not the majority of the faithful.

3. The Buddhist rejection of the idea of a creator god is simple: such a god must be either immutable or not—if it is immutable, it cannot change and thus is unable to decide or act to create; if it is not immutable, it is within the realm of change and thus did not create the realm of change but needs an explanation as much as anything else in the realm of change.

4. One common generalization is that the "modern mind" informed by science forms worldviews in a different way than does the "traditional mind" informed by religious experiences and mythology. The former starts with the natural world as given and looks for what knowledge we can attain through sense-experience and reason. The latter starts with the primacy of transcendent realities as given; it sees the natural world as a product of supreme transcendent realities and sees human beings as capable of participating directly in transcendent realities through experiences or rituals. Through the traditional approach, societies come up with competing, comprehensive metaphysical views. Through the modern approach, we need not end up with a metaphysical system that denies all transcendent realities (i.e., naturalism), but all metaphysical systems require defense in terms of reasons other than revelation.

5. The physicist Paul Davies has suggested a "turtle loop": the universe is in a self-consistent and self-supporting ontic loop. But one can still ask why that loop is there.

6. Theologians have come up with versions of unchangeable and simple transcendent realities that survive this problem, but the results are not the loving, active, personal god of theism. If being a designer is an attribute of any theistic god, then the problem of an infinite chain of designers is an argument against there being a theistic god. The same problem occurs with the Cosmological Argument if being the source of everything and not just the phenomenal universe is an attribute of a theistic god.

7. Alvin Plantinga also once argued that *the devil* is responsible for natural suffering. But this would not exonerate God from moral culpability: God would have created the devil and would also have permitted him to cause the suffering of his creatures. If it is argued that God permitted this in order to preserve the devil's free will, it would exhibit a gross lack of concern for the suffering of billions of his victims.

8. If salvation is a matter of being a member of a particular religion or holding a particular belief, there is also a moral problem: whatever is the "true religion," more than three quarters of the world's population are not members and thus are condemned to hell for eternity—most for no

other reason than that the true religion was not a live option where they were born. If there is predestination, the problem is aggravated: why would a moral god permit billions and billions of people to be born if he knew that their fate would be only to end up being tortured in hell for eternity?

9. One common theistic defense is that God does not want to make his existence known so that we will remain free to accept him or not. But in the book of Job, Satan has conversations with God: Satan knew with absolute certainty that God exists, and yet he still could exercise the self-will to rebel or whatever it was that earned him a spot in hell. So too with his minions. (Also note that angels with free will cause a problem for theologians about the need for any material creation with its suffering to produce beings with free will.) Thus, just knowing God exists is not enough, and one can ask why God would purposely hide and jeopardize billions of his creatures going to hell for eternal suffering. That God is so hard to detect is in fact an argument *against* his existence: the "absence of God" argument—an all-loving god would not want to condemn the majority of human beings to eternal suffering in hell, and so he would make his existence plainly knowable to all human beings; that this has not occurred must mean no god exists.

10. The multiverse hypothesis may aid theists here: if a sufficient number of miniverses exist with different features, then the amount of suffering would differ in every world having conscious beings, and the amount of suffering in our part of our miniverse would then be no mystery. A being "greater than which nothing can be conceived" may well prefer a multiverse to a single "best of all possible worlds." (If the point of the universe is only to produce beings that can be saved, and we are the only conscious beings in the universe, then even our galaxy alone is wasteful on a truly cosmic scale. The theists' reply is that vast regions with no conscious beings is inconsequential to a transcendent reality.) But, as noted in chapter 9, the possibility of a multiverse also harms the Teleological Argument: a creator god could, of course, create a multiverse as easily as one miniverse, but the possibility of other miniverses ruins the thrust of order or complexity in this world as pointing to the need of a transcendent designer—our order and complexity is only to be expected to exist somewhere if there are a sufficient number of miniverses with different laws. This also points to a problem for the Teleological Argument: it is too flexible—no matter how much or how little order or complexity or suffering there is in our world, God is invoked to explain it. Whatever there is, "God did it." But anything that explains every possible state of affairs regardless of what they are is not an explanation of any particular state. A multiverse also neutralizes all perceived value in our world: our world with its values is only here because every possible world is probably somewhere.

11. One might think that theists would at least converge on the idea that

they all worship the one creator of the natural universe. But apparently things are not that simple today. Conservative Wheaton College recently suspended a tenured professor for saying that Christians and Muslims worship the same god. She and the college finally agreed that she would leave.

12. In the survey cited in chapter 2, 62 percent of the philosophers accepted atheism and 11 percent leaned toward it. Many claim that in the absence of convincing positive evidence for God, one should be an atheist. Theists can argue the opposite. But the absence of convincing arguments for atheism or for theism only leads to agnosticism. The faithful and atheists may reject agnosticism and argue that they know the answers, or they can accept that they are not in a position to answer the question and simply state what they believe.

15
Is There an Objective Meaning to Our Lives?

My life has no purpose, no direction, no aim, no meaning, and yet I'm happy. I can't figure it out. What am I doing right?

       —Charles Schulz, author of "Peanuts"

For the general public, probably the most important philosophical question is about the meaning of life. Robert Solomon called it *the* Big Question—"the hardest to answer, the most urgent and at the same time the most obscure." Probably everyone has asked about it at some point. Why am I here? Why do I exist? Do I have a purpose? How do I fit into this world? How can anything I do on this tiny planet have any significance or lasting value in the big picture of things? Is all that I do as we "strut our hour on the stage" no more than "a tale told by an idiot, full of sound and fury, signifying nothing"? If our world comes to an end, must all our pursuits be deemed worthless? In sum, does anything I do matter? Are we just animals with no purpose beyond our own pleasure or reproduction of our genes? If we are inherently a social creature, is meaning necessarily social rather than individualistic? Can a society survive if most of its members see no meaning to life? So too, what makes a life meaningful or gives the world meaning? Is there any objective way to determine what is truly worthwhile to devote our lives to? When we look back on our lives, have we wasted so much time on frivolous pursuits, or are all human pursuits merely frivolous in the end? We should not sweat the small stuff, but in the end, is everything small stuff? Is the author of *Ecclesiastes* correct that we should enjoy whatever work comes our way because all is in vain? And why do I suffer? What happens at death? Must we have some greater purpose? Why are we obsessed with the demand that our lives have meaning? Is the demand that humanity must have some meaning only a cosmic form of solipsism? Also, what about the universe as a whole?[1] What is it doing here? Does it have a transcendent purpose or other principle that makes my life meaningful? Must it have some purpose? Can we have a well-lived life without some meaning to the cosmos? Do we simply fabricate a meaning to our lives to keep us going in the face of all our hardships and knowledge of our ultimate demise, or is there an objective, real meaning to the universe and our place in it? Is there a plan to life? In short, what's it all about?

Such questions arise both from our awareness of our own mortality (as Arthur Schopenhauer emphasized)—death shows us our limits—and from our sense of being small, finite, and overwhelmed by a universe so much vaster than our own little world. Concern with our happiness or flourishing (Gk., *eudaemonia*) once was central to philosophy: philosophy was seen as a contemplative way of life leading to the best possible life based on knowledge.[2] But today analytic philosophers rarely deal with this, although the issue of a meaningful life has recently begun to regain attention. Indeed, the low point of linguistic analysis was dismissing these questions as meaningless since "meaning" is only a matter of *semantics* and thus only words have meaning—in short, life is not a word and thus has no meaning. So too, for most philosophers the only purpose something can have is a functional purpose in the interaction between things—the world as a whole has no purpose. But to existential philosophers the central philosophical issue is: is life worth living? For Albert Camus, the most urgent issue is the meaning of life—in fact, the only important question in philosophy is why should we go on and not commit suicide?

Psychologists have long recognized the importance of having a sense of meaning to one's life. Viktor Frankl considered it as central as any biological need for human life: we need to trust reality, and seeing a purpose to the world provides that assurance. "To live is to suffer, to survive is to find meaning in the suffering." The anthropologist Clifford Geertz concurred: our need for meaning is as real and as pressing as our more familiar biological needs. The physicist John Wheeler asserted that more important than the deepest scientific question is finding a significance to our life—the most fundamental question we can ask in life is how we fit into the scheme of the things. For the sociologist Peter Berger, we have a deep need to know that we have significance and worth: we cannot accept meaninglessness, and religion protects us against that terror by conceiving the entire cosmos as humanly significant. To make the contingencies of life understandable and thus more bearable, religions offer narratives that show our place in the scheme of things—one then can lead a meaningful life. For example, with hope of an eternal reward, all labor and suffering, no matter how harsh, can be withstood. We have something to fall back on in moments of crisis when our self-image is shattered. As Friedrich Nietzsche said: "He who has a *why* to live for can stand almost any *how*."

Overall, there are four types of responses: God or another transcendent reality is necessary to provide meaning to our lives; there is an objective natural meaning to the universe; all senses of meaning are subjective, but that is sufficient; the only intellectually honest answer is to realize that there can be no meaning whatsoever to all this.

Transcendent Meanings

For the traditionally religious, transcendent meaning is necessary for there to be a meaningful life and cosmos. The religious are, as John Hick and Huston Smith noted, "cosmic optimists"—life is meaningful and there are grounds for ultimate trust and confidence. There must be a "because" for our plaintive "why," and so there must be a meaning to all this. And only a meaning from outside the natural universe itself can give a real meaning to the world *in toto* and to us individually: nothing can give meaning to itself, and the same applies to the natural universe as a whole. Helping one another with our suffering or trying to make things easier for those who come after us may make one's life meaningful, but it would not explain why we are here and why we suffer—there must be some more significant end that we achieve, and only answering these "why" questions by accepting the existence of something transcendent gives a final picture of the meaning of life. As Aristotle pointed out, all teleological explanations must end with something that is an end in itself. Theists may see the universe as "fine-tuned" to evolve conscious life. For all religions, human beings are not just an evolutionary accident of a pointless universe. The entire universe, including the sources of suffering, can be cast within a transcendent framework. In the words of Alfred North Whitehead: "The final principle of religion is that there is wisdom in the nature of things." All the Big Questions of life—why misfortunes befall us, why we live, why we die, what happens at death—are answered in terms of transcendent realities. Thus, life has a transcendent meaning, and our *summum bonum* is to align our lives with the reality providing that meaning, however salvation is defined in a given tradition.

For theists, only by seeing the natural world as a creation of God can it have any meaning at all. So too, we can only have meaning if God intentionally made us individually or at least created human beings as a species. What this meaning is varies depending on the revelations and teachings of a tradition. (The Bible has rules on diet and haircuts but does not specify what the meaning of life is.) But even if they do not know exactly what the meaning is, most theists are satisfied that God created the universe and thus it must have a meaning. With the universe as a creation, suffering is given meaning—we may not know what that meaning is, but God has some purpose for permitting suffering. The vicissitudes of history also gain meaning. Nontheists such as those Hindus and Buddhists who are transcendent realists can downplay the idea of creation and history as a venue of meaning: this world of change and suffering is eternal but meaningless.[3] For many Hindus, the eternal cycle of the emanation and absorption of phenomenal worlds is the "play" (*lila*) of a creator god or a nonpersonal reality (Brahman): emitting a world is simply the act of its nature, like breathing is to us, with no plan. It is done without motive or desire or further purpose—there is no "why" to the universe. But the transcendent goal of escaping this meaningless realm still gives our life a purpose.

However, there are problems with what theists identify the purpose of the world to be. The usual proffered answers always place *human beings* at the center of God's purpose—indeed, since we are looking for the meaning of things *for us*, it is difficult for us to think otherwise. But this makes all attempts at setting forth a purpose sound dubious. Consider some traditional purposes: God created the world to become known, loved, or glorified; or, in the words of Bernard of Clairvaux, man and the world only exist because God needed to both express his love and to be loved. But if the goal of humanity is to know, love, or otherwise please God, that could have been accomplished if we were placed in heaven and did not have to go through the suffering of a physical world. (Bertrand Russell in his retelling of the Biblical creation story suggested that God got tired of angels worshiping him and wanted to see if he could get beings who suffered to worship him.) Moreover, it also raises a moral issue: if God could have accomplished his purpose without creating a world of suffering, then was creating a universe with so much suffering really a moral act, no matter how much good is also created? This illustrates the problem: theological attempts to articulate the point of the universe, as the theologian John Haught notes, "inevitably sound flat and inconsequential." He adds that it is not necessarily our business to know the purpose of the universe (although this may only be a theological rationalization for our inability to know any transcendent purpose or meaning). Perhaps it is impossible to know God's plan—perhaps God's purpose is so alien that any beings within the universe could not comprehend it. Many believers find faith in God sufficient and leave the matter to God—in short, believing "God has his purpose" is enough for them.

More generally, naturalists would raise the problem that we are uncertain about the existence of transcendent realities or life after death. But for theists, naturalism can give no real meaning for the world or our lives—nihilism is the naturalist's only option.[4] Theists do not deny that naturalists can have a *meaningful life* in the sense of having a rich, full life dedicated to pleasure, creating art, helping others, leaving the world a better place for human beings, or whatever one is passionate about—but they believe that no act, no matter how noble or heroic, has meaning without God. Perhaps one can have a good life even in the pursuit of something trivial, such as becoming a checkers champion.[5] (Can one have a meaningful life being a mass murderer, or must morality be part of any meaningful life?) So too, naturalists can be struck with awe and wonder at the universe. But, theists contend, naturalists cannot provide a *meaning of life* in the sense of an objective meaning of the entire scheme of things. Naturalists must realize that the meaning they see is merely subjective— they must know that they are making it up and thus that it cannot truly give real meaning to their lives. For traditional theists, naturalists must believe we are only cogs in a cosmic machine of no significance—for naturalists, there is no valid reason to live, and they should envy children who avoid suffering by dying young.

Naturalism and the Meaning of Life

But naturalists do not see things that way. They believe that natural suffering and the convoluted course of the evolution of both the universe *in toto* and life on this planet shows that no transcendent reality is guiding things: the world is directionless except for an increase in complexity, and the bottom line is that our world of tsunamis and cancer just does not look like a world designed by a transcendent source, benevolent or otherwise, and we simply must accept that. Living with a sense of cosmic purpose is no doubt very comforting, but that does not make it real.

In addition, naturalists also think that merely fulfilling another being's planned-out purpose—simply slavishly doing a task that we are assigned by God in order to avoid ending up in hell—is not a goal worthy of free beings. We are not the Deltas of Aldous Huxley's *Brave New World*, created to do only tasks assigned to us—performing the tasks might give the Deltas' lives meaning, but this does not make their lives or the world objectively meaningful. Indeed, simply doing an assigned task is not even *moral* unless we can know what God's purpose is and can see that it is moral and valuable in itself.

Nor is it obvious that any afterlife necessarily makes this life meaningful. As Ludwig Wittgenstein asked: "Is some riddle solved by my surviving forever? Is not eternal life itself as much of a riddle as our present life?" Unless we know what awaits us in the next life, life after death would not per se answer the question of the meaning of this life— for example, simply sitting around praising God for eternity is not a meaningful life in the eyes of most people. Thus, extending life indefinitely does not per se make life meaningful. Indeed, some argue that only a finite life could have meaning: only knowing that we come to an end makes what we do matter—otherwise, we would have eternity to change the outcome of our acts. In fact, eternity in general presents a problem. For example, if you are a scientist, in heaven perhaps teachers will teach you about how the universe works in as much detail as you want and religious teachers will teach you why the universe was set that way. So now what do you now do for the next billion years? And the next billion billion years? Think of whatever you believe gives life meaning, and then think of doing it, not for a year or even a billion years, but for eternity. Indeed, every possible thing that could be done would be done an infinite number of times over and over and over again. Upon realizing that the billion times you have done something is only a drop in the bucket, the tedium of the endless repetition and knowing it is our permanent state would drain all meaning from it (as Buddhists note). Others argue that it is possible that an inexhaustible amount of new experiences, valuable things, and new inventions may await us that would keep us occupied for eternity; or perhaps changes in our personality over time would keep weariness and boredom away.

In any case, since we do not know what will transpire in the distant future, the question remains whether life is meaningful now. Naturalists also ask why meaning has to be connected to fulfilling some transcendent purpose rather than something inherent in the natural universe itself. For naturalists, the meaning that the religious claim is actually subjective and depends only on their interests and values—the religious simply do not realize that they project a meaning that they themselves have concocted onto a nonexistent transcendent reality and mistakenly think that it is objective. A transcendent source and a transcendent part of ourselves (a soul) is only their own invention. It is a matter of "terror management," to cope with death, but the search for such meaning is illusory. In addition, even if there is a transcendent source to this universe, this does not guarantee that our lives have meaning: the source may have created us just to watch us suffer or had some self-serving purpose that we do not know. Thus, merely invoking a source cannot still our disquiet over the meaning of life. There is also an *Euthyphro*-type problem here: does God confer an intrinsically valuable meaning upon the universe, or is the meaning valuable merely because God confers it? If the latter, then the meaning may be arbitrary and not really render life meaningful at all; but if the former, no god is needed since its value is independent of God.

Moreover, naturalists can rightly argue that to give a complete answer to the meaning of reality, the religious must provide a meaning for the transcendent source itself. The question "What is the meaning of God?" may not arise for theists since the question of meaning ends for us with a reason for our existence. But theists are merely pushing the problem of objective meaning back one step: human beings would have a purpose—being the obedient servants fulfilling God's plan, or whatever—but reality as a whole may not. What is the meaning of the totality of the natural realm plus its source? If God has no further source of meaning, the mystery of the meaning for the totality remains. If by definition what gives meaning to something must transcend it, our picture will always be incomplete: there can be no meaning transcending the totality that gives it meaning— there cannot be something outside "all there is" that gives it meaning. If so, there can be no meaning transcending God giving him meaning, and thus there is no final explanation of our purpose or value. Or does this render the question of the "ultimate meaning of everything" senseless? Or can meaning instead be internal to reality? Theists may argue that God is the source of his own meaning, but whether this is any more successful than the idea of something being the source of its own reality is doubtful. Moreover, if something can be its own source of meaning, why can't it be natural universe itself? Why can't the vibrant, complex universe as a whole give meaning to our lives?

Realizing that we will die may be a stimulus to leave some mark on the world, to engage with others, or to be creative. We may want to be alive at the end of the story, but living somewhere in the middle may be satisfying as long as we contribute to the plot. This is connected to the idea that we need to cast a mark that lasts for eternity to be significant— that our actions must "echo through eternity." For what is the difference between someone who leaves no trace and someone who never existed at all? Indeed, many think that all our achievements are meaningless since our world is only temporary. Leo Tolstoy believed that. Thereby the fate of the universe becomes crucial to the question of personal meaning for many people. And in fact, all of our possible impact will vanish in the future: how do we find meaning in the world knowing that it will come to an end? Our planet or miniverse will come to an end, and nothing of any of our achievements will leave a lasting dent in the universe's history unless our lives are somehow recorded in the fabric of the universe in a way that we do not see. In four or five billion years, our sun will expand and engulf the earth, destroying everything. Before then, we may be replaced by another species. But does that make our lives meaningless? Nothing has to last forever to be valuable—all pieces of music come to an end, but that does not render them worthless. So too, most people would prefer to be a flower that blooms beautifully and dies than a swarm of quarks that lasts forever. Thus, death does not completely undermine the possibility of value and meaning. But the fact that our world will come to an end means to naturalists that we must find meaning in how we live in the present.

Nor is it clear that only what is left at the end of history is all that matters. Each segment can still be significant even if there is an infinity of time before and after. Only our human hubris demands a permanent effect of our actions for them to have any value at all.[6] Perhaps there is no universal death—perhaps the universe continues through an endless series of miniverses. But even if each of us is forgotten in an eternal universe, it does not mean that human life must be meaningless or that we cannot make a significant contribution enriching what is real today. (There is also a logical problem: if the universe is itself of infinite value, then we cannot add any value—it is already infinite.) That we may be superseded by another species or otherwise not last forever is irrelevant. Certainly, leaving traces of good or improvement to humanity's lot is enough to give an objective meaning even if it does not last for eternity.

For naturalists, we must be ends in ourselves to be of value, not mere vehicles to fulfilling some transcendent purpose. Nor can meaning be put off to an indefinite future of humanity since we do not know what that holds. We are integral to the world, not thrown into it: we are *of* the world, not *in* it—only religion alienates us from our true home by making us believe that our true existence is transcendent.[7] Any human need for transcending ourselves must be satisfied by the natural world by giving up our sense of self-importance—for example, by being willing to sacrifice ourselves for some greater welfare of others. Indeed, if we are an inherently social animal, any meaning of life may not be individualistic. We are all made of the same dust from some dead star, and our biological connectedness with every person, animal, and plant is quite enough for many naturalists—enough even to overcome a sense of loneliness. Naturalists such as Paul Feyerabend too can say that all that matters is love. Just being part of the fascinating unfolding evolution of the universe and of life on earth is enough to give our life purpose and meaning. Naturalists do not need a meaning to the totality of reality any more than theists do. Indeed, naturalists can take the world more seriously than do theists since their focus is not being divided between this world and a purported transcendent realm. So too, naturalists can treat our one brief life as more precious: if immortality were awaiting us, this life is not as significant, and dying is not really dying.

Objective Natural Meaning

For Freeman Dyson, no open, eternally expanding universe with intelligent beings is pointless. There must be an objective value to our being here even if the meaning is internal to the universe itself. Indeed, many antireductive naturalists find the mere fact that the universe has produced conscious beings with free will is enough to conclude that we are an integral part of reality, not a fluke, and that in itself indicates that there must be some reason for all this: we are purposeful beings who are in a position to take an active role in the course of the universe's development. The deep structure of the universe is somehow programmed to produce life and conscious beings, and that is enough to guarantee meaningfulness—there is rationality behind all of this, and no external source is needed to make the universe meaningful. Such value is not arbitrary or subjective but as objective as any other feature of the universe.

However, naturalists who are committed to structural reductionism have a problem finding any objective meaning to the universe: meaning requires the originality that only free conscious beings can provide, and to reductionists consciousness is a mere fluke, if it is accepted as real at all, and not integral to the universe as antireductive naturalists believe. (For eliminationists, we are only nonconscious robots, which would be extremely depressing if we had consciousness.) That is, it is difficult to see how there could be any meaning to the universe in any sense without conscious beings with free will or some other source of originality—a deterministic world that simply plays out a fixed, predictable course would be meaningless even if a transcendent agent created it. Indeed, one can ask why a creator would bother creating such a world. So too, consciousness seems necessary if the beings within the universe are to have meaning. A universe without consciousness would be swirling along meaninglessly—like Mozart's sheet music existing with no one playing or hearing the music. For reductionists, all we are and all we do are nothing but the fixed result of the accidental collision of atoms. Random events on the quantum level would not significantly alter the picture.

That conscious beings with free will are necessary for there to be meaning to the universe does not mean that the universe has no objective value, any more than the fact that we need a certain sensory apparatus for the universe to register its colors and sounds. Nor does this mean that making conscious beings is the central purpose of the natural world. But the structures of the universe may provide an objective meaning, and part of that may be that conscious beings must be there at some point to ask whether there is such a meaning. The presence of conscious beings asking about the meaning of it all certainly does not make any such meaning subjective.

In fact, naturalists can argue that it is the religious who have the problem of finding some genuine meaning to the natural universe since they do not fully integrate human beings into the universe but believe that the most important part of us transcends the universe and that our real home lies outside of the natural universe. Indeed, any transcendent purpose may render this world *meaningless* in the end since salvation in all traditional religions involves existence *outside* of this world. Thus, it is difficult for the religious to show any ultimate value to the natural universe itself at all. Moreover, for naturalists, theists mistakenly start with human beings as central to the scheme of things rather than looking for whatever meaning there may be to the existence of the natural cosmos as a whole and in the evolution of all life. Naturalists can also take ending suffering more seriously than can the religious who have to have an explanation making suffering palatable. For naturalists, natural suffering is simply part of our lot, and to look for a transcendent meaning to it is misguided. Only someone already committed to a theistic point of view thinks something is missing from the naturalists' picture.

However, any meaning of the universe beyond producing conscious beings remains a mystery for naturalists. (To speak of "purpose" implies a transcendent or at least a natural objective to the universe and thus gets us off on the wrong foot.) For Philip Kitcher, we are only cogs in a vase machine whose point exceeds our comprehension, and how our condition confers meaning on what we do remains a mystery. For secular humanists, human beings are the sole source of meaning, and developing human potentials to their fullest is the only objective to be achieved. (Not all secular humanists are as antireligious as Richard Dawkins; some such as Kitcher and Ronald Dworkin can find value in religion, at least as matters of ethics, in countering reductive naturalism.) As noted in the last chapter, there also are today "religious naturalists" who find meaning while denying transcendent realities. Don Cupitt can even exclaim: "That existence is purposeless is to me religiously wonderful." Christian religious naturalists may attempt to establish the "Kingdom of God" on earth, as the Bible mentions, even if it is not a matter of the return of a transcendent Christ from a transcendent realm. But most naturalist philosophers prefer their worldview straight up without any religious sugarcoating even while acknowledging a mystery to all this.[8] They also point out that the difficulty the religious, traditional or naturalist, have in specifying a transcendent meaning to the world. But, as Kitcher acknowledges, the religious have a confidence that secularists cannot enjoy.

Subjective Responses

However, many naturalists reject such objective natural meaning. According to Friedrich Nietzsche, both the world and life are meaningless, but we can create meaning for ourselves and thus lead a meaningful life. Naturalists claim that any meaning that we make up is subjective, but the meaning is nevertheless sufficient to make their lives worthwhile. The need for meaning is only a human phenomenon and inherently subjective. As noted above, they see theists as fabricating meaning in transcendent terms to give their life meaning. When the astronomer Owen Gingerich says, "Frankly, I am psychologically incapable of believing that the universe is meaningless," he is saying more about himself (and many other religious believers) than anything about the universe itself. In fact, to require a transcendent meaning only diminishes the glory of the universe.

It may be natural to see ourselves as central to the purpose of all this, just as it is natural to see an unmoving earth as the physical center of the universe. But science has shown us otherwise—we live in a truly vast universe of billions of galaxies (and perhaps in a multiverse), and our world will come to an end. For reductionists, reality is purposeless and void of value or meaning, merely the actions of physical particles in space-time governed by the laws of physics—there may be consciousness but no true novelty. Nothing suggests that human beings are special. Nature, as Stephen Jay Gould put it, did not know we were coming and does not give a damn about us now. For Richard Dawkins, the universe that we observe has precisely the properties we should expect if there is at its bottom no design, no purpose, no values of good and evil—nothing but blind pitiless indifference. We are evolved products that are not *for* anything except to propagate our genes. We are alone on an insignificant planet in a cold, uncaring, pointless universe with no god to help us. Our aging and declining bodies are telling us our fate. We see our loved ones die, and we know we too are sentenced to death.[9] In the words of Robert Solomon, the universe does not care about our plans, and we are not part of a cosmic plan that would give our lives a permanent value. And if this is one of few planets with conscious beings in our universe, it shows how incredibly unlikely conscious beings are the objective of the universe rather than only an odd fluke. And as the physicist Steven Weinberg infamously said: "The more the universe seems comprehensible, the more it also seems pointless." Members of prestigious scientific societies indicate that the best scientists are less likely to believe that there are transcendent realities. So too, as our lives become more comfortable, the question of why we live becomes less pressing: we do not ask if life is meaningful when we are happy—we can keep ourselves busy with work and family, distract ourselves with friends and amusements, and not worry about how it all hangs together.[10] For many people, theism slides into a deism, and almost without notice this slides into religious indifference. It is not that today many more people are embracing atheism—many of the religiously unaffiliated (the "nones") still seek a meaning to life, but many are simply too uninterested in religious matters even to bother calling themselves "atheists."

Still, in such circumstances one can accept a subjective meaning and find life worth living—a Jamesian "leap of faith" is appropriate. It must be in accord with how one believes reality to be, but we can accept a meaning that one believes may in fact be objectively true even if we realize it is only a subjective guess. So too, the bar for a meaningful live may not be very high. Perhaps Paul Thagard is correct when he argues that a live filled with fulfilling work, relationships with other people, and a sense of autonomy is enough to satisfy our psychological needs for meaning, although transcendent realists do not think that would suffice to bear all the troubles we go through.

Nihilism

However, the attitude that we must create our own values and meaning in order to make our individual lives meaningful can also lead to embracing nihilism—the denial that there is any meaning to the world. God is dead, and nothing matters. There is no value except perhaps pleasure. The only intellectually honest response is to face the meaninglessness of life and the futility of it all. The existentialist Albert Camus thought that we should defy the meaninglessness and fight the abyss with dignity and courage by helping others—Sisyphus may have to spend eternity pushing the same boulder up the same mountain again and again, but we can imagine him being happy with his lot. However, nothing we do matters. Jean-Paul Sartre thought life was a tragedy: "Everything is born without reason, prolongs itself out of weakness, and dies by chance." (Sartre actually had a more optimistic view of life than that may sound, since we have the freedom to invent our own meaning.) The novelist Nikos Kazantzakis found life meaningful only in searching and struggling—his epitaph reads: "I hope for nothing. I fear nothing. I am free."

Since the cosmos has no objective transcendent or natural meaning, there is no point even in projecting a subjective meaning onto it. We come from nothing and go to nothing—in the end, what we do in between to fill our lives has no significance. The absurdity of the human condition comes from our perceived need to find a meaning in what is meaningless. We are an animal with a conceptualizing mind that creates a problem of meaning where there is none, only natural events. Even to imagine that there could be a meaning or purpose is misdirected: we are thinking in terms of concepts that only distort what is truly here and only making ourselves miserable. But without the illusory idea of an eternal afterlife misleading us, death loses its horror: like miscarriages and birth defects, it occurs, but a transcendent standpoint magnifies the loss. We may love the world and life so much that the prospect of no longer existing is horribly sad, but the end of our existence is our natural lot.

However, one must ask how nihilists *know* that the world is meaning-less. Or why should choosing the most hopeless option be the default position? It is difficult to see how nihilists can be so certain they know the answer. Granted, science does not show us any purpose or meaning to the world, but all that scientists produce is an abstraction of reality in terms of efficient causes and material—that is, only a skeleton of the full world. Science by its self-imposed focus on *causes* is not designed to find *meaning*. (And it should be noted that many scientists in America are theists or deists.) One may adopt science as ideally providing the complete picture of things—thereby eliminating all purpose and meaning—but one has to defend such naturalism on philosophical grounds since science itself does not demand it. Indeed, it is hard to see how a transcendent purpose could be established by any scientific finding—for example, finding any teleological activity in nature will be ascribed to natural principles by naturalists. Even if science could rule out any teleological mechanisms being active in reality, this does not rule out a meaning to reality in terms other than a goal to be achieved. So too, a transcendent purpose may be achievable without such mechanisms operating in nature—for example, scientists may one day be able to show that life and consciousness are the products of purely physical natural forces, but a god still could have set up the general order of things in a reductive manner that accomplishes that purpose. Science may eliminate any anthropocentric view of meaning, but science cannot prove there is no transcendent meaning to the universe *in toto*. That is, science "makes sense" of the world only in the sense of explaining *how* it works—it says nothing one way or the other about the "meaning" of the world in the sense of *why* the world exists or is as it is. (Nor does finding the universe to be at least partially comprehensible to us through our discovery of laws and patterns mean that it must have a transcendent purpose or other meaning.) All in all, we cannot be surprised that scientists do not find any transcendent or natural meaning to the universe when science is not designed to find meaning in the first place. Thus, there may be a meaning to all this, regardless of what scientists find.

In sum, as noted by philosophers from Socrates to Wittgenstein, the entire issue of meaning is screened out of scientific approaches, and thus scientists can succeed completely in what they do—describing and explaining nature's workings—and the questions of the meaning of why the universe exists and of our place in it will still remain open. Is there any other way to determine if there is a transcendent or natural objective meaning to all this? There does not appear to be. The "sense of the world" may, as Wittgenstein said, lie outside the world, but we are foreclosed from that perspective. Theists may rely on revelations and teachings, but there is no neutral way to determine if any of them are anything more than the subjective products of our mind. It may be that seeing a transcendent meaning leads to greater well-being or that belief in an afterlife leads in general to a happier life, but this does not prove that some meaning is objectively real but only that because of how we are constructed such a sense meaning is positive or perhaps even necessary. At least for nonpragmatists, the question is whether a meaning of life is true is not only a matter of whether endorsing one such meaning leads to healthy effects.

Values

What of our values? Are our moral, intellectual, and aesthetic values objective? Can something have value in itself, or is value inherently relational and thus requires a conscious being who values? Are goods such as pleasure, love, and moral worth only what we subjectively favor or are they objective features of reality? Is there some objective standard of positive and negative values? Is beauty innate to nature or merely a sense that has evolved in us? (Even naturalists such as Steven Weinberg can admit that "nature seems more beautiful than is strictly necessary.") Why are we aware of beauty at all, and why do we value it so? Were we created to respond to it? Does the impact that music has on us indicate something about what is real apart from our subjective reactions? Are all values merely products of our emotional responses? Are they any less real because of that? So too, William Barrett can ask: "Why should the pulse of life toward beauty and value not be a part of things?" In fact, are values the reason that a universe exists at all? That is, does value somehow cause there to be a physical universe with free conscious beings?

It is hard to determine how such questions could be answered. The dispute in metaethics between noncognitive antirealism (e.g., moral values are only projections of our own personal or social likes and dislikes) and realism (i.e., normative and evaluative values are objective facts of reality, like mathematical facts) is continuing with no end in sight. Morality seems to have an objective demand on us. But even if basic moral principles (e.g., against murder), if not all ethical precepts, are universal we still cannot determine whether these are any more than cultural products that are necessary for any society to flourish that our species has developed through our social evolution, even if they seem more objective than a "social contract" tacitly entered into in order for the ethics to work. People also disagree over whether moral concern should extend to only our own social group, all human beings, or all sentient animals. Skepticism concerning values as well as beliefs cannot be refuted. This does not mean that nihilists are correct, but only that no ultimate justification of our value choices can be established. Moral values and values in general are not necessarily unreal simply because their basis is a mystery, but we have to accept them as such.[11]

The Mystery of Meaning

Once again we have a Big Question that we are not in a position to answer: we cannot know whether life and the universe has an objective meaning. It is hard, despite what reductionists and existentialists claim, not to think that if there are conscious beings here there must be reason for all this (especially if the beings have free will). But this may be only an instance of the philosopher's disease—our mind demands a "because" to a "why" question even if we cannot answer it. And even if we accept that there must be some reason for all this, we must admit that we are not in a position to determine what the reason is or whether our subjective meaning reflects how things really are. Thus, we do not know if there is some unknowable meaning or no meaning at all. For a naturalist like Robert Solomon, realizing that this "why" has no answer is "the singular fact that now defines our existence." For Viktor Frankl, our concern about a meaning of life is "the truest expression of the state of being human." But we are doomed to live with this deepest personal mystery of all.

Adopting agnosticism once again is the most rational position: we are not in a position to know whether there is any objective meaning to reality or not. Perhaps no finite being within the phenomenal universe is in a position to see the true big picture of it all. But once again, we can both adopt agnosticism and endorse an objective meaning or meaninglessness, although we must accept that we may well be wrong concerning it.

If liberal religious people need a meaning to go on, many may be able to rest comfortably, agreeing with Arthur Koestler that merely knowing that life must be meaningful—that there *must be* a reason for all this or we would not be here—is enough, even if we cannot know what that meaning is. It is not merely a wish or hope that there is meaning but a deep-seated conviction that there is. The mere fact that there is conscious life is enough to lead many to an optimistic view of the universe, and such an attitude is reasonable even if we do not know whether there is a meaning to this world or what happens at death (although this optimistic attitude does not support any one particular religious way of life). In a quest for a more intellectually satisfying position, other religious people may speculate on the meaning of things, but they must admit that "we now see through a glass darkly" (I Cor. 13:12).

Still, no one can fault anyone else on philosophical grounds who accepts another answer, whether it is a transcendent one, a natural one, or nihilism. We cannot have great confidence in any answer. However, agnosticism does damage the commitment one can have to that meaning—it is difficult to live in a web of meaning once one recognizes that we cannot determine if it is true—but agnosticism remains the most intellectually honest action in this area of mystery.

In the end, the question of meaning is not so much a matter of knowledge as ethical belief related to living a certain way. Meaning gives a sense of well-being. Even adopting a meaning that we know is only subjective can make life worth living in such circumstances. Nevertheless, one may live without supplying a "because" for the "why" of the universe or with a minimal sense that there must be some unknown reason. Not knowing a "why" need not lead to anxiety, nausea, and despair as existentialists assert. Admitting that we can never fully comprehend our place in the universe leads to despair only if we demand that the universe must be fully comprehensible to us. But if we reject the philosopher's disease and its demand for answers, it can be exciting simply to know that we are part of a wondrous universe evolving more and more complex forms without knowing what the meaning of it all is or even if there is a meaning (and despite its many sources of suffering). Any anthropocentric meaning is difficult to maintain in light of science—conscious beings may be vital to the scheme of things and even uniquely valuable in the universe, but we have no reason to believe that we on this minor planet are the unique crown of creation. Yet we can still be open to the possibility of meaning of all this.

For Ludwig Wittgenstein the solution to the problem of life is seen in the vanishing of the problem. That is, we continue to live even if we have no answer to this question and despite our apparent deep psychological need to believe that our lives are essential to the cosmic scheme of things—we stop worrying about any possible meaning of life and simply get on with living. This may be possible to do while accepting that the question of meaning remains a mystery by being agnostic here and simply giving up the search for a meaning.

Notes

1. Even though the question of meaning is of the meaningfulness of life *to us*, the questions of a *personally meaningful life* and of an *objective meaning to reality* are distinguishable: one can have a "meaningful life" in the sense of leading a full, purpose-driven existence even if the universe has no objective meaning. Conversely, one's life may be empty and meaningless even if the universe has an objective meaning that we are missing.

2. Happiness may be necessary to a meaningful life, but that happiness is not the same as meaningfulness can be easily seen: if we had a drug that permanently put us in a state of ecstasy, we may be permanently happy, but few would consider such a life meaningful. So too, as John Stuart Mill pointed out, one can be happy without being aware of the issue of a meaning to life. Happiness is a byproduct of a meaningful life.

3. The Buddhist claim that "all is suffering (*dukkha*)" should not be taken to mean that all is painful or unpleasant—there are pleasures in this life. Happiness is a byproduct of a meaningful life. Rather, the idea is that even pleasurable experiences are only temporary and thus ultimately unsatisfying—pain and disappointment is inevitable. Eventually even pleasure become boring in countless rebirths. Thus, "all is unsatisfying or unfulfilling" is a better rendition of the idea. The Buddhist quest is to find an end to the *dukkha* inherent in the realm of rebirth by ending our rebirths. Any meaning to the world or life other than escaping it is hard to find with this view.

4. Most people see what they value as something all people should value and thus essential to a meaningful life. So, philosophers naturally think intellectual pursuits and an examined life are necessary to a meaningful life. But, not to sound flippant, a joke from Emo Philips is worth repeating: "I used to think that the brain was the most wonderful organ in my body. Then I realized who was telling me this." Perhaps an unexamined life is in fact meaningful for many people, and an overexamined life is not a full life at all.

5. "*Carpe diem*"—"seize the day"—in America has come to mean party 'til you drop, but it can also mean to be fully engaged in whatever you deem important or not to waste time.

6. Those who want fame and want their name to be remembered should consider what the Stoic Marcus Aurelius said in his notes to himself: most of the people he encountered in court as emperor of Rome were, to paraphrase, jerks, and he saw no reason to believe that people in a thousand years will be any different, so of what value is lasting fame?

7. Albert Camus spoke of our conceptualizing mind as alienating us even from the natural world: "If I were a cat among animals, this life would have a meaning, or rather this problem would not arise, for I should belong to the world. I would *be* this world to which I am now opposed by my whole consciousness." Nor does the question of meaning arise in such an animal consciousness.

8. Mystical experiences do not per se give a meaning to the cosmos. They may give a sense of the beingness of reality free of the conceptualizing mind, but bare being does not explain why we are here. Mystical experiences may overcome a sense of isolation or alienation from the world and other people that our conceptualizing mind generates and replace it with a sense of connection. This can lead to life seeming to make sense or to everything seeming all right as is, even if no concrete message of a meaning to life is given when the mind is empty of all conceptual content. When one is totally engaged in any activity, there is no inner distance to consider the issue of the meaning of life, and in the mystical enlightened state one is always totally engaged in the present with the activity at hand, and thus the issue never arises. In this way, the quest for meaning ends with the disappearance of the question.

9. The harshness of life presents a problem even without the question of life's meaning. A story from India's *Mahabharata* illustrates this: a man is chased through the jungle by a herd of wild elephants and jumps into an abandoned well to escape; he clings to a vine, but the herd is still outside, so he cannot leave; he looks down and sees a snake at the bottom waiting for him to drop; he looks up and sees mice gnawing away at the vine that he is clinging to; over the well, there is a beehive and angry bees are swarming him, stinging him; through all this, a drop of honey falls from the beehive and the man catches it on his tongue—the secret of life is to be able to enjoy that drop of honey in those circumstances.

10. In arguing that meaning is to be found in living our everyday lives, Will Durant related a story about an ant who in her travels discovers that there is no Great Ant ruling over us and that their colony is only one of millions of ant hills made out of mud in an endless universe. She tries to convince her fellow ants to stop being slaves because life is pointless. But a young ant replies: "This is all very well, sister, but we must build our tunnel."

11. William Lane Craig is not alone in believing that there are no objective moral values if there is no god. But even ignoring the *Euthyphro* problem, it does not take a god's commandment to know that gratuitously torturing a baby is morally wrong—it is morally wrong simply because it needlessly inflicts suffering on another human being. Craig also argues that we need belief in life after death and postmortem rewards and punishments to be moral. But if we act solely out of self-interest (here, fear of hell or hope for heaven), we are not being moral at all but simply looking out for ourselves—it is only a matter of prudent self-interest, not of a genuine moral concern for others. But Craig believes that anyone who does not believe in a postmortem reward or punishment is being "just stupid" to act any way but selfishly—for them, there is "no reason to be human." However, does he really believe that (to use his example) a mother who risks her life to save her children is being "just stupid" unless she believes that she will be rewarded for it after death? Nor is it obvious why a naturalist should feel compelled to adopt selfishness over concern for others: one can be selfish, but one does not need to be once one realizes that we are dependent upon others for our survival and that all life is connected. "No man is an island." Indeed, concern only for oneself conflicts with how things really are in an interconnected naturalistic world. In this way naturalism can ground morality. Without a heaven or hell awaiting us for our conduct, Craig apparently can see no reason to help others or to be human, but naturalists may believe otherwise for reasons connected to their metaphysics and act out of a genuine moral concern for others, not out of self-interest.

16

The Mystery of the Ordinary

Philosophy begins in wonder. And, at the end, when philosophic thought
has done its best, the wonder remains.

—Alfred North Whitehead

The upshot of all this is this: we know that something exists, but we also know that our world has known aspects, currently unknown aspects, and unknowable aspects. We have to recognize the limitations to what we can ever know, both from our finite cognitive abilities and our place in the universe and from possible limits in the universe itself. We must accept that it is very likely that we can know only a very tiny sliver of the total universe, even as reality flows in us. That mysteries surround all the Big Questions must be accepted—we will always lack closure on fundamental aspects of ourselves and our world. The religious once claimed all mystery as exclusively their own (although the mystery is not often mentioned in religion today), but even with the most ordinary things we participate in mysteries of a philosophical kind. Indeed, we are engulfed in mysteries: we cannot separate ourselves from our lives and the universe, and thus we cannot gain the necessary cognitive distance between us and the mysterious in order to make what is mysterious into objects that we could analyze or experiment upon and thus perhaps open to defeat. Our quest for comprehensive knowledge ends consigned to failure. To be sure, science in the future, as in the past, may well reduce some things that we currently consider "how" mysteries to manageable problems and solve them—scientists may devise procedures in the future that we do not have the conceptual and technical background today even to imagine. But as discussed, our lot is also to be stuck with some intractable mysteries no matter how far science goes in explaining the how-ness of things.

Some will find the fact that there is more to reality than we can know (and thus that our quest for knowledge leads to mysteries) exhilarating, and some will find it depressing. However, acknowledging a barrier to our claims to knowledge is a defeatist view of science and philosophy only if we believe that all of reality must be transparent to beings with our particular evolved brains, but there is no reason to believe that. There is also the very real possibility that science, at least when it comes to the Big Questions, may come to an end one day. Science may in these matters be, in effect, only a phase we are going through. But even if this happens, scientists should not be depressed that the quest for knowledge that they have devoted their work lives to cannot in principle be completely fulfilled any more than they should be depressed over the fact that their work is likely to superseded in the future—they are making valuable contributions to our knowledge of reality, and that should be enough for a meaningful life.

Nor is affirming mystery the height of irrationality: accepting limitations to our ability to know and that there may be aspects of reality that are in principle unknowable to any beings like us seems irrational only to those who suffer from the philosopher's disease of demanding an answer to a question even when we unable to supply one due to our circumstances—indeed, that disease would only stifle our sense of reality by imposing some false closure to questions where none is possible. Bryan Magee points out that sensory data cannot be "like" something that is categorically different from them—thus, they cannot correspond to objective world as it is independent of our experience. We cannot even form conceptions of the independent world: what exists exists without the characteristics that are dependent upon us—when it comes to the world independent of us, we are like airline pilots flying by instruments in a fog.

But today we seem to have lost any sense of mystery to reality. Modern science's "disenchantment of nature" has led to the spiritual impoverishment of many who value science. And it is certainly the case that in our everyday lives we can focus only on the known. Nevertheless, what is currently unknown and unknowable in principle cannot be forgotten and should play a role in our lives: we know less than we like to think, and our predicament must be given its due. It is not a matter of wandering around constantly gawking in awe and wonder, although Thornton Wilder's *Our Town* reminds us of the wonder and beauty of ordinary things that we do miss every day. Nor is it to ignore the fixable problems we have with the world. Rather, it is realizing in moments of reflection that what we know is framed by more of reality: there is a fuller picture of reality, and the permanent feature of mystery in our basic picture of reality should be brought into the light. When we ponder the full range of reality in light of our situation, we see how little we do know and see how tentative what we do know is.

Fundamental things related to the being of the world and our consciousness—matters that we are all but constantly aware of—enclose us without our ability to comprehend them in any complete sense of the word. We may agree with G.E. Moore's common-sense position that the existence of ourselves and the world does not need proving, but these still confront us as having fundamental mysteries at their foundations: we know they exist, but we do not know their basic nature. That is important to remember in order to realize what we are and what the world is. It is not only that we cannot control all that happens to us, but that we are surrounded by brute facts even in our everyday lives that we will never comprehend.

A sense of mystery adds another dimension to our lives: no matter how at home we feel in the universe, there is a strangeness to our being here that we cannot get around. Because of the conceptualizing mind that we have evolved, we are probably the one creature on our planet that is able to see the strangeness of there being such a reality, wonder about it, and formulate questions concerning it. But unfortunately, we are unable to answer all the questions that the strangeness of our situation provokes. Nevertheless, simply to ignore the mystery of all of this is to leave us with a truncated view of reality and not with the realization of our true place in the world. The more we increase our knowledge, the more we are aware of the presence of our ignorance and the limits of our knowledge, and that in the final analysis we have no certain fundamental knowledge beyond that something exists. Thereby, we can be more open to reality if we recognize that we live on the shoreline between the known and the unknown. Both sides of that shoreline are part of our world. Thus, living with mystery means balancing openness with the closure provided by our conceptual systems. It involves utilizing our science and our conceptual attempts at closing off the unknown while treating them as just that—our all-too-human attempts at dealing with what is ultimately beyond our grasp.

Perhaps the professional life of quantum physicists is the exemplar of how to lead a fuller human life in the world: they are constantly encountering the unknown, but they can live without closure with tentative theories despite their problems—indeed, it is only by remaining beyond the control of those theories that they can advance their science by seeing things in a new light. As physicist Richard Feynman put it: "I can live with doubt and uncertainty and not knowing. I think it much more interesting to live with not knowing than to have answers that might be wrong." He notes that in order to make progress in science, we "must leave the door to the unknown ajar." (It is worth noting that he also said that he was not frightened by being in a universe that has no purpose.) In a similar way, a sense of mystery can be very valuable to all our lives without the sense of not knowing overwhelming us. We can remain open by asking the Big Questions and not settling with any proposed answers as closure. The loss of certainty in our answers need not be seen as a loss at all but as a type of liberation. Indeed, life can be more interesting when we live with this openness to the fullness of reality.

Accepting that we are not in a position to answer some or all of the Big Questions— agnosticism—is in fact the most rational approach to take. Agnosticism does not mean indifference: it is not lack of interest in the Big Questions, but a reasoned-out epistemic position on what we can and cannot know based on the study of the issues surrounding mysteries. Nor is it simply the acknowledgment that all well-articulated positions on any philosophical issue probably will eventually be shown to have problematic premises that would not command the assent of all reasonable people. Rather, agnosticism is a matter of seeing that we are not in a position, due to limitations resulting from our evolution and our situation in the world, to resolve certain fundamental questions that we can formulate.

However, agnosticism is not very popular today. Most people from theists to reductive naturalists believe that they know more about basic questions than agnostics would admit as justified. Most philosophers may grudgingly acknowledge that agnosticism is all that is ultimately justifiable, but this does not discourage them from speculating. Such speculations provide closure and thus quiet our minds, and some may in fact be correct. However, we must accept such speculations as only that— guesses that are only based on our experiences and ways of thinking— and we must admit that we are not in a position to determine if our intuition-inspired speculations are correct. But this does not mean that the questions are not worth asking or have been shown to be illegitimate through a philosophical analysis—indeed, they are vital to understanding what we are and what the world we live in is like. Nevertheless, our position should be to accept, however reluctantly, that we cannot have much confidence in our speculations since we do not actually have the resources to answer the questions with any definitiveness. As Bryan Magee concludes, agnosticism is the only honest way to live without evasions or self-indulgence—it is the fullest acknowledgment of our ignorance.

But again, emphasizing mystery clearly goes against the spirit of our age. Today, most people, if they note the mysteries of reality at all, understandably focus on what is known and at best pay lip service to the mysteries. However, philosophy, as Plato noted, begins in wonder, but it also ends in wonder. Embracing mystery can lead naturalists to having more reverence for the ordinary and lead transcendent realists to being more humble toward all of reality. Philosophers today should continue to analyze problems to see if we have generated mysteries where there are none by how we conceptualize problems. And metaphysicians today will no doubt continue to try to penetrate the mysteries that remain standing after such an analysis by advancing speculative answers. But the foundations of all philosophical explanations are not secure, and it is best that we understand our situation in the world. The ground that philosophers walk on is soft, with no sure footing.

Thus, we must live with this acceptance of mystery. Philosophy can play a role today that is at least as important as speculation simply in exposing our epistemic situation by bringing mysteries to light and showing where they came from, even if this throws a little discomfort into our lives by bringing uncertainty to our claims of knowledge. Charles Darwin told the story that illustrates much of science: as a young man, he spent a day near a river and noticed nothing about the rocks, but after ten years of study he returned to the spot and noticed obvious evidence of glacial activity. Something like that also occurs in philosophy: no new empirical facts may be revealed, but by the end of the journey our understanding of where we stand in reality may be increased. In that way, philosophy can fulfill its claim to be the "love of wisdom."

Further Reading

Chapter 1

For more on this and the other subjects in this book, see Jones 2009. Also see Solomon 1999 on the lost joy of philosophizing and Magee 2016. On wonder and awe, see Fuller 2006. For a survey on wonder in philosophy, see Rubenstein 2008: 1–24. For introductions to the Big Questions, see Van Inwagen and Zimmerman 1998. On types of senses of mystery, see Verkamp 1997. On "why" questions, see Edwards 1967. On the classic account of the distinction between an irremovable "mystery" and a solvable "problem," see Gabriel Marcel 1950–1951.

Chapter 2

Analytic philosophers have written little on mystery in the last hundred years—see Foster 1957, Ross 1984, Cooper 2002, Jones 2009, and Rhodes 2012. On the complexity of concepts, see Wilson 2006. On the law of noncontradiction and paradoxes, see Fogelin 2003: chap. 2.

Chapter 3

On other logical and conceptual limitations to our knowledge, see Williamson 2002. For skepticism, see Unger 1975 and Stroud 1984. On agnosticism, see Joshi 2007. On reason and evolution, see Nagel 2003: chap. 7 and Sterelny 2003. On the paradox of knowability, see Kvanvig 2006. For a contemporary version of the Clifford/James debate, see Feldman and Warfield 2010.

Chapter 4

On current metaphysics, see Van Inwagen and Zimmerman 1998. On naturalized "scientific metaphysics," see Ross, Ladyman, and Kincaid 2015. For metametaphysics, see Chalmers, Manley, and Wasserman 2009. On being, see Munitz 1986: 181–235 and 1990: 192–208; on being and language, see Jones 2016: chap. 6. Also see Lawson 2001 on "closure" versus the "openness" of reality and Rubenstein 2008.

Chapter 5

See Munitz 1965, Nozick 1981, Parfit 1992, Rundle 2004, Holt 2012, and Goldschmidt 2013. For Stephen Hawking's view, see Hawking and Mlodinow 2010 and Krauss 2012. See Leslie 1989 for the idea that values are the source of the phenomenal universe.

Chapter 6

On whether there actually is causation in the world, see Field 2003.

Chapter 7

For a fuller treatment, see Jones 2013. See Anderson 1972 for a classic take on the issue by a physicist. See Morowitz 2002: 25–38 for a delineation of *twenty-eight* levels of emergence. On the new emergentists, see Clayton and Davies 2006. On metametaphysics and conceptual reductionism, see Sider 2009.

Chapter 8

On the sciences, see Gleiser 2014. On limits in mathematics and science, see Yanofsky 2013. See Davies 2003 for the suggestion that mathematized theories in science are unlikely to survive long.

Chapter 9

On the Big Bang, see Craig and Smith, 1993. On TOEs, see Lindley 1993. On fine tuning, see Rees 2000 and Stenger 2011. On string theory, see Greene 1999 (pro); Smolin 2006 and Woit 2006 (con). On the multiverse controversy, see Rubenstein 2013. On the end of science as we know it, see Baggott 2013.

Chapter 10

See Kaufmann 1993 on an order rather than natural selection that generates effects as the reason why genes tend to settle into recurring patterns. On alternatives to neo-Darwinism, see Corning 2005. For a reductionist view of evolution, see Dawkins 1986. For antireductionist views, see Davies 1987, Morris 2003, and Nagel 2010.

Chapter 11

On the elimination of the self, see Parfit 1984 and Dennett 1991. On the self as causal, see Flanagan 1992. On Advaita and the self, see Jones 2014.

Chapter 12

For a current overview of the mind/body field, see Chalmers 2003. Also see Dennett 1991, Searle 1997, McGinn 1999, and Nagel 2012. For a defense of dualism, see Foster 1991. On the rebirth of hylomorphism, see Jaworski 2016. On recent work on consciousness and quantum physics, see Tuszynski 2006. On John Searle's "Chinese Room" argument, see Preston and Bishop 2002. On panpsychism, see Strawson 2006.

Chapter 13

For compatibilism, see Dennett 1984 and Koch 2012; against it, see Honderich 2002. On free will debate, see Russell and Deery 2013. For the denial of free will, see Wegner 2002. For agent causation, see Chisholm 1966. On Libet's experiments and free will, see Libet 1999.

Chapter 14

On the arguments for the existence of God, see Peterson and VanArragon 2003. On atheism, see Martin 2002. On mysticism, see Jones 2016. On the absence of God argument, see Howard-Snyder and Moser 2002. On religious agnosticism, see Gutting 2013. For an evangelical Christian take on God as being both revealed and an impenetrable mystery, see Boyer and Hall 2012.

Chapter 15

See Klemke and Cahn 2007 and Baggini 2005. See Munitz 1993 on being-ness and meaning. On value, see Nagel 2012: 97–126. On religion and meaning, see Smith 2001 and Runzo and Martin 2000. On whether immortality must be boring, see Williams 1973 (pro) and Chappell 2007 (con). For existentialism, see Kaufmann 2004.

Bibliography

Alston, William. "Two Cheers for Mystery!" In Andrew Dole and Andrew Chignell, eds., *God and the Ethics of Belief: New Essays in Philosophy of Religion*, pp. 99–114. New York: Cambridge University Press, 2005.

Anderson, Philip W. "More is Different: Broken Symmetry and the Nature of the Hierarchical Structure of Science." *Science* 177 (August 4, 1972): 393–396.

Atkins, Peter W. *On Being: A Scientist's Exploration of the Great Questions of Existence*. New York: Oxford University Press, 2011.

Baggini, Julian. *What's It All About? Philosophy and the Meaning of Life*. Oxford: Oxford University Press, 2005.

Baggott, Jim. *Farewell to Reality: How Modern Physics Has Betrayed the Search for Scientific Truth*. New York: Pegasus, 2013.

Barrow, John D. *Impossibility: The Limits of Science and the Science of Limits*. New York: Oxford University Press, 1998.

———. *New Theories of Everything: The Quest for Ultimate Explanation*. New York: Oxford University Press, 2007.

Beckermann, Ansgar, Hans Flohr, and Jaegwon Kim, eds. *Emergence or Reduction? Essays on the Prospects of Nonreductive Physicalism*. New York: Walter de Gruyter, 1992.

Benatar, David, ed. *Life, Death & Meaning: Key Philosophical Readings on the Big Questions*. Lanham, MD: Rowman & Littlefield, 2004.

Boyer, Steven, and Christopher A. Hall. *The Mystery of God: Theology for Knowing the Unknowable*. Grand Rapids, MI: Baker Academics, 2012.

Brockman, John, ed. *This Explains Everything: Deep, Beautiful, and Elegant Theories of How the World Works*. New York: Harper Perennial, 2013.

Burrell, David B. *Knowing the Unknowable God: Ibn-Sina, Maimonides, Aquinas*. Notre Dame, IN: University of Notre Dame Press, 1986.

Byrne, Peter. *God and Realism*. Burlington, VT: Ashgate, 2003.

Camus, Albert. *The Myth of Sisyphus, and Other Essays*. Translated by Justin O'Brien. New York: Vintage Books, 1991.

Carroll, Lewis. "What the Tortoise Said to Achilles." *Mind* 4 (1985): 278–280.

Chalmers, David J. *The Conscious Mind: In Search of a Fundamental Theory.* New York: Oxford University Press, 1996.

———. "Consciousness and its Place in Nature." In Stephen P. Stich and Ted A. Warfield, eds., *The Blackwell Guide to the Philosophy of Mind*, pp. 102–142. Oxford: Blackwell, 2003.

———. "Why Isn't There More Progress in Philosophy?" In Ted Honderich, ed., *Philosophers of Our Times*, pp. 347–370. Oxford: Oxford University Press, 2015.

Chalmers, David J., David Manley, and Ryan Wasserman, eds. *Metametaphysics: New Essays on the Foundations of Ontology.* Oxford: Clarendon Press, 2009.

Chappell, Timothy. "Infinity Goes Up on Trial: Must Immortality Be Meaningless?" *European Journal of Philosophy* 17.1 (2007): 30–44.

Chisholm, Roderick. "Freedom and Action." In Keith Lehrer, ed., *Freedom and Determinism*, pp. 11–44. New York: Random House, 1966.

Clayton, Philip, and Paul Davies, eds. *The Re-Emergence of Emergence: The Emergent Hypothesis from Science to Religion.* New York: Oxford University Press, 2006.

Cooper, David E. *The Measure of Things: Humanism, Humility, and Mystery.* Oxford: Oxford University Press, 2002.

Corning, Peter A. *Holistic Darwinism: Synergy, Cybernetics, and the Bioeconomics of Evolution.* Chicago: University of Chicago Press, 2005.

Cottingham, John. *The Search for Meaning.* New York: Routledge, 2003.

Craig, William Lane. "The Indispensability of Theological Meta-Ethical Foundations for Morality." *Foundations* 5 (1997): 9–12.

Craig, William Lane, and Quentin Smith. *Theism, Atheism, and Big Bang Cosmology.* Oxford: Clarendon Press, 1993.

Crick, Francis. *The Astonishing Hypothesis: The Scientific Search for the Soul.* New York: Charles Scribner's Sons, 1994.

Davies, E. Brian. *Science in the Looking Glass: What Do Scientists Really Know?* New York: Oxford University Press, 2003.

Davies, Paul C.W. *The Cosmic Blueprint.* London: Heinemann, 1987.

———. *The Fifth Miracle: The Search for the Origin and Meaning of Life.* New York: Simon & Schuster, 1999.

Dawkins, Richard. *The Blind Watchmaker.* New York: Norton, 1986.

———. *Unweaving the Rainbow: Science, Delusion, and the Appetite for Wonder.* New York: Houghton Mifflin, 1998.

Dennett, Daniel C. *Elbow Room.* Cambridge: MIT Press, 1984.

———. *Consciousness Explained.* Boston: Little, Brown and Co., 1991.

Dewdney, A.K. *Beyond Reason: Eight Great Problems That Reveal the Limits of Science.* Hoboken: John Wiley & Sons, 2004.

Dworkin, Ronald. *Religion Without God*. Cambridge, MA: Harvard University Press, 2014.

Dupré, John. *The Disorder of Things: Metaphysical Foundations of the Disunity of Science*. Cambridge, MA: Harvard University Press, 1993.

Durant, Will. *On the Meaning of Life*. New York: Long & Smith, 1932.

Dyson, Freeman. *Infinite in All Directions: The Gifford Lectures, 1985*. New York: Harper & Row, 1988.

Eddington, Arthur. *The Nature of the Physical World*. Ann Arbor: University of Michigan Press, 1958.

Edwards, Paul. "Why." In Paul Edwards, ed., *The Encyclopedia of Philosophy*, vol. 8, pp. 296–302. New York: Macmillan, 1967.

———. "Life, Meaning and Value of." In Paul Edwards, ed., *The Encyclopedia of Philosophy*, vol. 4, pp. 467–477. New York: Macmillan, 1967.

Ferré, Frederick. "In Praise of Anthropomorphism." *International Journal for the Philosophy of Religion* 16 (1984): 203–212.

Feynman, Richard P. *The Meaning of It All: Thoughts of a Citizen-Scientist*. Reading, MA: Perseus Books, 1998.

Field, Hartry. "Causation in a Physical World." In Michael J. Loux and Dean W. Zimmerman, eds., *The Oxford Handbook of Metaphysics*, pp. 435–460. New York: Oxford University Press, 2003.

Fogelin, Robert. *Walking the Tightrope of Reason: The Precarious Life of the Rational Animal*. New York: Oxford University Press, 2003.

Ford, Dennis. *The Search for Meaning: A Short History*. Berkeley/Los Angeles: University of California Press, 2007.

Foster, John. *The Immaterial Self: A Defense of the Cartesian Dualist Conception of the Mind*. New York: Routledge, 1991.

Foster, Michael B. *Mystery and Philosophy*. London: SCM Press, 1957.

Fuller, Robert C. *Wonder: From Emotion to Spirituality*. Chapel Hill: University of North Carolina Press, 2006.

Galison, Peter, and David J. Stump, eds. *The Disunity of Science: Boundaries, Contexts, and Power*. Stanford, CA: Stanford University Press, 1996.

Gell-Mann, Murray. *The Quark and the Jaguar: Adventures in the Simple and the Complex*. New York: W.H. Freeman, 1994.

Gleiser, Marcelo. *The Island of Knowledge: The Limits of Science and the Search for Meaning*. New York: Basic Books, 2014.

Goldschmidt, Tyron, ed. *The Puzzle of Existence: Why Is There Something Rather Than Nothing?* New York: Routledge, 2013.

Greene, Brian. *The Elegant Universe: Superstrings, Hidden Dimensions, and the Quest for the Ultimate Theory*. New York: W.W. Norton, 1999.

Guthrie, Stewart Elliott. *Faces in the Clouds: A New Theory of Religion*. New York: Oxford University Press, 1993.

Gutting, Gary. *What Philosophers Know: Case Studies in Recent Analytic Philosophy*. New York: Cambridge University Press, 2009.

————. "Religious Agnosticism." *Midwest Studies in Philosophy* 37 (2013): 51–67.

Haeckel, Ernst. *The Riddle of the Universe*. Translated by Joseph McCabe. Buffalo, NY: Prometheus Books, 1992. (Originally published 1899.)

Haldane, John. "The Mystery of Emergence." *Proceedings of the Aristotelean Society* 70 (1996): 261–267.

Hasker, William. *The Emergent Self*. Ithaca, NY: Cornell University Press, 1999.

Haught, John F. "Mystery." In *What is God? How to Think About the Divine*, pp. 115–131. New York: Paulist Press, 1986.

————. "Science and Mystery." In *Christianity and Science: Toward a Theology of Nature*, pp. 19–33. Maryknoll, NY: Orbis Books, 2007.

Hawking, Stephen W. "Letter to the Editor." *American Scientist* 73 (Jan/Feb 1985): 12.

————. *A Brief History of Time*. New York: Bantam Books, 1988.

Hawking, Stephen W., and Leonard Mlodinow. *The Grand Design*. New York: Bantam Books, 2010.

Heidegger, Martin. *An Introduction to Metaphysics*. Translated by R. Manheim. New York: Doubleday, 1961.

Hepburn, Ronald. "Wonder." In *"Wonder" and Other Essays*, pp. 131–147. Edinburgh: University of Edinburgh Press, 1984.

Holley, David M. *Meaning and Mystery: What It Means to Believe in God*. Malden, MA: Wiley-Blackwell, 2010.

Holt, Jim. *Why Does the World Exist? An Existential Detective Story*. New York: Liveright Publishing, 2012.

Honderich, Ted. *How Free are You? The Determinism Problem*. New York: Oxford University Press, 2002.

Howard-Snyder, Daniel, and Paul K. Moser, eds. *Divine Hiddenness: New Essays*. New York: Cambridge University Press, 2002.

Jackson, Frank. "Mind and Illusion." In Anthony O'Hear, ed., *Minds and Persons*, pp. 251–271. New York: Cambridge University Press.

Jaworski, William. *Structure and the Metaphysics of Mind: How Hylomorphism Solves the Mind-Body Problem*. New York: Oxford University Press, 2016.

Jeans, James. *The Mysterious Universe*. Cambridge: Cambridge University Press, 1928.

Jones, Richard H. "The Religious Irrelevance of the Ontological Argument." In *Mysticism Examined: Philosophical Inquiries Into Mysticism*, pp. 149–166. Albany: State University of New York Press, 1993.

————. *Curing the Philosopher's Disease: Reinstating Mystery in the Heart of Philosophy*. Lanham, MD: University Press of America, 2009.

————. *Analysis and the Fullness of Reality: An Introduction to Reductionism & Emergence*. New York: Jackson Square Books/Createspace, 2013.

————, trans. *Early Advaita Vedanta Philosophy*, vol. 1. New York: Jackson Square Books/Createspace, 2014.

————. *Philosophy of Mysticism: Raids on the Ineffable*. Albany: State University of New York Press, 2016.

Joshi, S.T., ed. *The Agnostic Reader*. Amherst, NY: Prometheus Books, 2007.

Kant, Immanuel. *Critique of Pure Reason*. Translated by Paul Guyer and Allen W. Wood. Cambridge: Cambridge University Press, 1998.

Kauffman, Stuart A. *The Origins of Order: Self-Organization and Selection in Evolution*. New York: Oxford University Press, 1993.

————. *At Home in the Universe: The Search for Laws of Self-Organization and Complexity*. New York: Oxford University Press, 1995.

Kaufmann, Walter, ed. *Existentialism: from Dostoevsky to Sartre*. New York: Plume, 2004. (Originally published 1975.)

Kim, Jaegwon. *Philosophy of Mind*. 3rd ed. Boulder, CO: Westview Press, 2011.

Kitcher, Philip. *Life After Faith: The Case for Secular Humanism*. New Haven, CT: Yale University Press, 2014.

Klemke, E.D., and Steven Cahn, eds. *The Meaning of Life*. 3rd ed. New York: Oxford University Press, 2007.

Koch, Christof. *Consciousness: Confessions of a Romantic Reductionist*. Cambridge, MA: MIT Press, 2012.

Koons, Robert C., and George Bealer, eds. *The Waning of Materialism*. New York: Oxford University Press, 2010.

Kragh, Helge. *Higher Speculations: Grand Theories and Failed Revolutions in Physics and Cosmology*. New York: Oxford University Press, 2011.

Krauss, Lawrence. M. *A Universe from Nothing: Why There is Something Rather Than Nothing*. New York: Pocket Books, 2012.

Krishnamurti, Jiddhu, and David Bohm. *The Limits of Thought: Discussions*. New York: Routledge, 1999.

Kvanvig, Jonathan L. *The Knowability Paradox*. New York: Oxford University Press, 2006.

Ladyman, James, and Don Ross, with David Spurrett and John Collier. *Every Thing Must Go: Metaphysics Naturalized*. New York: Oxford University Press, 2007.

Lakoff, George, and Mark Johnson. *Philosophy in the Flesh: The Embodied Mind and its Challenge to Western Thought*. New York: Basic Books, 1999.

Landesman, Charles. *Skepticism: The Central Issues*. New York: Blackwell, 2002.

Laughlin, Robert B. *A Different Universe: Reinventing Physics from the Bottom Down*. New York: Basic Books, 2005.

Lawson, Hilary. *Closure: A Story of Everything*. New York: Routledge, 2001.

Leslie, John. *Universes*. New York: Routledge, 1989.

Lewis, David. *Plurality of Worlds*. Oxford: Blackwell, 1986.

Lewis, Hywel D. "God and Mystery." In Ian T. Ramsey, ed., *Prospect for Metaphysics: Essays of Metaphysical Exploration*, pp. 206–237. London: Allen & Unwin, 1961.

Libet, Benjamin. "Do We Have Free Will?" *Journal of Consciousness Studies* 6.8–9 (1999): 47–57.

Lindley, David. *The End of Physics: The Myth of a Unified Theory*. New York: HarperCollins, 1993.

Lowe, E.J. "Why is There Anything at All?" *Proceedings of the Aristotelean Society* 70 (Supplement 1996): 111–120.

Macquarrie, John. *Mystery and Truth*. Milwaukee, WI: Marquette University Theology Department, 1973.

Magee, Bryan. *Ultimate Questions*. Princeton, NJ: Princeton University Press, 2016.

Manley, David. "Introduction: A Guided Tour of Metametaphysics." In David Chalmers, David Manley, and Ryan Wasserman, eds., *Metametaphysics: New Essays on the Foundations of Ontology*, pp. 1–37. Oxford: Clarendon Press, 2009.

Marcel, Gabriel. *The Mystery of Being*. 2 vols. Translated by René Hague. Chicago: Henry Regnery Co., 1950–1951.

Margolis, Joseph. *The Unraveling of Scientism: American Philosophy at the End of the Twentieth Century*. Ithaca, NY: Cornell University Press, 2003.

Martin, Michael. *Atheism, Morality, and Meaning*. Amherst, NY: Prometheus Books, 2002.

McGinn, Colin. *Problems in Philosophy: Limits of Inquiry*. Oxford: Blackwell, 1993.

———. *The Mysterious Flame: Conscious Minds in a Material World*. New York: Basic Books, 1999.

Mead, George Herbert. *Mind, Self & Society*. Edited by Charles W. Morris. Chicago: University of Chicago Press, 2015 [1934].

Meheus, Joke, ed. *Inconsistency in Science*. Boston: Kluwer, 2002.

Messerly, John G. *The Meaning of Life: Religious, Philosophical, Transhumanist, and Scientific Perspectives*. Seattle: Durant & Russell Publishers, 2012.

Metz, Thaddeus. *Meaning in Life: An Analytic Study*. Oxford: Oxford University Press, 2013.

Miller, James B., ed. *Cosmic Questions*. New York: New York Academy of Sciences, 2001.

Morowitz, Harold J. *The Emergence of Everything: How the World Became Complex*. New York: Oxford University Press, 2002.

Morris, Richard. *The Big Questions: Probing the Promise and Limits of Science*. New York: Henry Holt, 2002.

Morris, Simon Conway. *Life's Solution: Inevitable Humans in a Lonely Universe*. New York: Cambridge University Press, 2003.

Moser, Paul K., and J.D. Trout, eds., *Contemporary Materialism: A Reader*. New York: Routledge, 1995.

Munitz, Milton K. *Cosmic Understanding: Philosophy and Science of the Universe*. Princeton, NJ: Princeton University Press, 1986.

———. *The Question of Reality*. Princeton, NJ: Princeton University Press, 1990.

———. *Does Life Have a Meaning?* Buffalo, NY: Prometheus Books, 1993.

Nagel, Thomas. *The Last Word*. New York: Oxford University Press, 2003.

———. *Secular Philosophy and the Religious Temperament: Essays 2002–2008*. New York: Oxford University Press, 2010.

———. *Mind and Cosmos: Why the Neo-Darwinian Conception of Nature is Almost Certainly False*. New York: Oxford University Press, 2012.

Needleman, Jacob, and David Appelbaum, eds. *Real Philosophy: An Anthology of the Universal Search for Meaning*. New York: Penguin Books, 1990.

Newberg, Andrew, and Mark Robert Waldman. *How God Changes Your Brain: Breakthrough Findings from a Leading Neuroscientist*. New York: Ballantine Books, 2009.

Nozick, Robert. "Why Is There Something Rather Than Nothing?" In *Philosophical Explanations*, pp. 115–164. Cambridge: Belknap Press, 1981.

Parfit, Derek. "The Puzzle of Existence: Why Does the Universe Exist?" *Times Literary Supplement* (July 3, 1992): 3–5.

Penfield, Wilder. *The Mystery of the Mind*. Princeton, NJ: Princeton University Press, 1975.

Peterson, Michael L., and Raymond VanArragon, eds. *Contemporary Debates in Philosophy of Religion*. New York: Wiley-Blackwell, 2003.

Placher, William C. *The Domestication of Transcendence: How Modern Thinking About God Went Wrong*. Louisville, KY: Westminster/John Knox Press, 1996.

Preston, John, and Mark Bishop, eds. *Views into the Chinese Room: New Essays on Searle and Artificial Intelligence*. New York: Oxford University Press, 2002.

Priest, Graham. *Beyond the Limits of Thought*. 2nd ed. New York: Cambridge University Press, 2002.

Quine, Willard van Orman. *Theories and Things*. Cambridge, MA: Harvard University Press, 1981.

Ramsey, Ian T. *Models and Mystery*. London: Oxford University Press, 1964.

———. "On Understanding Mystery." In Jerry H. Gill, ed., *Philosophy and Religion: Some Contemporary Perspectives*, pp. 295–308. Minneapolis: Burgess Publishing, 1968.

Rescher, Nicholas. *The Riddle of Existence: An Essay in Idealistic Metaphysics*. Lanham, MD: University Press of America, 1984.

———. *The Limits of Science*. Pittsburgh, PA: University of Pittsburgh Press, 1999.

Rhodes, Michael Craig. *Mystery in Philosophy: An Invocation of Pseudo-Dionysius*. Lanham, MD: Lexington Books, 2012.

Ross, Don, James Ladyman, and Harold Kincaid, eds. *Scientific Metaphysics*. New York: Oxford University Press, 2015.

Ross, Steven David. *Philosophical Mysteries*. Albany: State University of New York, 1981.

Rubenstein, Mary-Jane. *Strange Wonder: The Closure of Metaphysics and the Opening of Awe*. New York: Columbia University Press, 2008.

———. *Worlds Without End: The Many Lives of the Multiverse*. New York: Columbia University Press, 2013.

Rundle, Bede. *Why There is Something Rather Than Nothing*. Oxford: Clarendon Press, 2004.

Runzo, Joseph, and Nancy Martin, eds. *The Meaning of Life in the World Religions*. Oxford: Oneworld Publications, 2000.

Russell, Bertrand. *Why I am Not a Christian and Other Essays on Religion and Related Subjects*. New York: Simon & Schuster, 1957.

Russell, Paul, and Oisin Deery, eds. *The Philosophy of Free Will: Essential Readings from the Contemporary Debates*. New York: Oxford University Press, 2013.

Sartre, Jean-Paul. *Jean-Paul Sartre: Basic Writings*. Edited by Stephen Priest. New York: Routledge, 2001.

Schlesinger, George N. "Possible Worlds and the Mystery of Existence." *Ratio* 26 (June 1984): 1–17.

———. "The Enigma of Existence." *Ratio* n.s. 11 (April 1998): 66–77.

Schlick, Moritz. "Unanswerable Questions." *The Philosopher* 13 (1935).

———. "Meaning and Verification." *Philosophical Review* 45 (July 1936): 339–369.

Searle, John. *The Mystery of Consciousness*. New York: New York Review, 1997.

Sider, Theodore. "Ontological Realism." In David Chalmers, David Manley, and Ryan Wasserman, eds., *Metametaphysics: New Essays on the Foundations of Ontology*, pp. 384–423. Oxford: Clarendon Press, 2009.

Smart, J.J.C. "Sensations and Brain Processes." *Philosophical Review* 68 (April 1959): 141–156.

Smart, Ninian. "Paradox in Religion." *Proceedings of the Aristotelian Society Supplement* 32 (1959): 219–232.

———. "On Knowing What is Uncertain." In Leroy S. Rouner, ed., *Knowing Religiously*, pp. 76–86. Notre Dame, IN: University of Notre Dame Press, 1985.

Smith, Huston. *Why Religion Matters: The Fate of the Human Spirit in an Age of Disbelief.* San Francisco: HarperCollins, 2001.

Smolin, Lee. *The Trouble with Physics: The Rise of String Theory, the Fall of a Science, and What Comes Next.* Boston: Houghton Mifflin, 2006.

Solomon, Robert C. *The Joy of Philosophy: Thinking Thin versus the Passionate Life.* New York: Oxford University Press, 1999.

Sorensen, Roy. *A Brief History of Paradox: Philosophy and Labyrinths of the Mind.* New York: Oxford University Press, 2003.

Stannard, Russell. *Science and Wonders.* London: Faber and Faber, 1996.

Stenger, Victor. *The Fallacy of Fine-Tuning: Why the Universe Is Not Designed for Us.* Amherst, NY: Prometheus Books, 2011.

Sterelny, Kim. *Thought in a Hostile World: The Evolution of Human Cognition.* Malden, MA: Blackwell, 2003.

Strawson, Galen, et al. *Consciousness and Its Place in Nature: Does Physicalism Entail Panpsychism?* Charlottesville, VA: Imprint Academic, 2006.

Stroud, Barry. *The Significance of Philosophical Skepticism.* New York: Oxford University Press, 1984.

Swinburne, Richard. *Is There a God?* New York: Oxford University Press, 1996.

Templeton, John Marks, ed. *How Large is God? Voices of Scientists and Theologians.* Philadelphia: Templeton Foundation Press, 1997.

Thagard, Paul. *The Brain and the Meaning of Life.* Princeton, NJ: Princeton University Press, 2010.

Tillich, Paul. *The Courage to Be.* New Haven, CT: Yale University Press, 1952.

Trusted, Jennifer. *The Mystery of Matter.* New York: St. Martin's Press, 1999.

Tuszynski, Jack A., ed. *The Emerging Physics of Consciousness.* New York: Springer, 2006.

Unger, Peter K. *Ignorance: A Case for Scepticism.* Oxford: Clarendon Press, 1975.

Van Inwagen, Peter. "Why is There Anything at All?" *Proceedings of the Aristotelian Society* 70 (Supplement, 1996): 95–110.

———. "Free Will Remains a Mystery." In Robert Kane, ed., *The Oxford Handbook of Free Will*, pp. 158–177. New York: Oxford University Press, 2002.

Van Inwagen, Peter, and Dean W. Zimmerman, eds. *Metaphysics: The Big Questions.* Malden, MA: Blackwell Publishers, 1998.

Verkamp, Bernard J. *Senses of Mystery: Religious and Non-Religious.* Scranton, PA: University of Scranton Press, 1997.

Vernon, Mark. *Science, Religion and the Meaning of Life.* New York: Palgrave, 2007.

Wainwright, William J. "Theology and Mystery." In Thomas P. Flint and Michael C. Rea, eds., *The Oxford Handbook of Philosophical Theology,* pp. 78–102. New York: Oxford University Press, 2011.

Wallenstein, Immanuel M. *The Uncertainties of Knowledge.* Philadelphia: Temple University Press, 2004.

Wegner, Daniel M. *The Illusion of Conscious Will.* Cambridge, MA: MIT Press, 2002.

Weinberg, Steven. *The First Three Minutes of the Universe.* New York: Basic Books, 1977.

———. *Dreams of a Final Theory.* New York: Pantheon Books, 1992.

White, Curtis. *The Science Delusion: Asking the Big Questions in a Culture of Easy Answers.* New York: Melville House, 2013.

Williams, Bernard. "The Makropulos Case: Reflections on the Tedium of Immortality." In *Problems of the Self: Philosophical Papers 1956–1972,* pp. 82–100. New York: Cambridge University Press, 1973.

Williamson, Timothy. *Knowledge and its Limits.* New York: Oxford University Press, 2002.

Wilson, Mark. *Wandering Significance: An Essay on Conceptual Behavior.* New York: Oxford University Press, 2006.

Wittgenstein, Ludwig. *Tractatus Logico-Philosophicus.* Translated by David F. Pears and B.F. McGuinness. London: Routledge and Paul, 1961. (Originally published 1922.)

———. "A Lecture on Ethics." *Philosophical Review* 74 (January 1965): 3–12.

Woit, Peter. *Not Even Wrong: The Failure of String Theory and the Search for Unity in Physical Law.* New York: Basic Books, 2006.

Wolf, Susan. *Meaning in Life and Why It Matters.* Princeton, NJ: Princeton University Press, 2010.

Yonofsky, Noson S. *The Outer Limits of Reason: What Science, Mathematics, and Logic Cannot Tell Us.* Cambridge: MIT Press, 2013.

Young, Julian. *The Death of God and the Meaning of Life.* New York; Routledge, 2003.

Index